SCHIZOPHRENIA:
A Biopsychological Perspective

SCHIZOPHRENIA:
A Biopsychological Perspective

ANDREW CRIDER
Williams College

LEA LAWRENCE ERLBAUM ASSOCIATES, PUBLISHERS
1979   Hillsdale, New Jersey

DISTRIBUTED BY THE HALSTED PRESS DIVISION OF
JOHN WILEY & SONS
New York   Toronto   London   Sydney

Lawrence Erlbaum Associates, Inc., Publishers
365 Broadway
Hillsdale, New Jersey 07642

Distributed solely by Halsted Press Division
John Wiley & Sons, Inc., New York

Library of Congress Cataloging in Publication Data

Crider, Andrew.
  Schizophrenia, a biopsychological perspective.

  Includes bibliographical references and indexes.
  1. Schizophrenia.   I. Title.
  RC514.C75   616.8'982   79-17171
  ISBN 0-470-26833-6

Printed in the United States of America

Contents

ARRR ITS THE BLOB.

Hello all. I'm in my third year and I have
5 weeks until I leave. I have England
beckoning. 3 years in wales has
taught me one thing. Anne Robinson
should have thrown welsh people into
room 101. Its the best place for them,
Sorry but its true.   2001

Fuck You
- All of Wales

you are not
completely wrong (2028)

Preface

Schizophrenia has been a major challenge to clinical and scientific understanding since it was first described a century ago. However, recent developments in a variety of allied fields—descriptive psychiatry, psychopathology, neurochemistry, the genetics of mental disorder, life history research, and institutional practice—have markedly reduced the bounds of our ignorance. Because the specialized literature of these fields is fast approaching overwhelming proportions, the time is ripe for a more concise treatment of these developments. I have therefore attempted to organize and to evaluate current concepts and findings in each of these areas with a view toward the integrative possibilities they suggest. In length and complexity the book stands midway between the necessarily more limited treatment available in omnibus texts of psychopathology and the articles, monographs, and edited volumes addressed to the specialist. Its intended audience is therefore advanced undergraduate and graduate students in psychology; students in psychiatry, psychiatric nursing, and clinical social work; and teachers and professional workers who wish to renew or begin their acquaintance with the subject.

The first three chapters describe schizophrenia from differing but related perspectives. Chapter 1, *Clinical Schizophrenia,* deals primarily with diagnostic issues, including a discussion of the classical contributions of Kraepelin and Bleuler, the evolution of the current nomenclature, and recent attempts to improve diagnostic reliability and validity. Chapter 2, *The Schizophrenic Psychosis,* describes the altered state of consciousness in schizophrenia by use of first-person accounts of those who have experienced this state. This chapter also discusses the schizophrenic attention dysfunction revealed by experimental studies. Chapter 3, *Biochemical Models,* approaches schizophrenia on a neurochemical level. It assesses the evidence generated by three major biochemical hypotheses, indicating how each is derived from a particular pharmacological model of the schizophrenic psychosis.

Chapters 4 and 5 are devoted to more specifically etiological issues. Chapter 4, *Genetic Factors,* discusses methods and data supporting the hypothesis of a heritable component in the etiology of schizophrenia. It also examines the as yet unresolved issues of the schizophrenic spectrum and of genetic models of the mode of inheritance. Chapter 5, *Life History Factors* concerns attempts to isolate life history precursors to schizophrenia. It deals with research on the characteristics of the preschizophrenic child and the search for environmental potentiators of the genetic predisposition.

Finally, Chapter 6, *Patienthood,* deals with rapidly changing conceptions of the appropriate disposition and treatment of schizophrenic individuals. Following an exposition of epidemiological findings, the chapter analyzes the therapeutic, political, and legal forces behind the decline of the mental hospital and the rise of community-based care.

In organizing this material I have tried to tell one story rather than many. A synthetic understanding of the nature, causes, and consequences of schizophrenia remains elusive, yet a final answer will surely require contributions from many disciplines and levels of analysis. As is now more than ever apparent, no single approach is adequate to the complexities of the subject. Thus I have throughout assumed an ultimate compatibility among diverse clinical, psychological, and biological concepts and findings. My choice of title, *A Biopsychological Perspective,* reflects this assumption.

ANDREW CRIDER

Acknowledgments

I am grateful to several colleagues who gave me the benefit of their expertise in reviewing one or more draft chapters: George R. Goethals, Dennis S. Klos, Thomas E. McGill, Paul R. Solomon, and especially Richard O. Rouse, Jr. Their knowledge and good judgment have spared me many embarrassments. A special word of thanks to Angelina Giusti, who with customary skill and graciousness saw the manuscript through more drafts than either of us cares to recall. My wife and children, Anne, Juliet, and Jonathan, greatly alleviated the burdens of writing with constant interest, encouragement, and good humor.

Many authors and publishers have generously allowed me to reproduce or adapt passages, tables, or figures from their own work on schizophrenia. These contributions are acknowledged in the text by parenthetical reference to the bibliography. In addition, I would like to thank the following publishers, according to their requests, for use of the indicated materials:

American Association for the Advancement of Science: Figure 1 from Barchas, J. D., Akil, H., Elliott, G. R., Holman, R. B., & Watson, S. J. "Behavioral neurochemistry: Neuroregulators and behavioral states." *Science,* 1978, *200,* 964–973. Copyright 1978 by the American Association for the Advancement of Science. Also, Table 2 from Carpenter, W. T., Strauss, J. S., & Bartko, J. J. "Flexible system for the diganosis of schizophrenia: Report from the WHO international pilot study of schizophrenia." *Science,* 1973, *182,* 1275–1278. Copyright 1973 by the American Association for the Advancement of Science.

American Medical Association: Figure from Hogarty, G. E., Goldberg, S. C., Schooler, N. R., & Ulrich, R. F. "Drug and sociotherapy in the aftercare of schizophrenic patients." *Archives of General Psychiatry,* 1974, *31,* 603–618. Copyright 1974 by the American Medical Association.

American Psychiatric Association: Excerpt from Lang, J. "The other side of hallucinations." *American Journal of Psychiatry,* 1939, *96,* 423–430. Copyright 1939 by the American Psychiatric Association.

American Psychological Association: Table 1 from Kantor, R. E., Wallner, J. M., & Winder, C. L. "Process and reactive schizophrenia." *Journal of Consulting Psychology,* 1953, *17,* 157–162. Copyright 1953 by the American Psychological Association. Reprinted by permission. Also, Table 2 from Watt, N. F., & Lubensky, A. W. "Childhood roots of schizophrenia." *Journal of Consulting and Clinical Psychology,* 1976, *44,* 363–375. Copyright 1976 by the American Psychological Association. Reprinted by permission.

Canadian Medical Association: Excerpt from MacDonald, N. "Living with schizophrenia." Originally published in *Canadian Medical Association Journal,* 1960, *82,* 218–221.

W. H. Freeman & Co: Figure I.1 from Julien, R. M., *A Primer of Drug Action.* © 1975 by W. H. Freeman & Co.

Grune & Stratton, Inc: Table 12 of Cole, J. O., & Davis, J. M. "Antipsychotic drugs." In L. Bellack & L. Loeb (Eds.), *The Schizophrenic Syndrome.* New York: Grune & Stratton, 1969. Reprinted by permission. Also, excerpts from Sechehaye, M. *Autobiography of a Schizophrenic Girl.* New York: New American Library, 1970. Reprinted by permission.

Holt, Rinehart & Winston, Inc: Excerpts from *The Eden Express* by Mark Vonnegut. Copyright 1975 by Praeger Publishers, Inc. Reprinted by arrangement with Holt, Rinehart & Winston, Inc.

Springer Publishing Co., Inc: Excerpts reprinted from Lopez-Ibor, J. J. "The delusional schizophrenic mutation" and from Mendel, W. M., "A phenomenological theory of schizophrenia." In A. Burton, J. J. Lopez-Ibor, & W. M. Mendel (Eds.), *Schizophrenia as a Life Style.* Copyright © 1974 by Springer Publishing Co., Inc., New York. Used by permission.

Systems Science Publications: Figures 11 and 12 from Gerard, R. W. "The nosology of schizophrenia: A cooperative study." Reprinted from *Behavioral Science,* 1964, *9,* No. 4, 311–333, by permission of James Grier Miller, M.D., Ph.D., Editor.

To Anne

SCHIZOPHRENIA:

A Biopsychological Perspective

1
Clinical Schizophrenia

The presentation of clinical details in the large domain of dementia praecox *meets with considerable difficulties, because a delimitation of the different clinical pictures can only be accomplished artificially.*

—Emil Kraepelin (1902)

Prior to the development of psychiatry in the nineteenth century, psychological deviance was often dealt with in highly inhumane ways that form an unfortunate chapter of Western history. In the late middle ages, European cities routinely ostracized those we would now call mentally ill by placing them on "ships of fools" to traverse the canals and rivers of Europe homeless and unwelcome. The Renaissance is notorious for the persecution and execution of thousands of mentally ill as supposed religious heretics. In the seventeenth century, the mentally ill became victims of the so-called "great confinement." Because of unprecedented levels of urban poverty, European states incarcerated a variety of unproductive persons—vagrants, debtors, petty criminals, in addition to the mentally ill—in *quasi*-penal institutions euphemistically known as general hospitals on the Continent and workhouses or houses of correction in England (Foucault, 1965; Rosen, 1968).

Although many notable scholars, physicians, and humanitarians protested the attitudes and values that engendered these actions, it was only with the liberation of progressive forces in the French Revolution at the end of the eighteenth century that matters improved. The one person who best exemplifies this change was Phillipe Pinel, a revolutionary psychiatrist-physician credited with reforms of French general hospitals and the promotion of medical care of the mentally ill. It is a measure of our progress

1

that less than 200 years ago Pinel could generate controversy by proposing that people with psychological disabilities should be treated with the compassion due illness rather than the punishment accorded criminality.

Because proper medical treatment depends on an accurate diagnosis of the patient's condition, a good deal of the energy of the developing field of psychiatry in the nineteenth century was devoted to devising a workable diagnostic system to describe and classify the various forms of mental illnesses. Many such systems, or *nosologies,* were proposed, but few found wide acceptance. They ranged from Pinel's four "fundamental types"— mania, melancholia, dementia, and idiotism—to highly elaborate systems containing dozens of categories arranged into classes, families, genera, and species in the fashion of biological taxonomies (Menninger, 1963). It was not until the end of the century that a nosology developed by the German psychiatrist Emil Kraepelin gained international adherence. Kraepelin was a great systematizer and teacher whose famous textbook, published in nine editions between 1883 and 1927, culminated a century of nosological effort and established the pattern for all subsequent psychiatric classifications (Menninger, 1963).

KRAEPELIN'S *DEMENTIA PRAECOX*

The 1899 (sixth) edition of Kraepelin's textbook differentiated two major forms of mental illness in terms of their contrasting clinical pictures and their probable outcome, or prognosis. Under the heading of manic-depressive psychosis, Kraepelin described a disorder of mood marked by extreme states of depression or elation, but with an ultimately favorable prognosis. In contrast, he described *dementia praecox* as essentially a disorder of attention, thought, and emotional expression, which tended to appear in late adolescence or early adulthood and to continue on a worsening course to an irreversible state of mental deterioration, or dementia.

Nineteenth-century psychiatrists employed the term *dementia* much as we do today to describe impairments of memory, intelligence, judgment, orientation, and emotional modulation that often accompany old age or damage to the brain caused by disease, trauma, or toxic substances. Toward the middle of the century, however, psychiatrists began to describe cases of apparent dementia appearing before old age (a precocious or *praecox* form) and not obviously secondary to brain damage. Kraepelin's end of the century nosology transmuted the purely descriptive term "early dementia" to the status of a mental disease of unknown etiology but with specific symptoms and a predictable course. In effect, Kraepelin invented *dementia praecox* by conceptually linking a syndrome of clinical symptoms with an early-life onset, on the one hand, and an unfavorable prognosis, on the other, and by then classifying the entire complex as a disorder of central diagnostic importance (Kraepelin, 1899; Menninger, 1963; Wender, 1963).

Kraepelin's description of the early symptoms of *dementia praecox* emphasized a particular pattern of deficits in psychological functioning, (Kraepelin, 1904, in Altschule, 1976). Patients appeared unable to focus attention but were repeatedly distracted by momentary or accidental stimuli. Thought processes showed incoherence and looseness, seen in mild cases as rapid transitions from one thought to the other without any logical bridge and in more severe cases as a massive incoherence in speech. Patients often showed poor judgment, and Kraepelin felt this was the basis of another symptom: delusional beliefs (i.e., bizarre, irrational, or "silly" inferences about events or other people's motives). An early diagnostic sign was a decline in emotional attachments and expression: Patients showed a lack of interest, rarely expressed strong positive or negative emotions, and often stared vacantly and apathetically into space. Accompanying this affective blunting was a reduction in voluntary activity and a neglect of responsibilities, often progressing to a refusal to eat, dress, or otherwise care for oneself. The dementia was not complete, however, because patients showed little impairment of memory or intellectual abilities and were neither delirious nor disoriented. Perception was also intact, except as distorted by occasional hallucinations, most often of voices conversing with, commanding, or derogating the patient.

Kraepelin recognized three forms of *dementia praecox* depending on the relative prominence of the various symptoms in the clinical picture. (Here Kraepelin borrowed heavily from the nosological efforts of his contemporaries.) The *hebephrenic* form was marked by delusions and hallucinations early in its course, followed by a deterioration of thought processes and by affective blunting. In the *catatonic* form, the primary symptom was a stuperous immobility that often exploded into an excited, activated state marked by repetitive or stereotyped movements. Unlike the hebephrenic and catatonic forms in which hallucinations and delusions often disappeared with progressive deterioration, the *paranoid* form was characterized by the strength and persistence of these symptoms over many years. The delusions were generally of a persecutory nature in that the patient felt that others were watching him, conspiring against him, or otherwise rejecting and attempting to harm him. The accompanying auditory hallucinations were generally of threatening or accusing voices.

Kraepelin's delineation of *dementia praecox* and its variants was a masterly achievement of clinical description. His concept of *dementia praecox* drew attention to a large class of psychotic disorders appearing in adolescence and early adulthood without any known associated brain impairment, and it brought bits and pieces of earlier clinical description under a common rubric.

BLEULER'S *SCHIZOPHRENIA*

Yet Kraepelin's view of *dementia praecox* was relatively short-lived. In 1911, the Swiss psychiatrist Eugen Bleuler published his famous monograph *Dementia Praecox or the Group of Schizophrenias* and thereby ushered in not only a new diagnostic term but a new level of understanding of the disorder. Bleuler preferred the term *schizophrenia* ("split-mind") for several reasons. He first of all objected to the use of the term *dementia*. Kraepelin himself had noted that the degree of dementia was limited in such patients, and Bleuler emphasized that the lack of impairment of perception, memory, orientation, and intelligence were important criteria for differentiating schizophrenia from cases of brain tissue impairment in which the dementia was more complete. Thus matters could only be confused by speaking of schizophrenic patients as demented in the usual sense of the term. Bleuler also challenged the term *praecox* by pointing out that the onset of schizophrenia was not necessarily limited to adolescence and early adulthood but sometimes first appeared in later life. Finally, Bleuler (1950) argued that the course of *dementia praecox* was more variable than Kraepelin implied and that not all cases necessarily showed a progressive deterioration into an irreversible form of dementia: "By the term 'dementia praecox' or 'schizophrenia' we designate a group of psychoses whose course is at times chronic, at times marked by intermittent attacks, and which can stop or retrograde at any stage [p. 9]."

Bleuler's critique all but destroyed Kraepelin's marriage of dementia with an early onset, on the one hand, and a deteriorating course, on the other. Bleuler found that "dementia" poorly described the clinical picture, that "praecox" was belied by patients in whom symptom onset occurred later in life, and that inevitable deterioration was not a necessary part of the disorder.

Where Kraepelin's efforts were directed to the isolation of various forms of the disorder on the basis of symptom configurations, or syndromes, Bleuler (1950) was interested in that which united the variety of schizophrenia: "The disease is characterized by a specific type of alteration of thinking, feeling, and relation to the external world which appears nowhere else in this particular fashion [p. 9]." Bleuler accomplished this unifying effort by distinguishing "fundamental" from "accessory" symptoms. The former were symptoms held to be unique to schizophrenia and present in all cases. The latter were often shared by schizophrenia with other psychotic conditions and so could not serve as a primary basis for diagnosis. Interestingly, the accessory symptoms included many of the more striking features of clinical schizophrenia such as hallucinations, delusions, and catatonic stupor. Yet Bleuler insisted that cases of schizophrenia existed in which such accessory symptoms were muted or completely absent. Cases in which only the fundamental symptoms were present therefore belonged to a fourth variant—

simple schizophrenia—in addition to Kraepelin's hebephrenic, catatonic, and paranoid forms.

In coining the term *schizophrenia*, Bleuler intended to suggest the disconnectedness, or fragmentation, of thought, feeling, and interpersonal interaction that he considered the essence of the disorder. Although he was not dogmatic about the number of symptoms that might eventually be found to be fundamental, he at one time or another described the following, which have come to be known as Bleuler's "four A's":

> *Association disturbance:* The tendency for thought to become fragmented through the intrusion of bizarre, illogical, or irrelevant ideas.
> *Affect disturbance:* Incongruity between a thought and its accompanying emotion. In some cases emotion might be completely lacking; in other cases, emotional intensity might be disproportionate to the objective situation.
> *Autism:* Withdrawal from involvement with the external world into a strong fantasy life.
> *Ambivalence:* Psychological conflict, or the simultaneous arousal of mutually incompatible thoughts and feelings toward persons and situations.

In addition to the fundamental–accessory dichotomy, Bleuler also distinguished between primary and secondary schizophrenic symptoms. He defined primary symptoms as direct manifestations of the schizophrenic disorder, whereas the secondary symptoms represented adjustments or reactions to the primary impairments. Bleuler illustrated this distinction by several analogies to physical disorders. For example, a paralysis of lateral eye movements may be regarded as a primary symptom of an underlying lesion of the eye's abducens muscle. Compensatory contractions of the internus muscle and mistaken localization of visual images would then be categorized as secondary symptoms. Bleuler's distinctions between fundamental and accessory symptoms and between primary and secondary symptoms generates a fourfold classification of the clinical symptomatology in schizophrenia: (1) fundamental–primary; (2) fundamental–secondary; (3) accessory–primary; and (4) accessory–secondary. However, Bleuler never attempted a final categorization of schizophrenic symptoms into his theoretical fourfold scheme. Indeed, he was most often circumspect and tentative in his classificatory efforts. Yet he clearly indicated his conviction that the schizophrenic disorder of association was both fundamental and primary.

Bleuler argued that normal thought and speech require a purposive, sequential ordering of ideas (associations) into meaningful themes. To express this notion, Bleuler employed the metaphor of a chain of ideas connected by associative "threads." He argued that in schizophrenia thought and language were fragmented by a loosening of the associative threads normally connecting one idea to another in sequential units. In mild forms this associative weakening can be seen in a hodge-podge of disparate ideas with only tenuous relationships one to another, as in the response of one of Bleuler's patients to the question, "Who was Epaminondas?":

> He besieged the Acropolis with gun-boats and had the Persian garrisons put to the stake as living torches. The succeeding Pope Gregory VII . . . eh . . . Nero, followed his example and because of him all the Athenians, all the Roman-Germanic-Celtic tribes who did not favor the priests, were burned by the Druids on Corpus Christi Day as a sacrifice to the Sun-God, Baal. That is the Stone Age. Spearheads made of bronze [Bleuler, 1950, p. 15].

More severe forms of associative weakening allow the intrusion of illogical or irrelevant associates into the flow of speech. A woman patient, reporting on a walk with her family, began to describe her relatives as "Father, Son," and then added, "the Holy Ghost," and then proceeded to tack on "the Holy Virgin." Condensations of disparate ideas might produce apparently meaningless new words (neologisms), as in the patient who combined steamboat and sailboat into "steam-sail" [p. 26].

In even more extreme forms, patients might become stuck on one theme without being able to progress, producing long lists of perseverating associations to a single central idea:

> I wish you, therefore, a very happy, pleasant, healthy, blessed and fruit-crop rich year; and also many good wine-harvest years thereafter, as well as good potato-crop years; as well as fine potato years, and sauerkraut years, and sprouts years, and cucumber years, and nut years; a good egg-year, and also a good cheese year [Bleuler, 1950, p. 28].

Finally, all goal-directedness or communicative intent may disappear and be replaced by a disconnected, confused babble:

> Here in this smith-house it doesn't go very well. This is indeed no parish-house or even a poor-house but in this place there is noise, anger, grumbling—sunny—heavenly-knells all year round. Many a small and large landowner, wind-bag or poor drunk from Thalweil, Addisweil, from Albis, from Salz, from Seen, from Rorbach, from Rorbas have never again returned to their own homes [Bleuler, 1950, p. 31].

Kraepelin had noted affective blunting in *dementia praecox*, as seen in a decline of emotional attachments, apathy, and indifference, and Bleuler identified this pattern as a second fundamental symptom that was also probably primary. But where Kraepelin saw the problem largely in terms of withdrawal from the natural and social environment, Bleuler saw it in terms analogous to the associative disorder. That is, the affective life of schizophrenic patients could be described as fragmented, poorly modulated, and as lacking integration with the accompanying thought process or the immediate situation:

> In the severest cases emotional and affective expressions seem to be completely lacking. In milder cases we may note only that the degree of intensity of the emotional reactions is not commensurate with the various events that caused those reactions. Indeed, the intensity of the affective reactions may range from a complete lack of emotional expression to extremely exaggerated affective responses in relation to different thought-complexes. The affectivity can also appear to be qualitatively abnormal; that is, inadequate to the intellectual processes involved [Bleuler, 1950, p. 10].

Although most contemporary clinical workers join Bleuler in identifying the associative and the affective disturbances as distinguishing signs of schizophrenia, the current status of Bleuler's remaining two fundamental symptoms—ambivalence and autism—are much less clear. Even for Bleuler, ambivalence and autism were secondary problems (reactions or adjustments to the primary disorders of thought and affect) and therefore of lesser diagnostic importance. But many would also argue that they could hardly be fundamental in that ambivalence and autism are often seen as short-term adjustive reactions in a wide variety of psychiatric conditions. This is not to say that schizophrenia patients are not sometimes exquisitely ambivalent or autistic, but only that these behavior patterns are poor discriminating criteria for a diagnosis of schizophrenia.

The theoretical contributions of Kraepelin and Bleuler remain the foundation of current clinical views of schizophrenia. Kraepelin contributed the notion of schizophrenia as disease—that is, a pathological process that can be diagnosed by its outward signs and symptoms and that has a predictable course over time. From Bleuler, we have inherited a concern with the patient's mental state (the four A's) and a propensity to view certain symptoms, especially an associative or thought disturbance, as fundamental to the disorder. Bleuler is also responsible for amending Kraepelin's pessimistic view of prognosis by insisting that at least some degree of remission is possible in many cases.

THE CURRENT NOSOLOGY

The conceptual innovations of Kraepelin and Bleuler were quickly assimilated into psychiatric practice, perhaps nowhere more so than in the United States, where the nosology of schizophrenia evolved rapidly through the proliferation of subforms, or "types." In 1934, the American Psychiatric

Association (A.P.A.) added an *Other* type to permit a diagnosis of schizophrenia when the patient's symptoms did not fall readily into one of the four classic forms of Kraepelin and Bleuler. In 1952, the A.P.A. adopted an official nosology titled the *Diagnostic and Statistical Manual of Mental Disorders* (commonly known as DSM-I), in which schizophrenia was defined as one of three major forms of psychosis along with affective disorders and paranoid disorders. The DSM-I saw the addition of five further subcategories of schizophrenia: (1) *Acute episode;* (2) *Chronic undifferentiated;* (3) *Schizo-affective;* (4) *Childhood;* and (5) *Residual* types. The *Acute episode* and *Chronic undifferentiated* categories serve primarily to distinguish cases having an abrupt onset and a relatively brief course from cases with a more gradual onset followed by a course of long duration. The *Schizo-affective* category is employed for cases in which there is evidence of both a thought disorder and a pronounced elation or depression, signs that more conventionally indicate an affective psychosis. *Childhood* schizophrenia extends the general category downward in age from Kraepelin's original postpubertal criterion, and the *Residual* category covers cases in which a florid psychotic episode is followed by apparent remission.

A 1968 revision of the DSM (DSM-II) added a final category, the *Latent* type, to designate so-called "borderline" cases in which the person has never been obviously psychotic but whose intellectual and emotional life resembles in muted form the disordered thought and affective blunting of clinical schizophrenia. Latent schizophrenia had first been described by Bleuler, who maintained that it was many times more common than the classical forms of *dementia praecox.* With the inclusion of the *Latent* type, the DSM-II in effect distinguishes between individuals with schizophrenic character traits and individuals with such traits who also undergo psychotic episodes of greater or lesser duration.

This evolution can be seen in Table 1.1. The 11 categories of schizophrenia that appear in DSM-II are listed in the third column. The provenance of each type appears on the left with its associated date. Capsule summaries of the diagnostic criteria for each type, excerpted from longer descriptions in DSM-II, are included in the right-hand column.

PROBLEMS OF PSYCHIATRIC DIAGNOSIS

Diagnosis is essentially an act of classification, by which different patients are assigned to a common category because they share the same features or symptoms. If the diagnostic process works as it should, patients with common diagnoses should show similar symptom patterns, and those patterns should be different from the symptom patterns of patients with other diagnoses.

TABLE 1.1
Diagnostic Evolution of *Schizophrenia*

Date	Source	DSM-II Type	Diagnostic Criteria
1899	Kraepelin	Hebephrenic	Disorganized thinking, inappropriate affect, regressive behavior
		Catatonic	Excessive motor activity and excitement; or stupor, mutism, and negativism
		Paranoid	Persecutory or grandiose delusions, hostile and aggressive attitudes
1911	Bleuler	Simple	Reduction of external attachments and interests, apathy and indifference
1934	A.P.A.	Other	Any type of schizophrenia not otherwise described
1952	DSM-I	Acute episode	Acute onset of symptoms, confusion, perplexity, emotional turmoil
		Chronic undifferentiated	Mixed symptoms and definite schizophrenic thought, affect, and behavior
		Schizo-affective	Mixture of schizophrenic symptoms and pronounced elation or depression
		Childhood	Autistic, atypical withdrawn behavior; appearing before puberty
		Residual	Showing signs of schizophrenia but no longer psychotic
1968	DSM-II	Latent	Symptoms of schizophrenia but no history of psychotic episode; borderline

An immense amount of research has been devoted to examining the process of psychiatric diagnosis, and there is little question that it works poorly. The basic problem is that of poor agreement, or *reliability,* among psychiatrists in assigning patients to categories. The degree of agreement diminishes quickly as diagnosis moves from broad categories to more specific subtypes. There is relatively little disagreement that a given case falls into one of the three broad categories of functional disorders, mental retardation, or organic disorders. Agreement falls rapidly, however, in deciding which subcategory of the three broad designations is appropriate. And when the subcategory contains a series of variants or types (as in the case of schizophrenia), agreement is so poor that the diagnosis is virtually meaningless (Kendell, 1975; Zigler & Phillips, 1961).

The results of an analysis of six major studies of diagnostic reliability in psychiatry illustrate this problem well (Spitzer & Fleiss, 1974). In each study, at least two psychiatrists using standard nosological categories made independent diagnoses of a sample of hospitalized patients. For each study, Spitzer and Fleiss computed the proportion of cases in which above-chance agreement was reached in assigning a given diagnosis to a patient. For the broad categories of mental deficiency and organic disorders, the average proportion of agreement over the six studies was .72 and .77, respectively. The authors do not present data for functional disorders as a whole, but within this category the average proportions of agreement were .55 for psychoses, .40 for neuroses, and .32 for personality disorders. For the category of schizophrenic psychosis, the values in the six studies ranged from .32 to .77, with an average of .57. The authors concluded that reliability is satisfactory only for very broad categories like mental deficiency and organic disorders. It is no better than fair for schizophrenia and is poor for most other categories. Most reliability studies have not even attempted to probe the reliability of the 11 DSM-II schizophrenic types, but it must necessarily be lower than the reliability for schizophrenia as an inclusive category.

Two major consequences flow from unreliable diagnosis: (1) patients bearing the same diagnosis will not be homogeneous with regard to symptom pictures; and (2) patients bearing different diagnoses will show a degree of symptom overlap. A study by Wittenborn and Weiss (1952) illustrates the first point. The authors rated a group of patients diagnosed "manic-depressive, manic state" on a series of scales devised to measure the intensity of expression of a large number of psychiatric symptoms. The scale profile correlations yielded a data matrix that required six relatively distinct patient clusters to describe the symptom patterns of this supposedly homogeneous group.

Studying symptom overlap, Zigler and Phillips (1961) tallied the occurrence of 35 common symptoms among hospitalized patients broadly grouped into schizophrenic, neurotic, personality disorder, and manic-depressive categories. All 35 symptoms appeared in the case histories of at least one of the patients in both the schizophrenic and neurotic categories, 34 appeared at least once among the personality disorder patients, and 30 among the manic-depressive patients. It is of course true that certain symptoms *tend* to be associated with specific diagnosis. Yet Zigler and Phillips found that about half of the 35 symptoms did not appear differentially in any of the four categories, whereas the other half showed only weak specificity to a given category.

In sum, therefore, knowing a patient's official diagnosis will generally tell little about his or her actual behavior. Hence a diagnosis gives little indication to therapists as to proper treatment methods, nor any solid basis on which a researcher might choose patients for study. In the language of psychophysics, diagnostic labels have a low signal-to-noise ratio, which impedes communication and therefore limits the orderly accumulation of information on etiology and treatment.

The sources of diagnostic unreliability are not hard to isolate. Part of the problem is the lack of standardized definitions of terms used in the DSM-II. In diagnosing schizophrenia, for example, "thought disorder" might mean anything from raving incoherence to a slight conceptual slippage in responding to a projective test, depending on the diagnostician's theoretical proclivities and methods of eliciting information from the patient. A more important problem is the lack of fit between patient behaviors and textbook examples of diagnostic categories. Patients differ in the extent to which their behavior approaches diagnostic stereotypes, so that some cases will elicit more diagnostic disagreement than others. Many patients will present clinical pictures that could conceivably give rise to several different diagnoses, When constrained to specify just one, diagnosticians will disagree as to the predominant category. This lack of fit is in fact acknowledged in the DSM-II listings for schizophrenia. Subtypes like *Chronic undifferentiated* and *Other* allow for a diagnosis of schizophrenia when a patient does not in fact show the clustering of symptoms demanded by the remaining categories.

The descriptive problems of the DSM-II are often minimized in practice by a sort of benign neglect. In one diagnostic conference, a young psychiatrist began the discussion of his patient with the phrase, "Jones is a typical schizophrenic." An older and wiser chief psychiatrist chairing the conference quickly scotched this approach by replying, "Are you going to tell us about schizophrenia or about Jones?" It is unfortunate that DSM labels are applied to patients primarily for the record-keeping benefit of hospital administrators rather than for the descriptive information they convey to patients' families, to treatment personnel, or to researchers.

METHODS OF REFINING DIAGNOSIS

The case-by-case approach to treatment adopted by clinicians does not, however, solve the scientific problem of finding accurate means to describe the variousness of schizophrenia. We examine two major strategies for dealing with this problem. The first strategy attempts to identify aspects of clinical schizophrenia that can be reliably assessed by trained diagnosticians. The second strategy defines key clinical features in terms of their predictive validity. The distinction between refinement via *reliability* and refinement via *validity* is elaborated in the following discussion.

Refining Reliability

Through refined methods of observation, this strategy attempts to standardize the methods used to elicit, define, and categorize patients' symptoms. Because the symptomatic behavior of psychiatric patients is often situationally specific, it is important to standardize the observational context. In most cases, this means standardizing the clinical interview, but methods have also been developed for the observation of on-ward behavior patterns. A second step replaces ad-hoc clinical descriptions with rating schedules that require the diagnostician to indicate the presence, absence, and/or degree of intensity of a set of psychiatric symptoms specified in advance. To overcome terminological confusion the symptoms to be rated are defined as specifically as possible, and the diagnostician is trained in the appropriate application of terms to particular patient responses. Finally, the ratings are often summarized in numerical form to allow for computer reduction of the symptom profile into broader clusters or syndromes and then into standard diagnostic categories.

For example, the Present State Examination (PSE) is a standardized interview and symptom rating schedule developed over several years by Wing, Cooper, and Sartorius (1974). It consists of: (1) a glossary of lengthy definitions of 140 symptoms seen in neurotic and psychotic disorders; and (2) an interview schedule that allows the clinician to rate the presence, absence, or intensity of expression of each of these symptoms from direct observation or from the patient's response to interview questions. For example, the symptom of *worrying* is defined as "painful thought which cannot be stopped and is out of proportion to the subject worried about" and is rated in terms of the patient's response to such questions as "have you worried a lot during the past month?"; "how much do you worry?"; "what is it like when you worry?". The symptom of *distractibility* is rated if the patient "stops talking or changes the subject due to distraction by trivial noises or events outside the room or turns attention to furniture, etc."

The PSE system provides explicit rules for combining the 140 symptoms into 38 more general syndromes of related symptoms and thence to standard diagnostic categories. Reliability studies show high levels of interdiagnostician agreement on rating specific symptoms and a greatly improved agreement on diagnostic categories when judgments are made from PSE data. Using PSE information only, two diagnosticians agreed on the placement of 84% of 172 cases into one of 11 standard diagnostic categories. The two examiners also agreed 92% of the time that a given patient belonged in the combined category of possible, probable, or residual schizophrenia (Wing et al., 1974).

Among other uses, the PSE has figured in an ambitious attempt sponsored by the World Health Organization (WHO) to establish an empirical definition of the concept of schizophrenia. The subjects were over 1000 patients in nine countries who showed signs of psychotic behavior. Each was interviewed by a local psychiatrist and rated with an early form of the PSE containing 360 possible symptoms. Following the interview, each patient was given a diagnosis that could include schizophrenia or some other form of psychotic disorder. Finally, those symptoms most highly correlated with a diagnosis of schizophrenia were isolated (Carpenter, Strauss, & Bartko, 1973, 1974).

The nine most indicative symptoms are listed in the left-hand column of Table 1.2, with the right-hand column showing the PSE questions or behavioral observations by which symptom presence was elicited or judged. These nine symptoms provide a lowest common denominator for a diagnosis

TABLE 1.2
WHO Study of Schizophrenic Symptoms[a]

PSE Symptom	Interview Observation/Question
Incoherent speech	Free and spontaneous flow of incoherent speech
Restricted affect	Blank, expressionless face; very little or no emotion shown
Thoughts aloud	Do you feel your thoughts are being broadcast or transmitted? Do you ever seem to hear your thoughts spoken aloud?
Widespread delusions	How widespread are patient's delusions: How many areas in patient's life are affected?
Bizarre delusions	Are the delusions comprehensible?
Nihilistic delusions	Do you feel your body is decaying, rotting? Do you feel some part of your body is missing (e.g., head, brain, or arms)? Do you ever have the feeling that you do not exist at all, that you are dead, dissolved?
Poor insight	Overall rating of insight
Poor rapport	Did the interviewer find it possible to establish good rapport?
Unreliable information	Was the information obtained in this interview credible or not?

[a]Adapted from Carpenter, Strauss, and Bartko (1973).

of schizophrenia. Note that the world's psychiatrists tend to agree with Bleuler in their definition of schizophrenia. Both affective blunting (*restricted affect*) and thought disorder (*incoherent speech*) appear on the list. In addition, so-called accessory symptoms as seen in auditory hallucinations (*thoughts aloud*) and delusions (*widespread, bizarre,* and *nihilistic delusions*) also figure prominently. Finally, certain observations descriptive of the interaction between patient and interviewer (*poor insight, poor rapport, unreliable information*) are likely to be categorized as schizophrenic even though they do not figure in classical descriptions of the disorder.

A second important attempt to improve diagnostic reliability is represented by the Inpatient Multidimensional Psychiatric Scale (IMPS) developed by Maurice Lorr and his associates at the U.S. Veterans Administration (Lorr, Klett, & McNair, 1963). The device consists of 75 carefully worded items describing a broad sample of psychotic behavior observable in the conventional psychiatric interview. Following the interview, the patient's behavior and reports of feelings, thoughts, and beliefs are matched against the 75 items; applicable items are rated on numerical scales for their intensity of expression or frequency of occurrence. Illustrative items appear in the right-hand column of Table 1.3.

The 75 IMPS items may be reduced to a smaller number of clusters of interrelated symptoms. Specifically, the IMPS yields 10 syndromes of psychotic symptoms, as defined by a factor analysis of ratings on a large sample of hospitalized psychotic patients. Four of the 10 syndromes reflect patterns characteristic of manic-depressive psychoses and organic disorders. The remaining six, set out in Table 1.3, describe patterns conventionally regarded as schizophrenic. The left-hand column lists the titles given by Lorr, Klett, and McNair to the symptom clusters in the right-hand column.

The syndrome labeled *conceptual disorganization* appears to reflect schizophrenic thought disorder, while the typical affective blunting is seen in *retardation and apathy. Perceptual distortion* defines auditory and other forms of hallucination, and various types of delusions are seen in *paranoid projection* and *grandiose expansiveness. Motor disturbance* is best described as a syndrome of catatonic symptoms.

It would not be legitimate to compare the IMPS syndromes with the 11 subtypes of schizophrenia presented in DSM-II, because the former represent clusters of symptoms and the latter represents clusters of patients. The IMPS system does not constrain patients to fall into exclusive categories as is the case with DSM-II. A given patient may show symptoms from any or all of the six syndromes. This nicely eliminates an important source of diagnostic disagreement, and the reliability of the IMPS syndromes is quite high.

A more pertinent comparison—that between the IMPS syndromes and the WHO study using the Present State Examination—reveals impressive consistency. This is in spite of the fact that the WHO study took the diagnosis

TABLE 1.3
IMPS Schizophrenic Syndromes[a]

Syndrome	Illustrative IMPS Items
Conceptual disorganization	Gives answers that are irrelevant; gives incoherent answers; uses neologisms
Retardation and apathy	Indifferent to own future; apathetic to self or problems; fails to answer questions; slovenly appearance
Perceptual distortion	Hears voices that accuse or blame; hears voices that threaten punishment; reports tactual, gustatory or olfactory hallucinations
Paranoid projection	Preoccupied with delusional beliefs; believes people talk about him; believes people control his actions
Grandiose expansiveness	Believes he has a divine mission; believes he has unusual powers; believes he is a well-known personality
Motor disturbances	Exhibits peculiar, repetitive gestures; exhibits peculiar grimaces; exhibits peculiar, rigid postures

[a]Adapted from Lorr, Klett, and McNair (1963).

of schizophrenia as a given and isolated the defining symptoms, whereas the IMPS syndrome definition of schizophrenia emerges from the empirical associations among psychotic symptoms. Although the PSE and IMPS items are differently phrased, both clearly find Bleuler's disturbances of association (thought disorder) and affectivity (affective blunting) to be criterial. Hallucinations, especially of the auditory type, and a wide variety of delusions also appear in both. The IMPS, but not the WHO study, isolates a catatonic syndrome, whereas the WHO study includes judgments relating to the interaction between patient and examiner. These discrepancies are relatively minor and probably reflect differences in the basic items included in the two devices.

Refining Validity

With their emphasis on the delineation of symptoms and the clustering of associated symptoms into syndromes, the PSE and IMPS are heirs in modern dress to the nosological tradition inaugurated by Kraepelin. They differ from it less in intent than in method, which is that of psychological scaling and associated statistical methods. But the attempt to precisely define distinct groupings of clinical symptoms is identical to Kraepelin's approach to diagnosis. The notion of the symptom syndrome is a powerful one in psychiatry, yet there is no inherent reason that diagnosis need be based on clinical syndromes. Diagnosis should be essentially an act of classification by which different individuals are assigned to a common category because category membership predicts such factors as etiology, prognosis, or preferred treatment. In general medicine, such correlations are the norm, as in the recent discovery that the form of mental retardation known as Down's syndrome is linked to a chromosomal abnormality (trisomy-21), which in turn implies a predictable life history for affected persons. In the case of schizophrenia, however, it is not clear that differentiating, for example, hebephrenic from simple types in terms of clinical syndromes implies differences in etiology, course, or treatment.

In the absence of predictability based on syndrome similarity, other bases for differentiating the broad category of schizophrenia have been sought. Suggested differentiating criteria have included the presence of schizophrenia in family members, judgments of the severity of the clinical symptoms, response to drugs, and performance on various psychological tests. The test of any such criteria is that they be demonstrated to be valid predictors of other important aspects of the disorder. In this view, symptoms that correlate only with other symptoms in a common syndrome are thought to add relatively little to a more extensive understanding of schizophrenia.

A good example of a valid indicator in the domain of schizophrenia is the distinction between patients with and without paranoid features. Clinicians have long debated the question of whether paranoid schizophrenia ought to be considered a "true" form of schizophrenia at all. Aside from the presence of well-articulated and strongly held beliefs that he is being persecuted, conspired against, or otherwise prevailed upon, the paranoid schizophrenic patient often shows little evidence of psychosis. In many cases, the paranoid delusions are well controlled so that the patient manifests little behavior that could be considered deviant or unusual unless efforts are made to probe the delusional system. When hospitalized, paranoid patients are generally considered to be less disturbed and to have a more favorable prognosis than other schizophrenic patients.

Studies often show that paranoid patients not only differ greatly from nonparanoid patients but also often cannot be distinguished from non-psychiatric controls on the observation of interest. This is illustrated in Fig. 1.1, taken from a descriptive study of schizophrenia conducted at the University of Michigan's Mental Health Research Institute (Gerard, 1964). The study's goal was to isolate objective indicators of schizophrenia by measuring patients' responses to a series of psychological, physiological, and biochemical tests. In constructing Fig. 1.1, the average score of the entire

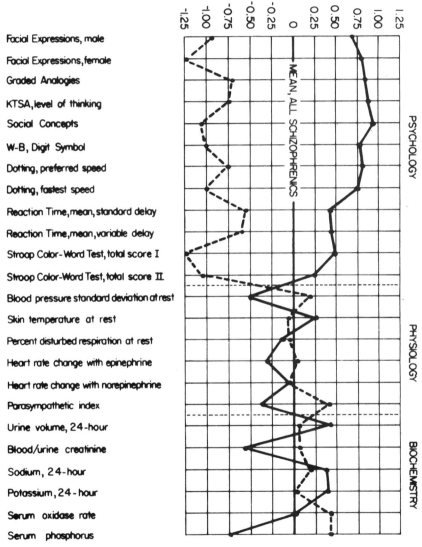

FIG. 1.1. Differential test profiles of nonparanoid (*dashed line*) and paranoid (*solid line*) schizophrenic patients. (Adapted from Gerard, 1964.)

schizophrenic sample on each test was first subtracted from each patient's scores, and the means of the resulting difference scores for paranoid and nonparanoid subgroups was then plotted. The substantive interpretation of these results is, for present purposes, secondary to the fact that the two groups differ markedly on most of the indices used. In other words, the presence or absence of paranoid features in the clinical picture is a valid diagnostic criterion. Because of such data, it has become routine for investigations of schizophrenia to divide patient samples into paranoid and nonparanoid subgroups.

The search for valid indicators has borne greatest fruit in the distinction between process and reactive schizophrenia. Although the terminology is fairly recent, the concept was implicit in Bleuler's original dissent from Kraepelin's view that cases of *dementia praecox* necessarily followed a chronic deteriorating course. In Bleuler's experience, a subset of patients was able to make a rather rapid and complete recovery from a schizophrenic psychosis clinically similar to *dementia praecox*. In later work, Bleuler distinguished between chronic schizophrenia—marked by a slowly developing clinical picture, severe disturbances of association and affect, and a poor prognosis—and what he termed "manifest" schizophrenia, characterized by an abrupt onset, a proliferation of accessory symptoms such as delusions and hallucinations, and a favorable prognosis (Bleuler, 1924). Subsequent workers have used such terms as "nuclear," "typical," "true" versus "benign," "atypical," and "schizophreniform" to make the same distinction. Schizophrenic-like psychoses with rapid recoveries were also reported frequently by military psychiatrists in World War II. Occurring under conditions of prolonged fatigue and combat stress, such cases were often dubbed "3-day schizophrenia" (Strecker, Ebaugh, & Ewalt, 1951).

Because clinical pictures are similar in both forms, researchers have sought premorbid (pre-illness) life history differences as defining criteria. In 1953, Kantor, Wallner, and Winder brought together a set of differentiating premorbid factors culled from the clinical literature (Table 1.4). Kantor et al. also introduced the terms "process" and "reactive," which have since become standard usage. Reactive patients usually have an onset in early adulthood. Symptom development occurs quite abruptly, often following an identifiable stressful life event. The premorbid history shows good psychological and social adjustment, and the clinical picture includes emotional components such as anxiety and depression. By contrast, process patients show a gradual development of the disorder stemming from early childhood. Premorbid social and psychological development is poor, distinguished by a constriction of interest, lack of zest, and avoidance of social interaction. It is as if the patient slides into clinical schizophrenia in the absence of any specific precipitating life crisis. The clinical picture is marked by affective blunting and a relative absence of emotionality.

TABLE 1.4
Differentiating Life History Criteria[a]

Process Schizophrenia	Reactive Schizophrenia
Birth to the fifth year	
a. Early psychological trauma	a. Good psychological history
b. Physical illness—severe or long	b. Good physical health
c. Odd member of family	c. Normal member of family
Fifth year to adolescence	
a. Difficulties at school	a. Well adjusted in school
b. Family troubles paralleled with sudden changes in patient's behavior	b. Domestic troubles unaccompanied by behavior disruptions; patient "had what it took"
c. Introverted behavior trends and interests	c. Extroverted behavior trends and interests
d. History of breakdown of social, physical, and mental functioning	d. History of adequate social, physical, mental functioning
e. Pathological siblings	e. Normal siblings
f. Overprotective or rejecting mother; "Momism"	f. Normally protective, accepting mother
g. Rejecting father	g. Accepting father
Adolescence to adulthood	
a. Lack of heterosexuality	a. Heterosexual behavior
b. Insidious, gradual onset of psychosis without pertinent stress	b. Sudden onset of psychosis; stress present and pertinent; later onset
c. Physical aggression	c. Verbal aggresssion
d. Poor response to treatment	d. Good response to treatment
e. Lengthy stay in hospital	e. Short course in hospital
Adulthood	
a. Massive paranoia	a. Minor paranoid trends
b. Little capacity for alcohol	b. Much capacity for alcohol
c. No manic-depressive component	c. Presence of manic-depressive component
d. Failure under adversity	d. Success despite adversity
e. Discrepancy between ability and achievement	e. Harmony between ability and achievement
f. Awareness of change in self	f. No sensation of change
g. Somatic delusions	g. Absence of somatic delusions
h. Clash between culture and environment	h. Harmony between culture and environment
i. Loss of decency (nudity, public masturbation, etc.)	i. Retention of decency

[a]From Kantor, Wallner, and Winder (1953).

A helpful way of thinking about the process-reactive distinction is to separate the domain of schizophrenia into two independent dichotomies. The first distinguishes patients in terms of a personality dimension of good versus poor premorbid adjustment. The second distinguishes between the presence or absence of an acute psychotic state (Bowers, 1975). Reactive schizophrenia can be seen as an acute but transitory psychotic state in an otherwise normal (good premorbid) personality. Process schizophrenia is defined in the first instance by poor premorbid adjustment, but such individuals may or may not be actively psychotic. In other words, psychotic states tend to be episodic, time-limited events imposed on a history of poor premorbid adjustment. Process patients will most often be hospitalized in an acute psychotic state, and their clinical picture itself will therefore be difficult to distinguish from that of reactive schizophrenia. When not actively psychotic, process patients may often be labeled with such terms as "*dementia praecox* proper" or chronic schizophrenia.

The fundmental validity of the process–reactive distinction is its ability to predict remission from hospitalization. In addition, an impressive number of correlates of the process–reactive distinction have appeared in psychological research on schizophrenia. A number of rating scales that readily distinguish schizophrenic patients on premorbid history factors have been developed (Higgens, 1964, 1969). As Garmezy (1970) points out, numerous studies have reported reliable differences between process and reactive cases in such diverse areas as learning, cognitive processes, language and verbal behavior, perception, motivation, and quality of parental relationship.

DSM-III

A recently proposed revision of the Diagnostic and Statistical Manual of Mental Disorders—DSM-III—takes into account many of the shortcomings of the DSM-II treatment of schizophrenia and sets the stage for future improvement of diagnostic practice (Task Force on Nomenclature and Statistics, 1978). Unlike DSM-II, the proposed revision sharply distinguishes between process cases (termed "schizophrenic disorder") and reactive cases (termed "schizophreniform disorder"). The distinction is based on the duration of clinically significant symptoms: A diagnosis of schizophrenic disorder may not be made unless the problem has lasted continuously for at least 6 months. A schizophrenic episode having a duration of less than 6 months is to be classified as schizophreniform disorder. The distinction reflects the accumulated evidence of differences in premorbid adjustment level, prognosis, and response to treatment of process and reactive forms of schizophrenia.

A diagnosis of either schizophrenic disorder or schizophreniform disorder requires the clear presence of at least one "characteristic symptom" from a list of 10. This list includes seven forms of delusion (e.g., somatic, grandiose, religious, or nihilistic delusions), two forms of auditory hallucination (e.g., hallucinations of voices commenting on the patient's behavior or thoughts), and Bleulerian thought disorder. Of diagnostic significance only if accompanied by one or more of the 10 criterial symptoms are: (1) forms of delusion and hallucination that are not listed; (2) affective disturbance; and (3) catatonic behavior. This degree of definitional specificity may discomfit many, but it should function to increase diagnostic agreement and thus the orderly accumulation of etiological, prognostic, and treatment information.

The sharp distinction between schizophrenic disorder and schizophreniform disorder marks a return to a more classical and European conception of schizophrenia among North American psychiatrists. This rapprochement is also seen in DSM-III's constriction of DSM-II's 11 subtypes of schizophrenic disorder to but five subtypes. Three are Kraepelin's original variants of hebephrenic (now called "disorganized"), catatonic, and paranoid schizophrenia. A fourth type, "undifferentiated schizophrenia," is diagnosed when the overall criteria for schizophrenia are met but when the symptom configuration does not conform to one of the classical subtypes. The fifth and final category of DSM-III, "residual schizophrenia," is reserved for patients who have had a schizophrenic episode but currently show only muted signs such as mild delusions or hallucinations, social withdrawal, or affective flattening. Excised are the questionable or infrequently used DSM-II categories of latent, childhood, simple, and "other" schizophrenia. DSM-III retains the concept of schizo-affective disorder, but as a separate major category in addition to schizophrenic disorder and schizophreniform disorder. Schizo-affective disorder is to be diagnosed when a depressive or manic syndrome precedes or develops concurrently with the criteria for schizophrenic disorder.

The DSM-III proposals are a major step toward conceptual clarity in the diagnosis of schizophrenia. In effect, they mark a halt to a long history of descriptive proliferation that threatened to render meaningless the concept of schizophrenia. The distinction between schizophrenic and schizophreniform disorders validates a generation of research distinguishing process from reactive cases. The specification of symptomatic criteria for the diagnosis of schizophrenic disorder, combined with a restriction on the number of available subdiagnoses, should act considerably to improve diagnostic agreement and hence the search for valid external correlates.

COMMENTARY

In the foregoing discussion, we have taken the concept of schizophrenia for granted while analyzing various clinical and scientific attempts to give it sound empirical definition. But it is only fair to point out that the concept itself is a cause of never-ending debate among mental health professionals. Few would deny that many patients suffer from associative disturbances, impaired emotional expression, bizarre delusions, or troubling hallucinations at different times, singly or in combination, and with varying degrees of intensity. But many take exception to the dominant tendency in psychiatry to apply a disease metaphor to such states. For antipsychiatrists Laing and Esterson (1964), it is "an assumption, a theory, a hypothesis, but not a *fact*, that anyone suffers from a condition called 'schizophrenia'. . . . we regard it as a palpable error, in the present state of the evidence, to take it to be a fact [pp. 11–12]." Nor should it be considered that such radical dissent is limited to a few *enfants terribles* among mental health professionals. Doubts about the meaningfulness of the term *schizophrenia* have probably occurred to all but the most stolid investigators when confronted with the inordinate complexities of the problem.

The notion of schizophrenia-as-disease originated with Kraepelin, who, in concert with prevailing views, felt that psychiatry could attain scientific respectability by reducing clinical syndromes to underlying brain pathology. Many syndromes could, in fact, be so reduced, as for example in dementias associated with traumatic injury to the brain or in general paresis following syphilitic infection. It was not a great leap of faith to assume that schizophrenia might follow a similar paradigm. Kraepelin's model of disease followed the then current doctrine of specific etiology made credible by nineteenth-century advances in microbiology and bacteriology. According to this model, a specific etiological agent is responsible for structural damage (a lesion) to bodily tissue that in turn results in symptom clusters by which the disease is clinically recognized. Treatment is then applied to arrest or reverse the natural course of the disease. In schizophrenia, the etiology and the lesion, if any, were unknown, but Kraepelin felt confident that a foothold could be achieved by a proper delineation of the clinical picture:

> Judging from our experience in internal medicine, it is a fair assumption that similar disease processes will produce identical symptom pictures, identical pathological anatomy, and identical etiology. If, therefore, we possessed a comprehensive knowledge of any one of these three fields—pathological anatomy, symptomatology, or etiology—we would at once have a uniform and standard classification of mental diseases. A similar comprehensive knowledge of either of the other two fields would give not only just as uniform and standard classifications, but all these classfications would exactly coincide. Cases of mental disease originating from the same cause must also present the same symptoms and the same pathological findings. [quoted in Price, 1972, pp. 65–66].

The problem with the application of this particular model of disease to schizophrenia is that it promises more than it has delivered in nearly a century of medical and psychological research. In the absence of demonstrated specific etiology or specific pathological anatomy, skeptics suspect that continued application of this model to schizophrenic states and behaviors is profoundly mistaken, if not downright perverse. Of course, many professionals would amend "disease" to "mental disease" in order to save the situation. But this only obscures the issue. According to Kraepelin's original model, schizophrenia is either a brain disease or it is not. If it is not, it is nonsensical to assert that the symptoms of schizophrenic patients are manifestations of a diseased mind, as if "mind" were a palpable entity rather than a theoretical construct (Ryle, 1949; Szasz, 1961).

Much acrimony has been generated over the disease model of mental illness, and it is not my intention to recreate the debate once again. But one wonders if the problem lies less in properly construing schizophrenia than in properly construing disease. The truth is that the doctrine of specific etiology current in Kraepelin's day is no longer adequate even for most medical disorders. Not only is it now appreciated that similar etiological agents can produce different clinical effects and that similar syndromes can be produced by different etiologies, but it is clear that people become ill and seek treatment for numerous and complexly interacting reasons. A given disorder may be the result of a variety of factors from many levels of observation, including genetic predispositions, pathogenic agents, biochemical and anatomical derangements, the number and degree of stressful events in the patient's life, his or her personality and coping style, and the degree of social support forthcoming. There is in fact no single contemporary model of disease that accounts for the manifold ills for which people seek professional help. Thus to assert that schizophrenic symptoms represent disease without at the same time specifying relevant predisposing and precipitating factors is in fact little more than a cover for ignorance. It says only that schizophrenic symptoms are of complex etiology, are generally distressful to those afflicted, and often require professional intervention or assistance. The controversy concerning the disease model of schizophrenia thus appears curious in the absence of any contemporary doctrine of disease. Or put slightly differently, contemporary concepts of disease are so broad as to exclude few if any views as to the nature and etiology of schizophrenia (Engel, 1977; Rabkin & Struening, 1976).

Demonstrations of the inadequacies of psychiatric diagnosis have also undoubtedly contributed to the theoretical difficulties surrounding the concept of schizophrenia. In many clinics and hospitals the label "schizophrenia" indicates no more than the staff's belief that the patient is severely disturbed. In his debunking style, Thomas Szasz (1976), the noted critic of current mental health practice, characterizes schizophrenia as an ill-defined, open-ended concept that is "often applied to almost any kind of behavior of which the speaker disapproves [p. 87]." The professional indifference to precise description that lies behind Szasz' comment in fact finds theoretical justification in the so-called unitarian school of psychiatry, which subscribes to the distinction between mental health and illness but regards various symptomatic expressions as points on an underlying continuum of severity. The contemporary American psychiatrist, Karl Menninger, proposes scrapping psychiatric nosology in favor of categorizing patients into no more than five "levels of dyscontrol." This echoes the aphorism of the nineteenth-century German psychiatrist Heinrich Neumann: "There is only one kind of mental disorder; we call it insanity" (Menninger, 1963).

Yet poor diagnostic reliability has been more of a problem in North America than in Europe, where a strong tradition of descriptive psychiatry has always existed. A telling study found that New York hospitals and clinics used the diagnosis of schizophrenia twice as frequently as their counterparts in London, in spite of the fact that the actual range of the behavior shown by the two populations of patients was virtually identical. The chief source of the difference was the disposition of the New York institutions to diagnose as schizophrenic many patients who would be considered manic-depressive in London (Gurland, Fleiss, Cooper, Sharpe, Kendell, & Roberts, 1970). Case conferences in North American institutions are often more notable for their flight into speculative etiological formulations than for their attention to the details of the patient's clinical picture (Meehl, 1973). But if professional indifference underlies diagnostic disagreement, it is hardly appropriate to take the observed disagreement as evidence for the impossibility of erecting rigorous diagnostic definitions.

Results from the use of such devices as the Present State Examination (PSE) and the Inpatient Multidimensional Psychiatric Scale (IMPS) are more positive: When conditions of observation are standardized, when diagnosticians are trained in the appropriate application of terms, and when observations are guided by a standard interview schedule, then perfectly adequate levels of interobserver agreement are possible at the level of symptom definition. Furthermore, research with such devices as seen in the WHO study of schizophrenia (Table 1.2) and the Lorr et al. factor analysis of IMPS ratings (Table 1.3) indicates that symptoms cohere in much the way that Kraepelin and Bleuler originally defined schizophrenia. However, there is little evidence that Kraepelin's classical subforms of schizophrenia exist as separate entities, to say nothing of the 11 types found in the DSM-II. On the other hand, distinctions between paranoid and nonparanoid forms and between process and reactive forms have proven to be valid ways of reducing the heterogeneity of the broader category.

A final cause of skepticism regarding the concept of schizophrenia is that the first detailed descriptions of the disorder appear abruptly in the work of Kraepelin and Bleuler at the end of the nineteenth century, when they systematized and elaborated fragments and partial descriptions that began appearing with increasing frequency at mid-century. Previous eras had not recognized anything like schizophrenia as a clinical entity. Menninger's (1963) collection of ancient and modern psychiatric nosologies shows clearly that disorders such as mania, depression, hysteria, and senile dementia have been known since antiquity and were described more or less as they are today by succeeding generations of scholars and physicians. But with the exception of acute toxic psychoses, no condition resembling what we today know as schizophrenia appears in these sources. This is indeed an historical enigma, which has not been fully dealt with in the scholarly literature on schizophrenia.

Given the perfectly valid descriptions of other disorders in earlier eras, it is not likely that the lapse can be attributed to the relatively unevolved state of prenineteenth-century psychiatry. Seen in the context of poor diagnostic reliability and an equivocal model of mental disease, however, these facts are more grist for the skeptic's mill. They can be used to further implicate the concept of schizophrenia as a myth, an invention of a profession striving for scientific respectability by elaborating distinctions without differences.

But another interpretation is possible. It is not beyond reason to suggest that schizophrenia did not in fact exist before the mid-nineteenth century, or was so infrequent as to be lumped with allied categories seen as "mania" or "dementia" when it did appear clinically. There is no necessary reason to assume that schizophrenia must be an ancient psychological disability. Other psychological disorders have changed in apparent frequency in modern times. The hysterical neuroses upon which Freud built his reputation are said to be fairly rare today; cases of "executive ulcers" appear to have peaked in the 1950s and to have mysteriously declined since (Arie, 1970). Thus it is quite possible that schizophrenia is a disorder of contemporary civilization, particularly in the West, where it was first described. Although historical research has scarcely even investigated this intriguing hypothesis, supporting evidence could provide important clues to questions of etiology.

CASE EXAMPLES[1]

These cases are drawn from a larger number provided by May (1968). All were first admissions to a state mental hospital judged to fall within the average range of prognosis for schizophrenia (i.e., neither excellent nor very poor treatment risks).

44-Year-Old American-Born Female of Japanese Descent

She was committed involuntarily to the hospital after she was found standing by a gas stove with the gas on, unlighted. Before her present illness she had been a happy, hardworking, energetic person, employed full time in a semiskilled occupation in addition to looking after her family of three

---

[1]From: May, P. R. A. *Treatment of schizophrenia.* New York: Science House, 1968.

children. Five weeks before admission she began to slow up and to complain of fatigue, exhaustion and headaches; a week later she started to neglect her household duties. Two to three weeks before admission she knelt and prayed in a corner for several hours, saying that someone was testing her brain and wanted to kill her. From then on she became rapidly worse, talked incessantly in a rambling nonsensical fashion and locked the house with the shades drawn, not permitting anyone to enter or to leave. She said she heard voices and complained that she was being gassed. Admitted to the hospital, she denied that she was in any way ill and demanded to be released instantly. She was untidy, depressed, uncommunicative, panicky, negativistic and resistive, stayed in bed and spat out any food that was given to her.

A 32-Year-Old White Single Male

He had always been lonely and isolated, but he first became aware that he was anxious around people fifteen years previously when he was in the army. However, the first sign of overt psychosis was nine years before admission, when he started to think that he was being (unjustly) suspected of being a homosexual and that he was being subtly kidded and humiliated; somewhere around this time he had a vivid hallucination of a fist coming at his face. During the following years wherever he went he felt that humiliating homosexual references were made about him, so that by six years before admission he was restless, unable to concentrate and always on the go. Although he did manage to complete some years of college, he was never able to do more than a little part-time work and was never able to support himself. One month before admission he got the idea that he was being questioned as an informer for the police and thought that people were looking at him, talking about him and making obscene gestures. Voices followed him in the streets, cars with prominent headlights trailed him and he suspected that the FBI was involved. He became frightened and unable to sleep, thought of suicide and then decided to ask for help. On the ward he was quiet, soft-spoken, emotionally unresponsive and seclusive.

A 23-Year-Old White Married Female

Her illness had started seven days before admission when she suddenly threatened to jump out of a window at work. Although she had always been quiet and kept things to herself, she had up to that time seemed entirely well. She had done satisfactorily at school and at work; according to her parents and her husband, the marriage was a success. No one was able to establish contact with her during the evaluation except that she would sometimes repeat automatically whatever the person said (echolalia). Her condition alternated between mutism and periods of excitement in which she would run at the wall and bang her head or attempt to injure herself in some other way. It was impossible to keep her clothing on; she was uncooperative, and had to be spoon fed; attempted to choke several nurses; almost killed the ward cat by choking it into unconsciousness.

A 21-Year-Old White Single Male

Although described as shy, frightened and quiet, enjoying music and art, he had been rebellious and in difficulty since age thirteen and had been placed in Juvenile Hall on several occasions. For a month before admission he had been behaving strangely and was finally brought to the hospital after the police found him walking down the white line in the center of a busy street. He informed them that he had received a radio message that Christ was coming and that his name had been called. On admission he was incoherent and in a state of panic: He felt that everyone was against him and trying to kill him, that there was a plot to control his mind and to make him do things by brainwashing. After the first week in the hospital he was able to put on a facade of normality, denying that he was ill and covering up his delusions. In brief contacts he appeared pleasant, talkative, likable and friendly, well-dressed, coherent and relevant, asserting that all he needed was a short rest. More extended interviewing revealed that he thought that people did not like him, that someone was trying to kill him because he was Christ, that this was not a hospital, that he could trust no one, that people were trying to control him and make him do things. Under pressure he would become angry and talk about visions and doing battle for humanity.

2 The Schizophrenic Psychosis

A hundred of the best shrinks in the world working day and night for years would be doing well to scratch the surface of a day in anyone's life. Schizophrenia multiplies the problem manyfold...

—Mark Vonnegut (1976)

Kraepelin's concept of *dementia praecox* was rooted in the nineteenth-century psychiatric doctrine that acute insanity was often a precursor to a chronic state of mental deterioration, or dementia (Menninger, 1963). The term *dementia praecox* was thus intended to summarize the course and outcome of the disorder rather than its active phase. Bleuler's "schizophrenia," in contrast, attempted to convey the essence of the active phase—the psychosis—while remaining noncommittal as to course and outcome. Bleuler's descriptive strategy was the sounder insofar as we now realize that an initial schizophrenic breakdown may be followed by a variety of courses and outcomes. Patients of the reactive or schizophreniform type may experience but one relatively brief psychotic episode and remit with few sequelae, if any. Other patients may experience a series of psychotic episodes over several years with varying degrees of restitution between episodes. Deterioration in the sense of failure to regain premorbid levels of functioning following a series of such episodes is not uncommon. Yet deterioration is not an inevitable outcome, and aggressive treatment may result in good recovery even after a history of psychotic episodes (M. Bleuler, 1970).

The single feature common to this variety of course and outcome is the episodic psychosis; this altered state of consciousness is the subject of the present chapter. Illustrations are drawn primarily from accounts written by former schizophrenic patients who have passed through this state. The exposition follows the lead of several excellent works: Bowers' (1974) structural analysis of psychotic states, Reed's (1972) remarkable *Psychology of Anomalous Experience,* Freedman's (1974) and Landis and Mettler's (1964) collations of first-person accounts of schizophrenia, and McGhie and Chapman's (1961) pioneering work on the phenomenology of the early stages of the psychosis.

Bowers (1974) divides the development of the schizophrenic psychosis into an early stage of heightened awareness, in which patients undergo an alteration of normal modes of experiencing themselves, others, and the world, and a later stage of self-fragmentation, in which they experience a loss of the unity and cohesiveness of the self as the executor of perception, thought, and action. The present discussion expands this scheme by dividing Bowers' first stage into an early phase of "Perceptual–Affective Enhancement" and a quickly supervening phase of "Loss of Volitional Control" over perception and ideation. Bowers' second stage of self-fragmentation is analogous to the present section headed "Dissociative Experiences." Because delusions occur throughout these three phases, they are treated under a separate final heading. The chapter concludes with a discussion of the problem of selective attention in schizophrenia, an issue arising from experimental studies of schizophrenic patients and happily consistent with many aspects of the phenomenology of the schizophrenic psychosis.

A word of caution is in order. The following picture is a composite of the experiences of many different individuals and is not necessarily characteristic of all patients. Indeed, it is unlikely that any given patient will show all of the elements of this idealized scheme (Freedman & Chapman, 1973). A taxonomy of the forms that the schizophrenic psychosis may take in different patients remains a challenge for the future.

PERCEPTUAL–AFFECTIVE ENHANCEMENT

For many patients, the onset of the schizophrenic psychosis is marked by a mood shift in the direction of mild to moderate euphoria. A sense of having been constrained, inhibited, or blocked is replaced by a sense of efficacy and well-being. This welcomed change is described variously by different commentators, but the major theme is that of a burden having been lifted, allowing for a fuller appreciation of the rich texture of experience. An anonymous report by a former patient puts it as follows:

> I experienced a sudden feeling of creative release before my illness, was convinced that I was rapidly attaining the height of my intellectual powers, and that for the first time in my life, I would be able to function up to the level of my ability in this direction [Anonymous, 1955, p. 678].

A frequently cited account by Norma MacDonald (1960) employs the metaphor of awakening from sleep to convey the contrast between her new-found expansiveness and her formerly more restricted range of interests:

What I do want to explain, if I can, is the exaggerated state of awareness in which I lived before, during, and after my acute illness. At first it was as if parts of my brain "awoke" which had been dormant, and I became interested in a wide assortment of people, events, places, and ideas which normally would make no impression on me [p. 218].

The heightened state of awareness in the early stages of the psychosis is most frequently assessed by patients in terms of an enhancement of both perceptual and affective reactions. The following account by Mark Vonnegut (1976) indicates the manner in which these two modes of reaction often coalesce into a more general state of exhilaration:

Things were still unbearably beautiful. I got this giddiness in my stomach and walked around completely overwhelmed by the incredible loveliness of the trees and the sky and the moss, infinitely delicate worlds within worlds, and people's faces and the way they moved and my own body and what a perfect machine it was and the stove and the floors and our funky house. And everything fit together so perfectly. It wasn't just in the way things looked. It was in the sounds of the wind and the stream and the way things felt, the ground gushing ever so slightly under my feet, the way everything smelled. It's everywhere, it's everywhere. And it keeps getting better and better. And I think to myself, look Ma, no drugs [p. 95].

On the other hand, perceptual and affective enhancement are clearly separable in the experience of other witnesses. John Custance (cited in Bowers, 1974) described with scientific detachment his experience of perceptual heightening in visual, tactile, and auditory modes:

If I am to judge by my own experience, this "heightened state of reality" consists of a considerable number of related sensations, the net result of which is that the outer world makes a much more vivid and intense impression on me than usual.... The first thing I note is the peculiar appearance of the lights.... They are not exactly brighter, but deeper, more intense, perhaps a trifle more ruddy than usual. Certainly my sense of touch is heightened.... My hearing appears to be more sensitive, and I am able to take in without disturbance or distraction many different sound impressions at the same time [p. 32].

Bowers (1974) presents two thumbnail cases that illustrate the case of affective heightening without apparent accompanying perceptual enhancement in early schizophrenia. The two cases are also interesting in that the affective shift follows directly on a period of despair over unresolved personal difficulties. It is as if the shift into psychosis were precipitated by a failure to master an important life crisis:

> A 21-year-old college student, concerned about his parents and about a love affair, became guilt ridden after a sexual experience with his girlfriend. Soon thereafter, he felt that his life was completely changed. He felt a sense of mission in the world which he now saw "as a completely wonderful place" and stated, "I began to experience goodness and love for the first time." Life for him took on an intense benevolent quality which he had never felt before. He talked with friends fervently about the "new life," and about the way he could now care for and understand people [pp. 26–27].

> A 38-year-old music teacher, depressed by debts and family problems and concerned with a very real national crisis, began to feel that life was taking on a new emotional intensity.... He felt close to nature, emphatically understanding human and subhuman life. A few nights later he described a sensation that "God actually touched my heart. The next day was horror and ecstasy. I began to feel that I might be the agent of some spiritual reawakening. The emotional intensity of the experience became overpowering" [p. 26].

By themselves these prodromal signs of emerging psychosis are not specifically schizophrenic. Indeed, one is struck by the similarity of many of these reports to commonly experienced states. The mildly euphoric quality of the accounts by Anonymous (1955) and by MacDonald (1960) are much like descriptions of happiness: Inhibitions are dissolved, senses are sharpened, and there is an opening out to the world and to others. The glowing account by Vonnegut (1976) might, in another context, be taken as the testimony of a young man in love; Bowers' (1974) first thumbnail case makes this analogy explicit. The difference between these more familiar states and incipient schizophrenia is not in their phenomenological quality but in their developmental course. Being happy or "in love" are conditions one moves in and out of from a base of ordinary waking consciousness; the psychologically similar state of the schizophrenic patient is merely a prologue to more profound alterations in consciousness that are properly called *psychotic*. The sense of release and broadened awareness described previously gives way, like an accelerating electric motor, to further disinhibition and an increasing sense of loss of volitional control over external sensory input and internal thought sequences.

LOSS OF VOLITIONAL CONTROL

Supervening rapidly upon the prodromal stage of the schizophrenic psychosis is a psychologically distinct phase of development in which the patient becomes increasingly perplexed because of an inability to control attention and ideation. If the former stage is experienced as a pleasurable broadening of awareness, this second stage is experienced as threatening because of a flooding of consciousness by external and internal stimuli. Although phenomenologically distinct, these two phases may in fact reflect only quantitative differences along a continuum of disinhibition. The mild euphoria correlated with disinhibition from habitual perceptual and affective responses in the first phase escalates to anxiety in the second as attention is involuntarily directed to a plethora of normally inhibited sensations, images, and thoughts.

Freedman and Chapman (1973) find that an inability to concentrate is a frequent complaint among psychiatric patients in general. However, nonschizophrenic patients differ from schizophrenic patients in character-izing the problem. Whereas the former tend to see it as secondary to a preoccupation with personal problems or daydreams, schizophrenic patients more often report an impairment in their ability to focus attention selectively on relevant stimuli or thoughts and to screen out or ignore irrelevant stimuli and thoughts.

This impairment is clearly seen in a series of now classic interviews with early schizophrenic patients reported by McGhie and Chapman (1961). A major problem reported by McGhie and Chapman's patients is a chronic inability to concentrate because of distraction from irrelevant external stimuli:

Patient 13. My concentration is very poor. I jump from one thing to another. If I am talking to someone they only need to cross their legs or scratch their heads and I am distracted and forget what I was saying. I think I could concentrate better with my eyes shut [p. 104].

Patient 2. I can't concentrate. It's diversion of attention that troubles me. I am picking up different conversations. It's like being a transmitter. The sounds are coming through to me but I feel my mind cannot cope with everything. It's difficult to concentrate on any one sound. It's like trying to do two or three different things at the one time [p. 104].

Increased distractability also appears to underlie similar complaints of a loss of intelligibility of speech sequences, especially if more than one person is talking or if the speaker uses complex constructions (McGhie & Chapman, 1961):

Patient 18. If there are three or four people talking at one time I can't take it in. I would not be able to hear what they were saying properly and I would get the one mixed up with the other. To me it's just like a babble—a noise that goes right through me [p. 105].

Patient 19. I can concentrate quite well on what people are saying if they talk simply. It's when they go into long sentences that I lose the meanings. It just becomes a lot of words that I would need to string together to make sense [p. 106].

Even more disconcerting is an inability to channel ideation in a sequential manner. Instead, patient's thoughts "wander off" as a given idea branches uncontrollably into a series of associated ideas, all of which clamor for conscious awareness (McGhie & Chapman, 1961):

Patient 9. My thoughts get all jumbled up. I start thinking or talking about something but I never get there. Instead I wander off in the wrong direction and get caught up with all sorts of different things that may be connected with the things I want to say but in a way I can't explain. People listening to me get more lost than I do [p. 108].

Patient 20. My trouble is that I've got too many thoughts. You might think about something—let's say that ashtray—and just think, oh yes, that's for putting my cigarette in, but I would think of it and then I would think of a dozen different things connected with it at the same time [p. 108].

Patient 18. I just can't concentrate on anything. There's too much going on in my head and I can't sort it out. My thoughts wander around in circles without getting anywhere. I try to read even a paragraph in a book but it takes me ages because each bit I read starts me thinking in ten different directions at once [p. 109].

This escalating loss of control over perception and ideation is often the basis of patients' complaints of "going crazy." The anxiety-provoking nature of such experiences is conveyed in these comments by two of McGhie and Chapman's (1961) patients:

Patient 2. You have no idea what it's like, Doctor. You would have to experience it yourself. When you feel yourself going into a sort of coma you get really scared. It's like waiting on a landing craft going into D-day. You tremble and panic. It's like no other fear on earth [p. 109].

Patient 7. When I am walking along the street it comes on me. I start to think deeply and I start to go into a trance. I think so deep that I almost get out of this world. Then you get frightened that you are going to get into a jam and lose yourself. That's when I get worried and excited [p. 109].

DISSOCIATIVE EXPERIENCES

The experiential shifts so far considered are characteristic of "early" schizophrenia, or, more precisely, the incipient stages of an acute schizophrenic psychosis. Because their appearance often antedates hospitalization, they have not been prominent features of classical descriptions of schizophrenia. Nor is it always possible to distinguish these early states of consciousness as specifically schizophrenic. Similar anomalous experiences may also occur in the manic excitement of an affective psychosis and, for that matter, in various drug-induced conditions. On the other hand, the particular dissociative experiences considered in the following have been central to clinical descriptions of schizophrenic psychosis. As we have already seen, the term "schizo-phrenic" was in fact coined by Bleuler to denote the splitting, fragmentation, or dissociation of normally integrated psychological processes, which he regarded as the core of the disorder.

Examples of schizophrenic dissociations are considered under several headings: (1) derealization, in which events external to the self are experienced as unreal or meaningless; (2) depersonalization, in which the sense of integrity or ownership of one's body is impaired; (3) thought dissociations, in which personal control over one's thoughts is impaired or lost in various ways; (4) hallucinations, in which internal images are perceived as external to the self; and (5) language disorder, in which the normally spontaneous flow of speech or writing is fragmented by involuntary verbal intrusions.

We have seen that the perceptual–affective enhancement of the early phases of the psychosis is not markedly different from normally occurring euphoric states and that even the early impairment of volitional control over perception and ideation is not unique to schizophrenia. Similarly, dissociative experiences also occur in other conditions. Under life-threatening conditions such as military combat or severe injury, psychiatrically normal individuals may undergo a dissociative phenomenon in which the self is experienced as separate from the body, a disinterested observer of the tribulations of the corporate "me." In hysterical neurosis, patients may also lose a sense of ownership of specific sensory or motor functions or, in cases of hysterical amnesia, memories of past events. Yet these dissociations are of a quite different quality from those of the schizophrenic patient. Normal or neurotic dissociations are usually interpretable as defensive attempts to master severe anxiety, at the cost of temporary or relatively minor loss of function. Throughout, a sense of self-identity remains intact. Schizophrenic dissociations, on the other hand, represent a more profound fracturing of the self. Not only do multiple forms of dissociation occur in any given patient, but they usually involve central aspects of self-identity. A loss of sense of control or ownership of one's body, one's thoughts, one's images, and even one's speech leaves increasingly little out of which to construct a sense of self. The experience of an increasing dissolution of self-identity is the phenomenological core of the schizophrenic psychosis.

Derealization

Freedman (1974) reports that autobiographies by former mental patients often contain descriptions of a "frightening, aphasic-like, diffuse loss of meaning from common words, objects, and people." This phenomenon, technically known as *derealization*, involves a basic dissociation between the self and the surrounding world. The patient's sense of self-identity remains intact, but he or she becomes an isolated observer of a world that has lost its familiarity. Derealization is not a question of altered sensory or perceptual functioning, which remains intact; rather, it involves an impairment of the normally automatic process by which perceptual events are reduced to familiar categories of meaning. Patients are often intensely conscious both of their impaired response to formerly familiar events and of their inability to rectify the situation. This in turn gives rise to secondary interpretations of the derealization experience, which is usually described as bizarre, uncanny, and threatening. An acute awareness of the alienation between the self and the external world is seen in the following two accounts by former schizophrenic patients. The first is from Jane Hillyer's *Reluctantly Told* (1926); the second is by Sechehaye's patient Renée in *Autobiography of a Schizophrenic Girl* (1970):

> I could feel the nurse's fingers, but she didn't seem there, herself. Beyond my reaction to her touch I was unable to project her into my consciousness. I could see her but it made little impression. Everything was like that. I was veiled. It was quiet and restful, but a little wearing after a time. I tried to brush something cobwebby from before me; it would not brush. Sounds came to my ears. They meant little besides just noise. I was unable to translate them into the milkman's cart, the doctor's machine, the ice cream freezer. They were just so many vibrations hitting my ear-drums [p. 51].

> In these disturbing circumstances I sensed again the atmosphere of unreality. During class, in the quiet of the work period, I heard the street noises—a trolley passing, people talking, a horse neighing, a horn sounding, each detached, immovable, separated from its source, without meaning. Around me, the other children, heads bent over their work, were robots or puppets, moved by an invisible mechanism. On the platform, the teacher, too, talking, gesticulating, rising to write on the blackboard, was a grotesque jack-in-the-box. And always this ghastly quiet, broken by outside sounds coming from far away, the implacable sun heating the room, the lifeless immobility [p. 24].

Depersonalization

Derealization may also extend to uncanny dissociations between self and body, in which case the phenomenon is known as *depersonalization*. This may involve delusional interpretations of discrete body areas, as in MacDonald's (1960) sense that her brain "became sore with a real physical soreness, as if it had been rubbed with sandpaper until it was raw," or as in Reed's (1972) description of a delusion known as "koro" in Far Eastern Chinese communities in which the patient is convinced that his or her genitalia are shrinking and will completely disappear. A number of patient accounts cited by Freedman (1974) focus on anomalous perceptions of the head and brain (e.g., that the brain "felt like a nut parched by hot sand," or that the head felt as if it were "filled with sawdust"). Another patient reported (Freedman, 1974): "I have at times the feeling of lines going through my head that were Indian lines. Sometimes they go to my eyes, coiling around in a not particularly unpleasant sensation. They feel about the size of a heavy cord [p. 339]."

In the extreme, the entire body is experienced as unreal, altered, or mechanical and is viewed as an alien entity by the perceiving self. Laura Jefferson (1947) wrote while hospitalized:

> Presently I shall wake up and be oh so relieved—to know that this has all been a dream. Then it will be only funny—and I can recall with horror the odd sensation I had on finding a crazy woman had moved into my body.... I shall shortly awake and remember how frail my strength felt and how helpless I was in trying to budge her gross and unseemly proportion.... She is not real —she is not I—I never saw her before I dreamed her [pp. 19–20].

Dissociation between self and body may occur in nonschizophrenic persons, especially under conditions of severe threat to self-esteem or to life and limb. In such cases, however, the phenomenological experience is qualitatively different from the schizophrenic experience. In typical nonschizophrenic depersonalization, the observing self experiences an embodied "me" as if from a distance. Although the experience is uncanny, it involves no particular distortion or alteration of the body image. For example, soldiers in the midst of combat may report that they "watched themselves" firing upon the enemy or taking evasive action. Some authors question whether this not uncommon experience should in fact be labeled depersonalization at all (Reed, 1972).

Among schizophrenic patients, depersonalization usually takes a more delusional form. Rather than an experience of physical separation between self and body, the schizophrenic patient tends to experience the body as a mere lifeless shell in which the self is contained, if not actually trapped. The phenomenology of schizophrenic depersonalization is sufficiently specific that some commentators see it as central to the altered state in schizophrenia. In his brilliant essay, *The Divided Self* (1960), R. D. Laing sees a chronic split between a "true" inner self and a "false" outer self as a precondition for later deterioration into frank psychosis. For Laing, the prepsychotic "schizoid" individual carries on a dual existence in which the disembodied inner self is split off from the actions, sensations, and perceptions of the embodied "false" self so that the true inner self is effectively excluded from direct participation with others and with the external world. He represents this schematically as follows:

Normal condition: (self/body) ↔ other
Schizoid condition: self ↔ (body/other)

Instead of feeling vital and engaged, the schizoid inner self exists as if in a vacuum; the behavior and perceptions of the embodied outer self are thus experienced as alien, unreal, and meaningless.

The following three accounts from among many collected by Mendel (1974) in his therapeutic encounters with schizophrenic patients carries some sense of the Laingian view of the schizoid existence:

> Nothing is me, nothing is mine.
> I don't live in my body.
> I don't live anywhere.
> My body just is.
> It is just like the strings are pulled
> And it is moved automatically
> But I haven't anything in it [p. 109].

> I feel like a thin, empty shell. There is a huge gaping hole in my body. No matter how much I pour into it, it never fills, it never gets any stronger. It is like an eggshell which is empty [p. 110].

> I look at my arms and they aren't mine. They move without my direction. Somebody else moves them. All my limbs and my thoughts are attached to strings and these strings are pulled by others. I know not who. I have no control. I don't live in me. The outside and I are all the same [p. 111].

Thought Dissociation

The sense of awakening and release characteristic of the onset of a psychotic episode is often accompanied by rushes of great energy, including an acceleration of thought processes. Mark Vonnegut (1976) reported that it was as if he were "thinking about a million miles an hour... cramming whole lifetimes of thinking in between sips of coffee":

> It's like I've discovered some sort of shorthand. I've got these little microdots of thinking. I just go "dit" and I've got years of thinking and then "dit" and another big hunk. Fitting it all together more and more. And it's not just my thinking, I'm tapping huge pools of other people's thinking. "Dit" and I've got the whole Bible. "Dit," all of Freud and then "dit" and the relationship of Freud and the Bible in one "dit." It goes forever in both directions. I'm getting closer and closer to having it all in one "dit" [p. 119].

As the psychosis progresses, however, a phenomenologically distinct phase may supervene in which the sense of personal control over one's thoughts is lost. Freedman (1974) cites the pertinent example of a patient who felt as if his mind led a separate existence:

My mind seemed almost to have a life and direction of its own. . . . I became increasingly aware of the separate life of my own mind. Without informing me of its intentions, without thinking, which seemed to me to be the means by which. . . my mind allowed me to participate. I found myself doing things impulsively, thinking things (except that it was not thinking in the usual sense, there was no process of conscious deliberate thought) [pp. 335–336].

The impression that one's mind is not one's own may expand into the delusional belief that one's thoughts are controlled by some external agency, a phenomenon technically known as "alienation of thought " (Reed, 1972). The following example, cited by Landis and Mettler (1964), is drawn from a letter written by a former patient to his psychiatrist:

On Saturday afternoon I thought you thought I ought to play croquet (I was thirty miles away), so I began, but could not go on, because it seemed as if you were definitely forbidding me to do so *by influencing my mind*. . . . I often see your thought as I go about, but if it is not in accord with what you have bidden me to do, it does not stop or confuse me. But this time it was different, and I *could* not go on. Please tell me if I did right to stop [p. 161].

Other patients may experience a loss of voluntary control over thinking in somewhat different ways. In "thought blocking," the patient suffers from an aphasic-like inability to recall words in a train of thought or speech. The patient may complain that an ongoing sequence of thoughts has been unaccountably interrupted as if siphoned off by forces beyond his control (Reed, 1972). The delusion of "thought broadcasting" is that one's private thoughts are transformed into sounds and transmitted to others. Some patients may react with embarrassment, whereas others experience a sort of wonderment at their new-found telepathic communication. For example, a patient wrote as follows (Landis & Mettler, 1964):

My difficulty is an outgo of my silent thought. It goes as it comes. I may think whatever I please, but whatever I do think goes as it comes. I suppose the constant irritation and annoyance they have kept up around me has affected the tension of nerve, so that unlike others who have the same phenomenal power, it goes as rapidly as my mind thinks. I have but to think a thought and it reaches other minds in sound without an effort on my part, and is sounded for a distance, I suppose, of two or three miles [pp. 160–161].

Hallucinations

A hallucination is conventionally defined as a "false perception," a definition that is also conventionally regarded as inadequate because of its ambiguity. If by "false perception" is meant an atypical interpretation of some external event, then the term "illusion" is more precise. An illusion is a misapprehension of a person or object due to incomplete information. For example, one may see a distant figure as an acquaintance but, on closer inspection, realize that the person is in fact a stranger. In the Müller–Lyer illusion, two lines of the same measurable length are interpreted by most people as of different lengths because of the distorting context in which they are embedded.

If, on the other hand, we take "false perception" to mean that some other psychological phenomenon is falsely interpreted as a perceptual event, we are closer to the clinical meaning of hallucination. An important distinction between an illusory perception and a hallucination is that the former involves a misperception of available stimulus information, whereas the latter is a perceptual-like event that occurs in the absence of a specific external stimulus. The perception of a whistling radiator as a disembodied voice is an auditory illusion; hearing voices in the absence of minimally adequate auditory stimulation is an auditory hallucination. Reed (1972) suggests that hallucinations are better regarded as strong internal images rather than as perceptions.

This suggestion is consistent with the layman's tendency to dismiss hallucinations as "figments of the imagination." In this view, hallucinations are akin to such everyday occurrences as carrying a tune in one's head, imagining the face of an old friend, or recalling in the dead of winter the sensation of a summer breeze. The reason that imagery is common and hallucination pathological resides primarily in the loss of a sense of personal control over the latter. Whereas one may self-consciously and voluntarily summon up images of past experience, the schizophrenic patient experiences hallucinations as external independent events. And it is this quality of foreignness that gives hallucinations the phenomenological status of perceptions of the external world. As a former schizophrenic patient wrote of his hallucinatory experience (Lang, 1939):

> If there is anything that I can say with certainty concerning the problem of hallucinations, it is that hallucinations are not the product of the activity of the conscious self, of the experiencing individual. The conscious self acts merely as a spectator. It does not anticipate; it does not initiate; it does not control the hallucinations. To the conscious self, hallucinations come as phenomena which it experiences. . . . At the time of their incidence, the self cannot distinguish them from normal sensory stimuli except through the presence of clues in the surrounding situation which indicates such separate identity. They reach it as already organized sensory configurations [p. 423].

Hallucinations may be associated with any of the sensory modalities— visual, auditory, olfactory, gustatory, or tactile. Intermodal mixing may also occur, as in a complex visual–auditory hallucination of people talking. Hallucinations are not, of course, specific to schizophrenia but may also occur in many other conditions, especially organic impairments, senile psychosis, alcohol and other drug intoxications, and psychotic reactions to toxic substances. Even so, auditory hallucinations are often diagnostic bell-ringers for schizophrenia, because they occur frequently in such cases and relatively infrequently in other conditions. In the interest of brevity, the following examples are limited to auditory hallucinations among schizophrenic patients.

A particularly vivid auditory hallucination occurred to L. M. Jayson (cited in Landis & Mettler, 1964) while he was sunbathing at the shore:

> Seated on a steamer chair on the boardwalk of Coney Island, I heard the voice for the first time. It was, I remember distinctly, a rough, deep bass voice that did not belong to my brother who was sitting quietly in the chair next to mine, nor to the middle-aged gentleman with whom I'd just picked up a talking acquaintance. It was a voice without any body at all. But it was as positive and persistent as any voice I had ever heard. It said slowly, "Jayson, you are worthless. You've never been useful, and you've never been any good." I shook my head, unbelievingly, trying to drive out the sound of the words, and as if I had heard nothing, continued to talk with my neighbor. He was nodding sympathetically, and I remember thinking it funny how blurred and misty his face looked—as if it were miles off—when suddenly, clearer, deeper, and even louder than before, the deep voice came at me again, right in my ear this time, and getting me tight and shivery inside. "Larry Jayson, I told you before you weren't any good. Why are you sitting here making believe you're as good as any one else when you're not? Whom are you fooling? You're no good," the voice said slowly, in the same deep tones. "You've never been any good or use on earth. There is the ocean. You might just as well drown yourself. Just walk in, and keep walking." As soon as the voice was through, I knew, by its cold command, I had to obey it [p. 36].

Jayson walked into the water beyond his depth and was restrained only with difficulty by lifeguards.

The first experience of auditory hallucinations in schizophrenic patients is not usually as abrupt and intense, however. As Mark Vonnegut (1976) recounts, they may be muted or incoherent at first, requiring some effort to "tune in":

> At first I'd had to strain to hear or understand them. They were soft and working with some pretty tricky codes. Snap–crackle–pops, the sound of the wind with blinking lights and horns for punctuation. I broke the code and somehow was able to internalize it to the point where it was just like hearing words. In the beginning it seemed mostly nonsense, but as things went along they made more and more sense. Once you hear the voices, you realize they've always been there. It's just a matter of being tuned to them [pp. 136–137].

Patients will also differ in the extent to which the hallucinations are externalized. Whereas Jayson clearly experienced his hallucinations as disembodied voices, others may speak of "voices in the head." A nineteenth-century account (cited in Landis & Mettler, 1964) is notable for the localization imposed on hallucinations of different qualities:

> The voices ... were mostly heard in my head, though I often heard them in the air, or in different parts of the room. Every voice was different, and each beautiful, and, generally, speaking or singing in a different tone and measure, and resembling those of relations or friends. There appeared to be many in my head, I should say upwards of fourteen. I divide them, as they styled themselves, or one another, into voices of contrition and voices of joy and honour. Those of contrition were, I think all without any exception, on the left temple and forehead; those of joy and honour on the right temple and forehead; but on each side of the head, as it were over the middle of the eyebrow, two spirits seemed always to sing or speak to a measure more quick and more flaunty than the others [p. 122].

Language Disorder

So-called "schizophrenic speech" is not an inevitable accompaniment of the schizophrenic psychosis, nor does it characterize all of the utterances of those patients in whom it does occur. Although not universal, it is unquestionably pathognomic of schizophrenia and, in addition, is clinically regarded as a sign of rather severe deterioration. Clinicians have little difficulty agreeing on the schizophrenic nature of a given speech sequence (or written passage) and on its degree of clinical severity (Maher, 1966).

The following two examples (the first is from Bowers, 1974; the second is from Maher, 1966) are from written documents spontaneously produced by schizophrenic patients. Characteristically, both begin rather auspiciously but quickly deteriorate into a barely comprehensible flow of words with seemingly little direction or communicative intent. Although neither is properly punctuated, this lapse is idiosyncratic and not necessarily typical of such sequences:

I don't think there is anything incomprehensible about this

> You go in and out deeper and shallower and you come back you always come back it's like a drug but without the excuse of being drugged drugs do do that they make you think you're going to know yourself and then make you forget yourself so they promise and then they take away promise and take away someone promised and took her the bitch Laura my mother my mother promised to love me and then took it away and gave it back to him and kept doing that taking it away and giving it back to him you can't trust them they're not to be trusted they give and then take back and they make you cry and leave you frightened and crying and watching from your crib as they walk away walk away back to their room bedroom her room [pp. 69–70].

If things turn by rotation of agriculture or levels in regards and "timed" to everything; I am re-fering to a previous document when I made some remarks that were facts also tested and there is another that concerns my daughter she has a lobed bottom right ear, her name being Mary Lou.... Much of abstraction has been left unsaid and undone in this product/milk syrup, and others, due to economics, differentials, subsidies, bankruptcy, tools, buildings, bonds, national stocks, foundation craps, weather, trades, government in levels of breakages and fuses in electronics too all formerly "stated" not necessarily factuated [p. 395].

Note that both passages have the mystifying quality of the so-called "double-talk" often used by entertainers for sake of amusement. Double-talk relies for its effect on being recognizable as speech yet at the same time being incomprehensible. More formerly, we might say that schizophrenic speech, like double-talk, is syntactically correct but semantically bizarre or deviant. Given a few appropriate punctuation points, the individual phrases in the two examples conform adequately to the grammatical rules of spoken discourse: Subjects, objects, verbs, and modifiers occur in recognizable forms. Yet the meaning of individual phrases and the entire passage is obscure and confusing. The passages can be described as allusive, tangential, and perseverative and without apparent focus, direction, or closure.

One theory of schizophrenic language holds that patients indeed engage in double-talk or, more precisely, that they speak in a linguistic code designed to obscure underlying communicative intent. R. D. Laing (1960) illustrates the code hypothesis by quoting a passage from a lecture by Kraepelin (1905). Kraepelin is addressing an audience of medical students on the signs and symptoms of schizophrenia seen in an 18-year-old patient on display:

The patient sits with his eyes shut, and pays no attention to his surroundings. He does not look up even when he is spoken to, but he answers beginning in a low voice, and gradually screaming louder and louder. When asked where he is, he says, "You want to know that too? I tell you who is being measured and is measured and shall be measured. I know all that, and could tell you, but I do not want to." When asked his name, he screams, "What is your name? What does he shut? He shuts his eyes. What does he hear? He does not understand; he understands not. How? Who? Where? When? What does he mean? When I tell him to look he does not look properly. You there, just look! What is it? What is the matter? Attend; he attends not. I say, what is it, then? Why do you give me no answer? Are you getting impudent again? How can you be so impudent? I'm coming! I'll show you! You don't whore for me. You mustn't be smart either; you're an impudent, lousy fellow, such an impudent, lousy fellow I've never met with. Is he beginning again? You understand nothing at all, nothing at all; nothing at all does he understand" [Laing, 1960, p. 30].

Kraepelin concludes that the patient "has not given us a single piece of useful information. His talk was... only a series of disconnected sentences having no relation whatever to the general situation [Laing, 1960, p. 30]." But,

as Laing wishes to demonstrate, Kraepelin has missed a great deal. The patient seems to be engaged in a parody of Kraepelin's authoritarian manner—"You there, just look! What is it? What is the matter? Attend, he attends not"—coupled with an angry dismissal—"You understand nothing at all, nothing at all; nothing at all does he understand." We might speculate that the patient's cryptic remarks are a means of expressing resentment at being displayed and objectified while at the same time avoiding the likely negative consequences of overtly insulting the great man.

Although brilliantly employed in this instance, the code hypothesis is a rather unsatisfactory general explanation of schizophrenic language. It requires postulating a degree of intentionality to schizophrenic behavior that is difficult to square with our previous examples of involuntary dissociations and feelings of loss of efficacy and self-control. The code hypothesis is also difficult to prove, because each case must be treated idiosyncratically. There obviously can be no single schizophrenic code, but rather different patients must be assumed to design private codes for fulfilling individual needs for disguise. And if a different interpretation is required for each case, no general principle can be sought (Maher, 1968).

Schizophrenic language is often described as autistic because it communicates so poorly. Yet it is not completely random. As already noted, schizophrenic language is rule-bound to the extent that syntax is generally preserved; rather, it is the choice of words within syntactical structures that is peculiar. A degree of predictability of word usage exists in normal language sequences. For example, there is a high probability that the deleted words in the sentence, "Students should attend _____ if they wish to receive a good _____," are "class" and "grade." Less probable choices might be "lectures" and "marks" or even less probable "carefully" and "education." The sentence begins to sound a bit schizophrenic when we insert the very improbable alliterative choices "attentively" and "God." Thus we may describe schizophrenic language as a series of lexical elements having low transitional probabilities between contiguous or near-contiguous elements. The unpredictability of schizophrenic word choice has been demonstrated in a number of studies employing a method known as the *Cloze Procedure*. Samples of schizophrenic and normal language are edited such that every *n*th word is deleted and judges are asked to guess the missing element. The probability of correct choices is routinely higher for normal than for schizophrenic passages (Maher, 1972; Salzinger, 1973).

The low transitional probabilities between elements of schizophrenic speech was exemplified in the previous chapter by Bleuler's patient who described her family members as "Father, Son . . . and Holy Ghost." Bleuler explained such idiosyncratic and bizarre intrusions as the result of a weakening of the associative bonds that normally connect one idea with another in communicable sequence. Yet the phrase "Father, Son, and Holy

Ghost" is a highly probable word sequence in a religious context, so that it would be more accurate to describe his patient's difficulty as an inability to inhibit or suppress a strong but contextually inappropriate association to "Father, Son." Another Bleulerian example is the unintended pun by another patient, "I have many ties with my home. My father wears them around his collar." Here the second phrase represents a strong association to "ties" as an article of clothing, while the use in the first phrase has the weaker meaning of "bonds."

The associative intrusion hypothesis of schizophrenic language proposes that speech sequences are disrupted by the arousal of contextually irrelevant associations to already uttered elements (Chapman & Chapman, 1973; Maher, 1972). The associations per se are not necessarily deviant; it is the patient's inability to edit out semantically nonsensical associations to previous elements that reduces communicability. In this view, the generation of normally communicative speech requires a successful inhibition of potentially disrupting associations to the elements in the utterance. A skillful speaker is one who "chooses" his words carefully, avoids "slips of the tongue," does not ramble, and is not distracted by the minor bypaths of his own thought. The schizophrenic speaker, then, is like the novice writer or lecturer who yields to sloppy construction such as "To appreciate modern art we must appreciate the artistic goals of modern artists," rather than mentally composing a more suitable phrase like "To appreciate modern art we must understand its aesthetic goals." The difference is that the poor word choice of schizophrenic language is, like other schizophrenic dissociations, beyond voluntary control or the reach of instruction.

Maher (1972) presents several examples of different forms of associative intrusions in schizophrenic language in addition to the pun-like confusions already cited. One form is a kind of "clang" or auditory repetition of phonemes, as in:

> The subterfuge and the mistaken planned substitutions for that demanded American action can produce nothing but the general results of negative contention and the impractical results of careless application, the natural results of misplacement, of mistaken purpose and unrighteous position, the impractical serviceabilities of unnecessary contradictions [p. 13].

In this passage, associative repetitions occur to the initial syllables of the following word pairs: subterfuge–substitution; unrighteous–unnecessary; mistaken–misplacement; contention–contradiction.

A second form appears in associative pairings between words or entire clauses in a sentence (Maher, 1972):

> See the Committee about me coming home for Easter my twenty-fourth birthday. I hope all is well at home, how is Father getting on. Never mind, there

is hope, heaven will come, time heals all wounds, Rise again Glorious Greece and come to Hindoo Heavens, the Indian Heavens [p. 13].

Like the examples that began this section, the passage begins auspiciously enough but soon degenerates. The first sentence is an intelligible request to come home for Easter, the patient's birthday. The second sentence is also adequate. However, Easter appears to trigger a series of associations having to do with rising again and with heaven. Further types of associative intrusion ensue. Heaven is repeated three times, Glorious Greece is an unusual alliteration, and Hindoo and Indian appear in close contiguity.

Repetitions of the same word or phrase is a primitive form of association in which the "stimulus" word is its own response. This sort of anomaly is quite frequent in schizophrenic language and is often clinically characterized as "impoverished." The following is a particularly good example (Maher, 1972):

Kindly send it to me at the hospital. Send it to me Joseph Nemo, in care of Joseph Nemo and me who answers by the name of Joseph Nemo will care for it myself. Thanks everlasting and Merry New Year to Metholatum Company for my nose, for my nose, for my nose, for my nose, for my nose, for my nose [p. 14].

DELUSIONS

Delusions form a category of schizophrenic experience separate from any so far discussed. Although they may supervene in the emergent stage of the schizophrenic psychosis, they are phenomenologically distinct from the diffusion of attention and ideation characteristic of this stage. Nor do they really fit into the broad category of dissociative experiences seen in the more advanced form of the psychosis, except insofar as they often have the quality of experiences imposed on the patient as a passive recipient. Delusions are often defined as false beliefs, or as false beliefs arising from a psychotic disorder. But neither of these simple definitions is adequate. The mistaken belief that children are brought by the stork is also a false belief, but it hardly qualifies as a delusion. And it is circular to define a delusion as a belief engendered by psychosis, when the delusion is taken as evidence of psychosis in the first place. We will obviously have to dig a bit deeper.

Lopez-Ibor (1974) recounts the following delusional experience of a schizophrenic woman:

Another patient, a woman, after remaining silent for several days, abandoning her work, and doing without sleep or food, said that on the first day, on returning home, she had seen a number on the door of a shop (corresponding to the numbering of the street). There were several figures, but only the number "7" attracted her attention, because that 7 "*was or signified*" the serpent—the sin which made her fall sexually. From that moment on, her sad and anxious behavior of the previous weeks was illuminated. Even though she told her mother what happened—she had had an amorous adventure—it failed to tranquilize her about the anomalous meaning of that number 7; instead, there now appeared, without the initial anxiety, a proliferation of multiple and diverse meanings that lasted several weeks [p. 8].

We may note two components of this experience. The first is an interpretive shift or slippage in which the percept "number seven" is more or less automatically and unreflectively imbued with the unconventional meaning of "serpent." Stated differently the perceptual event triggers an idiosyncratic concept or interpretive category. The second component of the experience is an elaboration of this idiosyncratic category in religious terms so that the serpent becomes a metaphor for sin, as in the fall from grace of Adam and Eve, and thus helps the patient account for her own amorous misadventure. The distinction between the primary shift in meaning of the numeral seven and its cognitive elaboration in a context of related symbols is conveyed by the terms *primary delusion* and *secondary delusion*. Secondary delusions arise out of primary delusional experiences and represent patients' understandable attempts to come to grips with the primary delusion. The latter, in contrast, is a fundamental, nonderivable psychological phenomenon that is particularly pathognomic of psychotic states.

Primary Delusions

Ordinary perception involves the selection of sensory information and its reduction to preexisting perceptual categories, as when a small four-legged animal of a particular shape, color, gait and behavioral disposition is perceived as a black cat. The perception of a black cat may be further embedded in a broader schema of memories and associations, such as a domestic pet, a mouse catcher, a sign of bad luck, or aloof animals. Each of these elements of the cat schema are perfectly comprehensible in terms of our own past experience with black cats or terms of acquired cultural stereotypes. In delusional perception, the same psychological sequence obtains, but unusual intrusions of schematic elements occur. Bowers (1974) speaks of a broadening of categories of relevance, and Reed (1972) speaks of a world of new meanings. Thus, in primary delusion, the black cat percept may take on an inexplicable meaning of, say, a sign from God or proof that the world will soon come to an end. As Reed (1972) points out, these meanings are not the result of any deliberative metaphorical thinking but arise immediately in the same way that a black-cat-as-house-pet might arise in normal perception. Nor do they have any identifiable relationship to the patient's cultural or personal experience. Mark Vonnegut (1976) relates the following example during his acute breakdown:

I have a fuzzy recollection of walking up to some doctor-looking person and being totally absorbed by his gold tie clip. I suspected it was the button to end the world so I didn't touch it. I'm pretty sure it was Dr. Dale. I don't know who else could be so tasteless as to walk around a mental hospital wearing the button to end the world [pp. 166–167].

In addition to their automaticity and unlikely content, delusional perceptions are marked by an extraordinary subjective certitude, a profound conviction of their validity. They are thus relatively immune to challenge or logical refutation. Indeed, many patients continue to maintain their delusions even after their psychotic episode has remitted; some learn simply to refrain from speaking of them in order to obtain a clean bill of health from their professional caretakers. At the same time, the patient may retain an awareness of the unusual nature of the content of the delusion. Instead of rectifying the belief, however, the patient often sees himself as the focus of a new world of meaning in which he is fated to play an important role. The intense feelings of self-reference in delusional perception are technically known as "ideas of reference." For example, Norma MacDonald (1960) stated:

Not knowing that I was ill, I made no attempt to understand what was happening, but felt that there was some overwhelming significance in all this, produced either by God or Satan. . . . The walk of a stranger on the street could be a "sign" to me which I must interpret. Every face in the windows of a passing streetcar would be engraved on my mind, all of them concentrating on me and trying to pass me some sort of message [p. 218].

And in the words of young Mark Vonnegut (1976):

One of the many worst things about being nuts was being so goddamned important. Who was I that such powerful mysterious forces were buggering around with my life? One team would come through cramming my head full of new knowledge, the next would sneak in and erase all the new stuff plus a lot of the old. I'd be crucified and resurrected several times a day [p. 161].

Secondary Delusions

Whereas primary delusions represent automatic, preemptory, and unreflective attributions of meaning, secondary delusions (also known as *paranoid delusions*) are elaborated, often highly complex systems of belief. Secondary delusions are among the most striking aspects of schizophrenia, and they are one of the chief symptoms indicative of a psychotic process. As we saw in the previous chapter, psychiatrists around the world link a diagnosis of schizophrenia to "widespread," "bizarre," and "nihilistic" delusions (Carpenter, Strauss, & Bartko, 1973). Among laymen, innumerable jokes are made about the madman who believes he is Jesus Christ, Napoleon, or some other prominent historical figure.

Secondary delusions are not, however, pathognomic of schizophrenia; they may occur in other psychotic conditions, particularly mania, psychotic depressions, and psychoses associated with organic impairments. But it is also the case that secondary delusions in schizophrenia tend to have predictable content. In delusions of persecution, the patient is convinced that he or she is the target of a threatening conspiracy, sometimes by particular organizations (e.g., the FBI, the telephone company, the Communist Party), sometimes by more mysterious forces. The persecutory delusion of Sechehaye's (1970) patient Renée exemplified the latter:

> Some time after, I discovered that the Persecutor was none other than the electric machine, that is, it was the "System" that was punishing me. I thought of it as some vast world-like entity encompassing all men. At the top were those who gave orders, who imposed punishment, who pronounced others guilty. But they were themselves guilty. Since every man was responsible for all other men, each of his acts had a repercussion on other beings. A formidable interdependence bound all men under the scourge of culpability. Everyone was part of the System. But only some were aware of being part [pp. 35–36].

In delusions of grandeur, the patient feels that he or she holds an extraordinary and unique place in the scheme of things. Landis and Mettler (1964) cite the following example from Schreber's famous autobiography, *Memoirs of My Nervous Illness:*

> I can put this point briefly: *everything that happens is in reference to me.* Writing this sentence, I am fully aware that other people may be tempted to think that I am pathologically conceited: I know very well that this tendency to relate everything to oneself, to bring everything that happens into connection with one's own person, is a common phenomenon among mental patients. But in my case the very reverse obtains. Since God entered into nerve-contact with me exclusively, I became in a way for God the only human being, or simply the human being around whom everything turns, to whom everything that happens must be related and who therefore, from his own point of view, must also relate all things to himself [p. 56].

Most commentators agree that secondary delusions are not abnormal per se, in spite of their apparent bizarreness. That is, given the presence of primary delusions, as well as other forms of altered consciousness previously exemplified, secondary delusions may be accounted for in terms of normal cognitive processes without recourse to the postulation of any pathological mechanism (Reed, 1972). In Maher's (1974) terms, strange events demand explanation; secondary delusions are hypotheses designed to explain unusual experience by cognitive activities not different in kind from those employed by nonpatients, by scientists, and by people in general. Bowers (1974) likewise suggests that secondary delusions are understandable constructs derived from experiences of heightened awareness, widened categories of relevance, and a push for closure or meaning. He cites the following example in which these elements combined to produce an articulated delusional system, which the patient found oddly reassuring. The patient was a Ph.D. in psychology and a third-year medical student who developed an acute psychosis. The account begins after a night spent fearing that something was wrong with him and that he might die (Bowers, 1974):

I got up at 7 a.m., dressed, and drove to the hospital. I felt my breathing trouble might be due to an old heart lesion. I had been told when I was young that I had a small ventricular septal defect. I decided that I was in heart failure and that people felt I wasn't strong enough to accept this, so they weren't telling me. *I thought about all the things that happened recently that could be interpreted in that light.* I looked up heart failure in a textbook and found that the section had been removed, so I concluded that someone had removed it to protect me. *I remembered other comments.* A friend had talked about a "walkie talkie," and the thought occurred to me that I might be getting medicine without my knowledge perhaps by radio. I remembered someone talking about a one-way plane ticket; to me that meant a trip to Houston and a heart operation. I remembered an unusual smell in the lab and thought that might be due to the medicine they were giving me in secret. I began to think I might have a machine inside of me which secreted medicine into my blood stream. Again I reasoned that I had a disease no one could tell me about and was getting medicine for it secretly. At this point, I panicked and tried to run away, but the attendant in the parking lot seemed to be making a sign to motion me back. I thought I caught brief glimpses of a friend and my wife so I decided to go back into the hospital. A custodian's eyes attracted my attention; they were especially large and piercing. He looked very powerful. He seemed to be "in on it," maybe he was giving medicine in some way. Then I began to have the feeling that other people were watching me. And, as periodically happened throughout the early stages, *I said to myself that the whole thing was absurd, but when I looked again the people really were watching me.* I felt that comments made in the elevator pertained to me. . . . All of a sudden I felt a warm glow. I felt these people were trying to help me. They seemed to be giving me helpful hints. I thought that all the doctors in a meeting I went to were psychiatrists and that they were trying to help me. Conversations had hidden meanings. *When someone told me later that I was delusional, though, I seemed to know it. But I was really groping to understand what was going on. There was a sequence with my delusions: first panic, then groping, then elation at having found out.* . . . There were times when I was aware, in a sense, that I was acting on a delusion. One part of me seemed to say, "Keep your mouth shut, you know this is delusion and it will pass." *But the other side of me wanted the delusion, preferred to have things this way* [italics in original, pp. 186–187].

A striking example of the production of a paranoid delusion in a psychiatrically normal person subjected to altered sensory experience is described by Kohler (1964). In a classic series of experiments, Kohler induced transformations of visual perception by having subjects wear spectacles containing distorting prisms for several weeks. In one such experiment, the prisms produced a slight lateral shift in the visual field so that the subject found it impossible to walk in a straight line and would, for example, find himself walking off the sidewalk into the street. Adaptation occurred with prolonged use of the spectacles, and the visual field slowly regained its veridicality. After the spectacles were finally removed, however, the subject again experienced a lateral shift in visual field, but this time in the opposite direction to the prism-induced distortion. And although the subject, unlike schizophrenic patients, was perfectly aware of the source of his altered perceptual experience, the resulting "delusion" occurred (Kohler, 1964):

> Writing about these first impressions in retrospect does not do them justice. The experience is most uncanny. You are walking along, not worrying about a thing, since you can clearly see which way the street ahead of you goes. Then, all of a sudden, you know something is wrong. You could swear some mysterious force is trying to play a mean trick on you by always changing everything around at the last moment. . . . You get to the point where you cannot take anything for granted anymore. It is not your vision you blame, though; far from it; your confidence in your vision has not been a bit shaken by all this. No, it is the world you blame, the world whirling at your feet, which is trying to make a fool out of you. As for the apparent movements—why should I think that they originate "inside of me" rather than "outside"? After all, don't they make the world look as if it were being shaken up by one earthquake after another? This is what makes those first impressions so unique [p. 90].

ATTENTION DYSFUNCTION IN SCHIZOPHRENIC PSYCHOSIS

The task of any purely psychological theory of schizophrenia is to account for the plethora of clinical symptoms and associated mental states with a fewer number of more general concepts. This was clearly Bleuler's intention in first distinguishing between fundamental symptoms, seen only in schizophrenia, and accessory symptoms, seen also in other conditions. Further distinguishing among fundamental symptoms in terms of those that were primary and those that were secondary adjustive reactions led Bleuler to identify disturbances of association and affect as the psychological core of the clinical condition.

In more recent years, a general hypothesis relating many aspects of the altered state in schizophrenia to anomalies of attention has stimulated a great deal of interest among experimental psychopathologists. This renewed attention to attention in fact harkens back to Kraepelin's early description of *dementia praecox,* in which he identified deficits in both "active" and "passive" attention as diagnostically relevant signs. By an active attention deficit, Kraepelin referred to patients' inability to voluntarily concentrate on external events for any length of time; a deficit in passive attention was seen in an undue susceptibility to distraction by peripheral or irrelevant features of the environment. Although the nineteenth-century distinction between active and passive forms of attention is no longer current, a similar distinction is today conveyed by the terms "focused" and "selective" attention. Contemporary work has curiously little to say about possible deficiencies in focused attention among schizophrenic patients; rather, most discussions of attentional deficits in schizophrenia are encompassed within the accommodating notion of selective attention.

Selective attention refers to what Reed (1972) calls our "puzzling talent" to follow one ongoing activity or source of information when there are many others competing for attention. Reed cites as everyday examples the ability to follow the action of one player in a football game, or the clarinet in an orchestra, while ignoring the multiplicity of other sights, sounds, and movements concomitantly impinging on our senses. Formal models of this process (e.g., Broadbent, 1958, 1971) postulate some central gating mechanism, or filter, that may be preset to receive and pass on for further processing a limited amount of sensory information while excluding or severely attenuating task-irrelevant inputs.

In a seminal paper, McGhie and Chapman (1961) offered a unified interpretation of the altered state among early schizophrenic patients in terms of a breakdown of the central mechanisms subserving selective attention. The hypothesis was presented in conjunction with a series of first-person accounts derived from interviews with acute schizophrenic patients in the early stages of their psychosis. McGhie and Chapman (1961) suggested that because of a breakdown in selective attention, the schizophrenic patient suffers from information overload, in which "consciousness is flooded with an undifferentiated mass of incoming sensory data [p. 112]." This generalization was but a small inference from many of the accompanying statements by patients (several of which were cited previously) of difficulties in concentrating and of continual distraction by normally disregarded sensations. McGhie and Chapman extended this generalization to account for the increasing loss of volitional control over thought sequences seen in the same patients. They suggested that associative intrusions into ordered trains of thought may be considered mentational analogues of distractibility by irrelevant sensory stimuli, both of which may be accounted for by a fundamental deficit in the normal mechanisms of selective attention. The very earliest stages of perceptual–affective enhancement, in which the patient becomes conscious of normally disregarded features of external and internal events, may similarly be interpreted as prodromal forms of attentional disinhibition.

At approximately the same time that McGhie and Chapman's analysis appeared, a former schizophrenic patient, Norma MacDonald (1960), arrived at a highly similar explanation of her psychosis. Whether or not MacDonald had received formal training in psychological analysis is not known. But her much-cited account is eminently compatible with contemporary notions of a selective attention deficit in schizophrenia:

> Now, many years later, I can appreciate what had happened. Each of us is capable of coping with a large number of stimuli, invading our being through any one of the senses. We could hear every sound within earshot and see every object, line, and colour within the field of vision, and so on. It's obvious that we would be incapable of carrying on any of our daily activities if even one-hundredth of all these available stimuli invaded us at once. So the mind must have a filter which functions without our conscious thought, sorting stimuli and allowing only those that are relevant to the situation in hand to disturb consciousness. And this filter must be working at maximum efficiency at all times, particularly when we require a high degree of concentration. What had happened to me in Toronto was a breakdown in the filter, and a hodge-podge of unrelated stimuli were distracting me from things which should have had my undivided attention [p. 218].

Distraction Studies

The McGhie and Chapman paper introduced two fundamental notions that have guided subsequent developments in the experimental psychopathology of schizophrenia. It emphasized the raw phenomenology of the patient as the primary data to be explained by any psychological theory of the schizophrenic psychosis, and it pointed to a deficit in selective attention as a key explanatory concept. In this analysis, the schizophrenic patient suffers from attentional disinhibition: He or she is unable to sort out relevant stimuli but instead attends to transient, peripheral, or minor aspects of the total sensory flux. A minor degree of attentional disinhibition is experienced as an exhilarating expansion of consciousness; at a more intense stage, however, the patient experiences a perplexing inability to concentrate or to voluntarily direct thought and action, so that the coordinated unfolding of adaptive sequences of behavior is degraded. An important corollary is that the schizophrenic deficit should be controllable by a reduction of environmental complexity to the point where only response-relevant information is available to the patient.

This general hypothesis has guided a number of experimental investigations known as *competing information,* or *distraction,* studies (McGhie, 1969; Neale & Cromwell, 1970). Experiments of this sort compare the performance of schizophrenic patients and controls under two major conditions. In the first condition, subjects are instructed to observe and report discrete items of visual, auditory, or verbal information presented against a noise-free background. In the second condition, the information is presented along with a similar series of irrelevant stimuli or is embedded in a context of irrelevant items. The general finding in such studies is that schizophrenic patients perform more poorly than controls only in the second instance—that is, when the task involves attending and responding to relevant input that is presented along with irrelevant input.

But as Chapman and Chapman (1973) point out, such results are merely consistent with an attentional-deficit hypothesis rather than being completely confirmatory. Because the detection of a stimulus in noise is a more difficult task than the detection of an isolated stimulus for all subjects, these results may only indicate that schizophrenic patients perform similarly to controls on easy tasks but more poorly than controls on difficult tasks. The poorer-than-normal performance of schizophrenic patients as a function of task difficulty may simply be secondary to the generalized debilitating effects of their disorder rather than being specifically attributable to an attentional deficit. To infer a specific deficit requires a demonstration that the performance decrement of schizophrenic patients relative to controls on selective attention tasks is greater than their performance decrement relative to controls on tasks of equal difficulty that do not require a separation of relevant and irrelevant information.

Neale and his colleagues report a series of results from a visual signal-detection paradigm that appear to meet this methodological stricture (Cash, Neale, & Cromwell, 1972; Neale, 1971; Neale, McIntyre, Fox, & Cromwell, 1969). On each of several trials, one of two letters—F or T—was tachistoscopically presented for approximately 100 msec. The subjects were asked simply to indicate which of the two letters appeared on any given trial. Such a "forced-choice" procedure, in which the subject is obliged to choose between predetermined response categories, yields a direct estimate of perceptual sensitivity uncontaminated by individual differences in task motivation or risk-taking propensities. Thus any differences between schizophrenic and control subjects would have to be explained by perceptual factors per se.

The first experiment in the series (Neale et al., 1969) compared the performance of acute schizophrenic patients and matched controls under two detection conditions. In the first, one of the two target letters was presented alone on each trial. In the second, the letters were embedded in a distracting context of seven additional letters arranged within the visual field. The results showed that both schizophrenic and control subjects detected the noise-free signal at a high level of accuracy and that the performance of both groups deteriorated in the signal-in-noise condition. However, this deterioration was significantly greater for schizophrenic than control subjects, an observation consistent with the presumed inability of the former to inhibit response to irrelevant aspects of a stimulus configuration. These results were replicated in a second study (Neale, 1971) that further found that the deficit among schizophrenic subjects was increasingly greater as the signal-in-noise array increased from four to eight to 12 letters. In this study, no difference was found between good or poor premorbid patients, whether paranoid or not, but all schizophrenic groups were found to differ from nonpsychiatric controls.

In a third study (Cash et al., 1972), the investigators attempted to determine whether these results were indeed due to a selective-attention deficit rather than attributable to a generalized performance decrement on difficult experimental tasks. As we have seen, this requires a demonstration that schizophrenic subjects show a lesser deficit on a control task of equal difficulty that does not involve selective attention for optimal performance. The control task chosen was a recall test in which subjects were presented with brief exposures of both eight- and 12-letter arrays and asked to name as many letters as possible. Although the task was not explicitly calibrated for difficulty with the previous signal-detection task, one's intuitive impression is that a store-and-recall format of this sort is at least as, if not more, difficult than the forced-choice recognition procedure. Indeed, control subjects are able to name an average of only 40% of the letters in any such array. Remarkably, schizophrenic patients were found to perform as well as controls in this particular situation. In other words, when all stimuli are relevant, no performance deficit is seen among schizophrenic patients. On the other hand, when the task requires identification of relevant stimulus embedded among a number of irrelevant items, schizophrenic patients show an increasing deficit as the number of distractors is increased. This deficit is seen in schizophrenic patients having a variety of subdiagnoses, hence the results are highly consistent with a hypothesis of defective selective attention in schizophrenia.

Shakow's Segmental-Set Hypothesis

David Shakow (e.g., 1962, 1963, 1977) has developed an influential hypothesis of the schizophrenic altered state that is in many respects similar to the McGhie–Chapman selective-attention deficit formulation, even though it is derived from a quite different empirical base. Whereas the McGhie–Chapman hypothesis grew out of a clinical analysis of patients' phenomenology, Shakow's hypothesis of "segmentalized set" was derived in the first instance from many years' observation of schizophrenic performance deficits on a variety of laboratory tasks. For Shakow, the impaired performance of schizophrenic patients relative to controls provides a microcosm for describing the multitude of dissociative processes that he sees as central to the schizophrenic psychosis.

Shakow's analysis builds on a basic distinction between generalized (or major) sets and segmental (or minor) sets. The concept of generalized sets is proposed to account for the ability to inhibit response to minor or irrelevant aspects of a situation and to focus on the principle or relevant aspects. Attention to relevant stimuli allows for the smooth integration of cognitive, affective, and motivational processes necessary for maximally adaptive response to task demands. In contrast, segmental sets are revealed in the disposition to respond to partial or minor aspects of a task or even to completely irrelevant thoughts, fantasies, and memory traces, resulting in degraded task performance. Shakow illustrates the breakdown of generalized sets and the intrusion of segmentalized sets in schizophrenia with a variety of data, among which observations of slowed reaction time and slowed electrodermal-response habituation are especially pertinent.

The reaction-time (RT) task requires the subject to respond as quickly as possible to the onset of a discrete auditory or visual stimulus. This "go" stimulus is usually preceded by a warning stimulus, which, in Shakow's terms, enables the subject to establish a generalized set to respond rapidly. A slower than normal speed of reaction among schizophrenic patients has been demonstrated many times over by various investigators; indeed, slowed RT is one of the most reliable observations in the entire corpus of experimental psychological research in schizophrenia. For Shakow (1962), "it is as if, in the scanning process which takes place before the response to a stimulus is made, the schizophrenic is unable to select out the material relevant for optimal response [p. 25]."

Slowed RT does not by itself prove an inability to maintain a generalized set, and Shakow provides a number of supplementary observations to bolster his interpretation. For example, nonschizophrenic subjects will generally show a slight slowing of response when the preparatory interval between warning signal and "go" stimulus is lengthened from about 2 to 10 seconds. The requirement to maintain a response set for increasingly long preparatory intervals has a major debilitating effect on patients' RTs, however. And whereas control subjects take advantage of a series of trials with consistent preparatory intervals to improve their RTs, schizophrenic patients do no better in this condition than they do when the preparatory interval varies from trial to trial (Rodnick & Shakow, 1940). Zahn, Rosenthal, and Shakow (1961) have demonstrated that one source of the slower response of schizophrenic patients in an irregular preparatory interval series lies in their inordinate tendency to be distracted by the preparatory interval on the trial *preceding* the trial in which RT is measured. When a series of trials with longer preparatory intervals (and thus longer RTs) precedes a series with shorter intervals, RTs in the shorter series are abnormally slowed among schizophrenic patients. Thus the perseveration on previous preparatory intervals produces an example of a segmental set that interferes with a more generalized set for quick response.

Another example of maladaptive perseveration is seen in impaired electrodermal response habituation among schizophrenic patients. In this test, the electrical activity of the palmar sweat glands is measured in response to repeated presentations of an innocuous stimulus such as a mild tone or a dim light. Nonschizophrenic subjects generally attend to the first stimulus in such a series and display a concomitantly large electrodermal response. With repetition of the same stimulus, however, the response amplitude rapidly habituates toward zero. Schizophrenic patients, on the other hand, continue to respond to each succeeding stimulus as if it were novel and thus fail to habituate. Because electrodermal response habituation requires an inhibition of response to an essentially irrelevant event, the failure of habituation among schizophrenic patients may be taken as an example of the breakdown of a generalized set.

Shakow (1963) employs a similar analysis to account for the bizarre clinical behavior of many schizophrenic patients:

> This immense variety of schizophrenic symptoms can in one sense be viewed as different expressions of only partial integration, or individuation, or breakdowns of major sets—in other words, of segmentalization.... There is an increased awareness of, and preoccupation with, the ordinarily disregarded details of existence—the details which normal people spontaneously forget— train themselves, or are trained rigorously to disregard. These, rather than the biologically adaptive functional aspects of the situation, appear to take on a primary role. It is only when a patient develops a persisting aversion to food because the cafeteria menu lists a common item which we read as "soup" but which he can only see in his excretory significance as "so-u-p," that we begin to realize how very many of the thousands of details of daily existence get by us ordinary normals [p. 303]!

Chapman and Chapman's Stimulus-Selection Bias Hypothesis

Shakow's segmental-set hypothesis of the altered schizophrenic state is obviously a close analogue of the McGhie–Chapman selective-attention deficit hypothesis. Both agree that schizophrenic patients suffer from an inordinate tendency to attend to peripheral or irrelevant aspects of the environment. Irrelevant stimuli are those not essential for the optimal execution of purposive behavior sequences. Stated differently, schizophrenic patients fail to screen stimuli for their relevance to task demands, and thus their behavior often appears inappropriate, idiosyncratic, or tangential. This deficit will be minimized in situations in which only response-relevant information is available and maximized in situations demanding a selection of relevant from irrelevant information and a corresponding inhibition of attention to the latter.

Yet schizophrenic task performance in distracting environments is not completely haphazard. Although less adequate than that of control subjects, performance is nonetheless patterned in that some prediction is possible of the type of error schizophrenic subjects will make in different tasks or across trials on the same task. As Chapman and Chapman (1973) point out, this regularity implies that potential distractors are not all equally likely to attract patients' attention; rather, schizophrenic subjects appear to prefer certain classes of task-irrelevant stimuli over others.

Chapman and Chapman propose that the stimuli to which schizophrenic patients will inappropriately attend are those to which nonschizophrenic subjects would also attend if they were not incompatible with task demands. Thus the errors of schizophrenic patients under distraction may be predicted from a prior knowledge of normal stimulus-selection biases. In the absence of situational constraints, for example, nonschizophrenic subjects will show a bias to respond to the stronger of two stimuli, to novel as opposed to familiar stimuli, and to recent as opposed to temporally remote stimuli. If, however, the situation or task is so constrained as to render such stimulus-selection biases incompatible with adequate performance, nonschizophrenic subjects are generally able to shift attention to weaker but task-*relevant* stimuli. Schizophrenic patients, on the other hand, continue to attend to strong but task-*irrelevant* features of the environment. In other words, the stimuli to which nonschizophrenic subjects preferentially respond are the same ones to which schizophrenic subjects show a greater than normal preferential response.

Consider, for example, a hypothetical task that requires subjects to explain the meaning of the phrase, "The chair called the meeting to order." In the absence of context, a highly probable or preferred response to "chair" might be "a piece of furniture." A correct interpretation of the phrase, however, requires that this selection bias be inhibited in favor of a less probable but situationally correct response such as "group leader" or "chairperson." Chapman and Chapman's hypothesis predicts that schizophrenic subjects will be unable to disattend from the stronger meaning and will thus give an incorrect and seemingly bizarre response such as "The chair spoke to the other people" or "Somebody taught the chair to speak."

Chapman and Chapman (1973) report an elegant experimental confirmation of this effect. The task was a four-alternative multiple-choice vocabulary test containing 60 items of the following form:

SHOOT means the same as
(a) rifle
(b) rug
(c) sprout
(d) none of the above

The first alternative, "rifle," is a strong but contextually incorrect association to the word "shoot." The second alternative, "rug," is an incorrect filler, and the third alternative, "sprout," is the correct choice. In order to ascertain that any poor performance of schizophrenic relative to nonschizophrenic subjects on the test represented a specific disability to disattend from strong selection biases rather than a simple performance deficit on difficult tasks, the authors prepared a similar, equally difficult test without associative distractors. In the following example of a control-task item, the first two incorrect alternatives have no particular associative connection with the stimulus word:

SCALE means the same as
(a) pin
(b) yell
(c) climb
(d) none of the above

The authors compared the performance, on experimental and control tests, of 42 chronic schizophrenic patients and an equivalent number of nonpsychiatric control subjects matched for age and education. As seen in Table 2.1, nonschizophrenic subjects were as accurate on the experimental test with associative distractors as on the control test, whereas schizophrenic patients were less accurate on the experimental than the control test. The greater difference between schizophrenic and nonschizophrenic subjects on the test containing associative distractors than on the control test indicates the presence of a specific inability to disattend from strong distractors over and above any generalized performance deficit.

TABLE 2.1
Mean Accuracy of Schizophrenic Patients and Nonpsychiatric
Subjects on Tests With and Without Associates[a]

	Associates	No Associates
Nonpsychiatric subjects	36.4	35.3
Schizophrenic patients	22.4	28.0

[a]Adapted from Chapman & Chapman (1973).

The tendency of schizophrenic patients to yield inappropriately to normal stimulus-selection biases can have a disastrous effect on verbal-communication sequences, as demonstrated in an experiment reported by Cohen, Nachmani, and Rosenberg (1974). Subjects were required to describe a colored disc (the referent) so that a listener could distinguish it from one or more differently colored discs in a display. The task could be varied in difficulty depending on both the number and the similarity of colors displayed. The authors describe the task as a two-stage process in which the speaker first samples one of a number of possible verbal associates to the referent color and then compares the ability of this word to distinguish referent from nonreferent colors. If the word adequately distinguishes referents from nonreferents, it is emitted. If the discrimination is poor, increasingly weaker verbal associates are sampled and compared until an adequate discrimination is achieved. Cohen et al. found little difference in the communication accuracy of acute schizophrenic and control subjects when the referent differed maximally from the nonreferent colors—that is, when the strongest verbal associate to the referent provided an adequate discrimination. For example, the following responses were obtained to a two-disc display in which the referent, a purple–blue, was 12 hue steps distant from the red nonreferent:

Normal Speaker 1: "Purple."
Normal Speaker 2: "Purple."
Schizophrenic Speaker 1: "Blue."
Schizophrenic Speaker 2: "The bluer."

In contrast, the following examples, taken from the same subjects in the Cohen et al. study were typical of those obtained when strong verbal associates to the referent did not adequately distinguish it from the nonreferent. Here the referent color was a red and the nonreferent a highly similar, slightly more yellow, disc only two hue steps distant:

Normal Speaker 1: "Both are salmon colored. This one, however, has more pink."
Normal Speaker 2: "My God this is hard. They are both about the same except that this one might be a little redder."
Schizophrenic Speaker 1: "A fish swims. You call it a salmon. You cook it. You put it in a can. You open the can. You look at it in this color. Salmon fish."
Schizophrenic Speaker 2: "Make-up. Pancake makeup. You put it on your face and they think guys run after you. Wait a second! I don't put it on my face and guys don't run after me. Girls put it on them."

The nonschizophrenic speakers, finding that an initial stronger associate such as "salmon" provides a poor discrimination, shift to other more precise descriptors such as "more pink" or "a little redder." The schizophrenic subjects, after very similar initial responses, are unable to produce an associate to the weaker but discriminating aspects of the target. Instead, they perseverate on the initial response, producing chains of loosely connected elements that degenerate into incoherence.

These examples of schizophrenic subjects' responses are remarkably similar to the ad-hoc communications of schizophrenic patients cited earlier under the heading of "Language Disorder." In producing such language under controlled conditions, Cohen et al. establish the important generalization that schizophrenic linguistic disruption will occur when ongoing communication requires disattention from normal stimulus-selection biases in favor of weaker features of a stimulus configuration.

3

Biochemical Models

Mental diseases are brain diseases.
—Wilhelm Griesinger (1845)

In the previous two chapters, we examined schizophrenia as a clinical phenomenon and the schizophrenic psychosis as a particular altered state of consciousness. The following exposition considers major attempts to link schizophrenia with underlying disorders of neurochemical functioning. The hypothesis that schizophrenia is associated with some impairment of central nervous system activity is as old as the diagnostic category itself. For example, both Kraepelin (1904) and Bleuler (1950) speculated about the possible nature of the "brain disease" underlying the clinical syndrome. As they implicitly recognized, the association of schizophrenia with a characteristic brain state is in one respect a foregone conclusion. Because all mental activity and behavior are mediated by the central nervous system, schizophrenic mental activity and behavior must also be so mediated. But this notion has gained widespread credibility only in recent years with the demonstration that certain pharmacological agents can induce psychotic states in psychiatrically normal subjects, whereas other agents can reverse or ameliorate the symptoms of schizophrenic patients.

It is important to realize that no specific neurochemical defect or defects have yet been demonstrated among schizophrenic patients. On the other hand, pharmacological models of psychotic states, coupled with an increasingly sophisticated understanding of brain chemistry, have produced substantial hypotheses regarding likely biochemical anomalies in schizophrenia. Current research is dominated by three major hypotheses, each of which commands the attention of competing groups of investigators. Each attempts to elucidate schizophrenia by reference to neurochemical mechanisms underlying a psychosis of known origin taken as a model of the schizophrenic psychosis. In order of their presentation here, they are: (1) the *transmethylation hypothesis,* suggested by the psychoticlike state produced by psychedelic drugs; (2) the *dopamine hypothesis,* suggested by psychotic reactions to amphetamine drugs; and (3) the *orthomolecular hypothesis,* suggested by the toxic psychosis associated with the vitamin deficiency disease pellagra. Because much of this material is somewhat complex, the discussion of these hypotheses is preceded by a brief overview of concepts basic to neurochemical research on schizophrenia.

NEURONS, SYNAPSES, AND NEUROTRANSMITTERS

The brain is essentially a lacy network of interconnecting nerve cells, or neurons, embedded in a supporting mass of glial cells, the whole having a custardlike consistency (Fig. 3.1). Each neuron consists of a cell body, or *soma,* whose contours form a large number of small extensions—the *dendrites*—which receive electrical signals from as many as several hundred other neurons. Signals from connecting neurons alter the target cell's internal electrical charge; when this charge reaches a critical level, the cell triggers its own signal. This signal is conducted along a fibrous extension of the cell, or *axon.* At its tip, the axon subdivides into numerous branches that form junctions with the dendrites and cell bodies of succeeding neurons. Each neuron thus receives and transmits information in the form of electrical signals from and to numerous other neurons. Junctions between adjacent neurons are known as *synapses.* Each synapse can be described in terms of the *presynaptic terminal* of the axon, the synaptic gap or *cleft,* and the *postsynaptic membrane* of the succeeding dendrite or cell body.

In the great majority of cases, communication across synapses is regulated by chemical substances. More than 40 such *neuroregulators* have so far been identified, and the number continues to grow with the evolution of knowledge regarding neuronal function. The neuroregulators may be divided into a smaller group of *neurotransmitters* and a larger group of *neuromodulators.* Neurotransmitters are the chief agents of synaptic communication, the means by which electrical signals are transferred between adjacent neurons. The role of neuromodulators is less well understood, but they appear to regulate the ongoing background level of neuronal activity. Some neuromodulators may act to influence the synthesis and metabolism of neurotransmitters; others appear to amplify or dampen the transsynaptic effectiveness of neurotransmitters (Barchas, Akil, Elliott, Holman, & Watson, 1978).

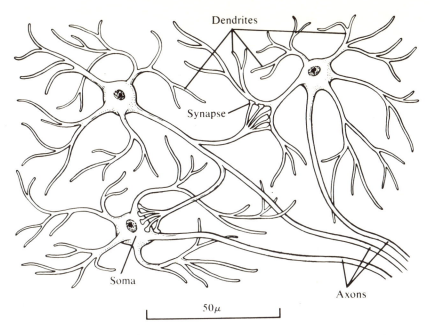

FIG. 3.1. A schematic representation of three nerve cells (neurons) illustrating the major subdivisions of such cells and the interactions between them. (From Julien, 1975, p. 214.)

Figure 3.2 schematizes the process of neurotransmission across a synapse. Neurotransmitter substances are synthesized within the presynaptic neuron and stored in *vesicles*, or *granules*, located in the axon terminal. When the axon signal reaches the terminal, storage vesicles migrate to the presynaptic membrane and fuse with it, releasing packets of transmitter molecules into the synaptic cleft. The molecules diffuse across the cleft and become attached to receptor sites on the postsynaptic membrane much in the way a key fits a lock. This causes a temporarily increased permeability of the postsynaptic membrane. At *excitatory* synapses, positively charged ions of sodium from the surrounding fluid flow into the postsynaptic cell, which maintains a normal resting voltage of approximately –70 millivolts. The ionic inflow reduces this negative voltage until a threshold between –60 and –40 millivolts is reached, causing the cell to discharge. At *inhibitory* synapses, the neurotransmitter acts to increase the flow of negatively charged ions of chloride into the cell, which increases its negativity and thus acts to impede discharge. Whether or not a given neuron discharges will therefore depend on the summative influences of the excitatory and inhibitory synapses impinging upon it.

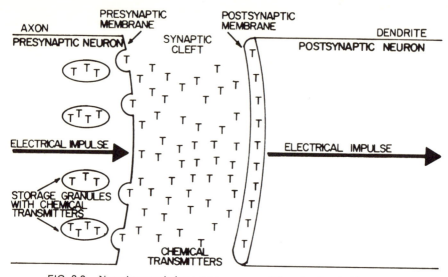

FIG. 3.2.   Neural transmission across a synapse: When the electrical impulse reaches the presynaptic membrane, the storage granules release their chemical transmitters. These chemicals flow across the synapse onto receptor sites in the postsynaptic membrane of the adjacent neuron. This changes the level of the membrane potential, either depolarizing it and favoring discharge of a nervous impulse, or hyperpolarizing it and inhibiting the discharge of an impulse. (From Schildkraut, 1974.)

Biochemical investigations of schizophrenia have thus far centered on three neuroregulators known or presumed to act as neurotransmitters: (1) *dopamine;* (2) *norepinephrine* (noradrenaline); and (3) *serotonin*. Because the molecule of each of these compounds terminates in an amino group (NH_2), they are known collectively as *monoamines,* or simply *amines*. Monoamines can be further differentiated in terms of their molecular structure. Dopamine and norepinephrine are highly similar in structure and fall into a class of compounds known as *catecholamines*. The simple structure of any catecholamine consists of a catechol nucleus [a six-carbon benzene ring with two adjacent hydroxyl (HO) groups] with a side chain terminating in an amino group. In contrast, serotonin belongs to the class of *indoleamines,* whose basic structure consists of an indole nucleus and a side chain terminating in an amino group:

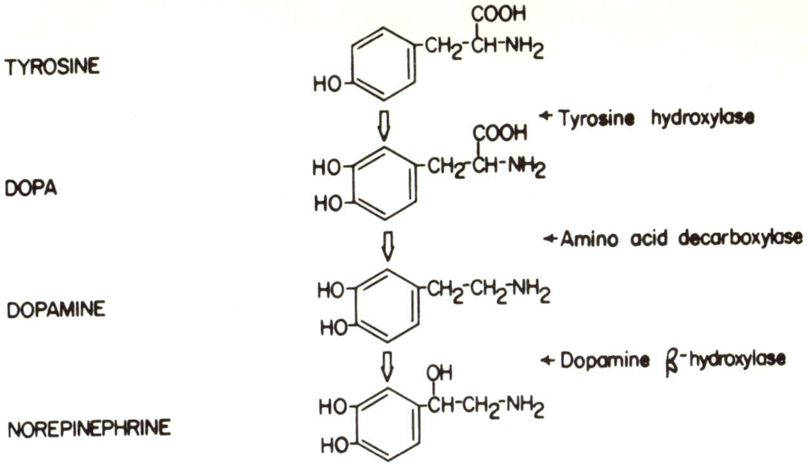

TYROSINE

DOPA

← Tyrosine hydroxylase

DOPAMINE

← Amino acid decarboxylase

NOREPINEPHRINE

← Dopamine β-hydroxylase

FIG. 3.3. Biosynthesis of dopamine and norepinephrine.

Dopamine, norepinephrine, and serotonin are each synthesized within the neuron by the action of intracellular enzymes on amino acids absorbed from the blood stream (Figs. 3.3 and 3.4). Dopamine and norepinephrine are derived from the amino acid *tyrosine*. The intermediate substance *dopa* is produced by the addition of a second hydroxyl group to the ring by the enzymatic action of *tyrosine hydroxylase*. Dopamine is then synthesized from dopa by the enzymatic action of *amino acid decarboxylase*, which removes

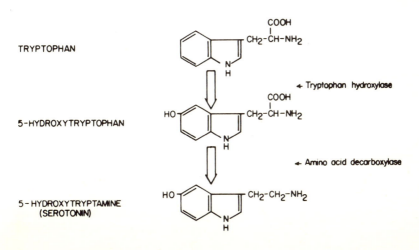

TRYPTOPHAN

← Tryptophan hydroxylase

5-HYDROXYTRYPTOPHAN

← Amino acid decarboxylase

5-HYDROXYTRYPTAMINE
(SEROTONIN)

FIG. 3.4. Biosynthesis of serotonin.

the carboxyl group (COOH) from the side chain. In neurons that utilize dopamine as the neurotransmitter, synthesis ends with the storage of dopamine in synaptic vesicles. In norepinephrine-utilizing neurons, however, the enzyme *dopamine-beta-hydroxylase* converts dopamine to norepinephrine by the addition of a hydroxyl group to the side chain.

Serotonin is synthesized from the amino acid *tryptophan* via the intermediary *5-hydroxytryptophan*. This latter compound is produced by the addition of a hydroxyl group to the tryptophan molecule via the enzyme *tryptophan hydroxylase*. 5-Hydroxytryptophan is then decarboxylated to produce serotonin, or 5-hydroxytryptamine (5-HT).

Figure 3.5 illustrates in some detail the process of neurotransmission at a dopamine (DA) synapse. Dopamine is synthesized within the presynaptic neuron from the amino acid tyrosine and stored in synaptic vesicles. At the point of transmission, it is released into the synaptic cleft and diffuses onto dopamine receptors of the postsynaptic neuron. Interaction of dopamine with its receptor increases postsynaptic membrane permeability to ions, initiating the regeneration of the electrical impulse. The figure also illustrates the subsequent fate of the released dopamine. Once the neurotransmitter has interacted with its receptor—a process that occupies no more than 1 or 2 milliseconds—it is rapidly inactivated by one or more of three mechanisms.

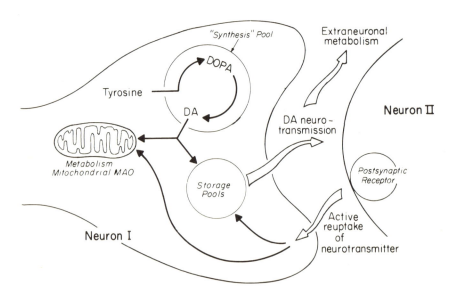

FIG. 3.5.   A model of a dopamine (DA) synapse illustrating neurotransmitter synthesis, storage, release, and subsequent inactivation. (Adapted from Barchas et al., 1978.)

The most important of these is the reabsorption, or *reuptake,* of dopamine molecules into storage vesicles of the presynaptic terminal, where they are available for subsequent release. Some of the neurotransmitter may be metabolized into breakdown products by enzymes in the extracellular fluid and ultimately excreted in the urine. Finally, some dopamine may diffuse from storage in the presynaptic terminal and be inactivated by the enzyme *monoamine oxydase* (MAO), which is located in the metabolic structures known as *mitochondria.* Similar processes characterize the synthesis, storage, release, and inactivation of the other amine neurotransmitters.

MAJOR BIOCHEMICAL HYPOTHESES

The Transmethylation Hypothesis

The Model.   In 1943, Dr. Alfred Hoffman, a chemist employed by the Swiss pharmaceutical house of Sandoz, ingested what we now know to be an unusually large dose of d-lysergic acid diethylamide. He and an associate had synthesized the compound 5 years earlier from ergot, a fungus that affects rye and other cereal grasses. Because this compound was the twenty-fifth lysergic acid synthesized at Sandoz, Hoffman had labeled it LSD-25 for short (Brecher, 1972).

Hoffman's now classic account of his reaction to the drug (Box 3.1) has been by and large confirmed by innumerable subsequent first person reports, as well as by controlled studies of the LSD state. The drug produces a rather confusing affective state. Relaxation and euphoria occur simultaneously with jittery, tense, dreamlike, excited, and giddy feelings. Logical thought and speech are impaired and movement slowed. Subjects report experiences of both derealization and depersonalization: Some become fearful of the loss of self-control; others revel in the discovery of previously unsuspected dimensions of consciousness (Katz, Waskow, & Olsson, 1968). Even at fairly low doses, the drug produces profound alterations in perception. Objects may appear vaguely outlined, and colors and textures often take on a depth and richness of ineffable beauty. The sense of time slows dramatically, which is probably secondary to an acceleration of mental activity. A brief inspection of the altered features of an object may be experienced as a long and careful scrutiny. Synesthesias occur, as when subjects "see" sounds or "hear" colors (Snyder, 1974). Subsequent studies of the LSD high have corrected Hoffman's rather negative description of his experience to a more neutral view. It is now appreciated that the drug produces a rather ambivalent state that may be interpreted in either euphoric or dysphoric terms.

Box 3.1—The Original LSD Trip

I asked my laboratory assistant to accompany me home as I believed that I should have a repetition of the disturbance of the previous Friday. While we were cycling home (a 4-mile trip by bicycle, no other vehicle being available because of the war), however, it became clear that the symptoms were much stronger than the first time. I had great difficulty in speaking coherently, and my field of vision swayed before me and was distorted like the reflections in an amusement park mirror. I had the impression of being unable to move from the spot, although my assistant later told me that we had cycled at a good pace....

By the time the doctor arrived, the peak of the crisis had already passed. As far as I can remember, the following were the most outstanding symptoms: vertigo, visual disturbances, the faces of those around me appeared as grotesque, colored masks; marked motoric unrest, alternating with paralysis; an intermittent feeling in the head, limbs, and the entire body, as if they were filled with lead; dry, constricted sensation in the throat; feeling of choking; clear recognition of my condition, in which state I sometimes observed, in the manner of an independent, neutral observer, that I shouted half insanely or babbled incoherent words. Occasionally I felt as if I were out of my body.

The doctor found a rather weak pulse, but an otherwise normal circulation....Six hours after the ingestion of the LSD, my condition had already improved considerably.

Only the visual disturbances were still pronounced. Everything seemed to sway, and the proportions were distorted like the reflections in the surface of moving water. Moreover, all objects appeared in unpleasant, constantly changing colors, the predominant shades being sickly green and blue. With closed eyes multihued, metamorphizing fantastic images overwhelmed me. Especially noteworthy was the fact that sounds were transposed into visual sensations so that from each tone or noise a comparable colored picture was evoked, changing in form and color kaleidoscopically.

—Adapted from Brecher (1972, pp. 246–347)
Originally published in F. J. Ayd, Jr. & B. Blackwell, *Discoveries in biological psychiatry*. Philadelphia: Lippincott, 1970.

LSD is the most widely investigated of many natural and synthetic substances such as mescaline, psilocybin, and dimethyltryptamine (DMT) that produce similar psychological effects, even though they may differ considerably in molecular structure. The term *psychedelic*—"mind-manifesting"—is perhaps the best rubric for these substances, simply because it is descriptively open-ended. "Hallucinogenic" fails to do justice to the plethora of effects produced, whereas "psychotomimetic" suggests too strongly that the effects are entirely homologous with naturally occurring psychotic states (Snyder, 1974).

Most investigators agree that psychedelic compounds do not in fact recreate the full range of symptoms of a schizophrenic psychosis. Yet as Bowers (1974) points out, there exist strong parallels between psychedelic phenomena and the early stages of schizophrenic breakdown. As was discussed in Chapter 2, early schizophrenic patients report a broadening of awareness and an altered way of perceiving themselves and the world around them. Sensory impressions become more vivid and intense, and relatively minor events take on an aura of special significance. Experiences of derealization and depersonalization are common. Emotional response is heightened and may fluctuate between feelings of creative release and joy or a vague, disquieting sense of dread. It is not necessary to assume a complete homology between the schizophrenic psychosis and psychedelic effects to pursue the similarities that do exist between these two altered states.

The transmethylation hypothesis is a result of the stimulation of scientific interest in psychedelic phenomena subsequent to Hoffman's report and of contemporaneous advances in basic neurochemistry. In 1952, an important paper by Osmond and Smythies, with an afterword by chemist Harley-Mason, pointed to the structural similarity between the molecule of a naturally occurring catecholamine, norepinephrine, and the molecule of a psychedelic substance, mescaline. Since then, many psychedelic substances have been found to be derived from the same nuclei from which the brain amines are synthesized. As indicated in Fig. 3.6, the catecholamines dopamine and norepinephrine are derived from hydroxylation (the addition of hydroxyl groups) of simple phenethylamine, and serotonin is the hydroxylated derivative of simple indoleamine. In contrast, many psychedelic compounds are derived from methylation [the addition of methyl groups (CH_3)] of the same nuclei. Figure 3.6 illustrates two such examples. Mescaline is a methylated derivative of phenethylamine; DMT (dimethyltryptamine) is a methylated derivative of indoleamine.

The methylation of brain amines is a normally occurring metabolic process. For example, the metabolic inactivation of both dopamine and norepinephrine proceeds via both methylation and the oxidation of the terminal amine group. But where normal metabolites are singly methylated, their psychedelic analogoues are dimethylated, as with DMT, or trimethylated, as with mescaline. The transmethylation hypothesis suggests that in schizophrenic persons, methyl groups may be transferred along normally suppressed pathways to synthesize an endogenous psychedelic substance from brain amines. Abnormal methylation would require an as yet unspecified enzymatic error at one or more stages of catecholamine or indoleamine metabolism.

The Evidence. If schizophrenic symptoms are due to an abnormal methylation of brain amines, one might expect that the administration of substances rich in methyl would exacerbate the symptoms of schizophrenic patients but have little effect on nonschizophrenic controls. Such an

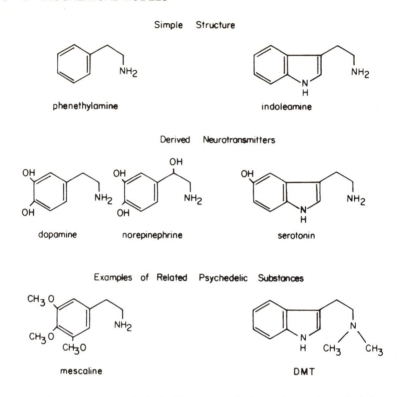

FIG. 3.6. Structural similarities among brain amines and psychedelic substances.

experiment was first performed by Pollin, Cardon, and Kety (1961), who administered the methyl-rich amino acid methionine to a group of schizophrenic patients. In a substantial fraction of patients, a brief intensification of their psychotic symptoms ensued. The effects included an increased flood of associations, incoherent speech, hallucinations, anxiety, and increased motor activity. This dramatic experiment has since then been repeated by at least 10 independent groups of investigators, all of whom have reported a similar worsening of patients' clinical status. Control subjects tend to respond quite differently to methionine, showing drowsiness, lethargy, fatigue, and anxiety (Wyatt, Termini, & Davis, 1971).

If methyl donor substances exacerbate schizophrenic symptoms, it should be possible to produce an amelioration of patients' symptoms following administration of methyl acceptor substances. This hypothesis was first tested in the early 1950s by the therapeutic administration of large doses of niacin (vitamin B_3), which at that time was thought to be a powerful methyl acceptor. The results of these and subsequent clinical studies are discussed with the orthomolecular hypothesis below. Suffice it to say that the question of the efficacy of niacin therapy for schizophrenia is highly controversial. Moreover, regardless of its clinical effects, Baldessarini (1967) showed that niacin is *not* an especially good methyl acceptor, so its use does not constitute an adequate test of the transmethylation hypothesis. Unfortunately, substances with stronger affinities for methyl have not been systematically tested in schizophrenic patients.

A second major method of testing the transmethylation hypothesis is to search for methylated amines in the body fluid of schizophrenic patients. This approach has many potential problems, however. For example, there is no assurance that any psychedelic substance would be sufficiently stable to appear in its active form in the blood, urine, or spinal fluid should it in fact be present in the brains of schizophrenic patients. Thus an inability to find a given substance can never be conclusive, because the possibility of rapid metabolic destruction always exists. If, on the other hand, a substance is isolated, it is necessary to demonstrate that its presence is correlated with schizophrenia per se, rather than with such nonspecific attributes of patienthood as long periods of hospitalization, drug treatment, or institutional diet. Such demonstrations require extensive, long-term, and detailed investigation. In spite of the skepticism that such problems might induce, a great deal of enthusiasm greeted the 1962 report of Friedhoff and Van Winkle that the psychedelic amine DMPEA (dimethoxyphenethylamine) was found in the urine of schizophrenic patients and not in that of nonschizophrenic controls. More precisely, Friedhoff and Van Winkle reported that on assay, a urinary metabolite showed properties analogous to those demonstrated by synthetic DMPEA. Because this metabolite appeared as a pinkish color on chromatographic testing, it has often been referred to as the "pink spot."

Early attempts at replication appeared to confirm this finding, but subsequent reports have produced a welter of confusing and contradictory data. Some investigations indicated that the pink spot disappeared when patients were placed on a plant-free diet; others attributed it to a metabolite of antipsychotic drugs. More refined methods of assay have shown that the pink spot contains a number of metabolic constituents in addition to DMPEA, and that DMPEA itself appears in the urine of both normal and schizophrenic individuals. A severe problem is caused by the observation that ingestion of synthetic DMPEA does not appear to produce schizophreniclike effects (Wyatt, Termini & Davis, 1971). Thus the early enthusiasm has been replaced by a great deal of disenchantment. Ironically, definitive studies with careful controls for nonspecific factors and advanced assay methods have yet to be carried out, so that the DMPEA hypothesis survives for want of definitive disconfirmation (Friedhoff, Park, Schweitzer, Burdock, & Armour, 1977).

Recent work has investigated the possible presence of methylated indoleamines in the body fluids of schizophrenic patients. One such compound, DMT, is known to be a powerful psychedelic, and there is enticing evidence that an enzyme capable of synthesizing DMT from tryptamine (a simple indoleamine) shows higher than normal levels of activity in schizophrenic patients (Matthysse & Lipinski, 1975). Some investigators have, in addition, reported DMT to be present in the body fluids of schizophrenic patients; yet other groups have not confirmed this, and the status of DMT research must be considered on a par with that of DMPEA.

In sum, the transmethylation hypothesis has been neither confirmed nor convincingly refuted. It rests primarily on the reliable observation that the administration of methyl donor substances worsens the clinical status of schizophrenic patients. But there is as yet no consistent evidence that this effect is produced by abnormal methylation of monoamines in schizophrenic patients.

The Dopamine Hypothesis

The Model. Admitting officers in mental hospitals are sometimes confronted with patients who present with symptoms of an acute episode of paranoid schizophrenia but who recover in a few days without any specific treatment. Upon investigation it is discovered that the patient had been ingesting or mainlining massive doses of amphetamine—perhaps 100–200 milligrams every 3 or 4 hours—for several days on end (Snyder, 1972). Although abuse of amphetamine compounds has been known since their commercial introduction in the 1930s, it was not until 1958 that Connell published a detailed study of 42 cases of amphetamine psychosis, in which he asserted that the clinical features of amphetamine psychosis might be such as to make it indistinguishable from paranoid schizophrenia (Angrist, Sathananthan, Wilk, & Gershon, 1974). In order to rule out the possibility that amphetamines simply trigger a psychosis in preschizophrenic individuals, studies conducted after Connell's monograph administered amphetamines to volunteer subjects with neither signs nor history of schizophrenia. For example, Angrist et al. (1974) administered as much as 50 milligrams per hour of various amphetamine compounds for as long as the volunteers would tolerate the regime. Some examples of the effects observed are presented in Box 3.2.

The predominant symptoms of amphetamine psychosis are florid paranoid delusions accompanied by a degree of excitement and belligerence. Visual hallucinations, as well as illusions of objects changing shape or being transmuted into frightening apparitions, are also frequent. The auditory hallucinations that are characteristic of acute schizophrenic episodes are less frequent but do occur in some cases.

Box 3.2—Amphetamine Psychosis

One subject who had taken 465 mg of racemic amphetamine over 22¾-hr abruptly experienced a florid paranoid psychosis. Before the experiment he had made a "deal" with an attendant on the ward, to whom he owed several dollars. As he became psychotic, he "heard" a gang coming on the ward to kill him (sent by the attendant). His paranoid feelings included the experimenter who he assumed had "set up" the "trap." He was at times quite hostile. Explanations that his experiences were amphetamine-induced were rejected with sardonic mock agreement (i.e., "Oh sure ha! Is that the way it's going to be?," etc.). At other times he would become panicky and tearful and beg the experimenter to explain what was "really going on." He had visual hallucinations of gangsters, and doors opening and closing in the shadows, and visual illusions, in which papers on the bulletin board "turned into" "a gangster in a white rain coat." He jumped at the slightest sound, assuming that it was the gang. He was so frightened he refused to investigate the ward to prove that no one was there. . . .

In a separate experiment, after 270 mg of d-amphetamine, he suddenly "realized" there was something "else" in the experiment that we would not tell him. A pile of tables and chairs in the hall was suddenly perceived as an operating table. He felt that the doctors planned to subdue and drug him and then operate on him or kill him. He became alternatively belligerent and hostile, panicky and tearful.

On yet another occasion, on l-amphetamine, he at first experienced gradually increasing euphoriant effects and then as these diminished (after 415 mg) "realized" that the experimenters had substituted a placebo, or a sedative or neuroleptic drug for the amphetamines without telling him. He became quite hostile and belligerent, stating, "I've been straight with you, why don't you be straight with me, why do you do this to me?" I asked him what he meant and he replied as follows: "I know my backside didn't open up and drop it out; my system can't be cleared that fast."

—Adapted from Angrist et al. (1974, p. 15)

A major limitation of amphetamine psychosis as a schizophrenic analogue is that the cardinal symptoms of affective blunting and thought disorder are generally absent. This may be partially a question of the amount and duration of amphetamine administration, because Angrist et al. (1974) did observe affective flattening accompanied by tangential, diffuse, and unfocused thinking in some subjects. On the other hand, paranoid schizophrenia is often diagnosed in the absence of these symptoms, so that amphetamine psychosis can at least be said to mimic this particular type of schizophrenia.

The ability of amphetamines to exacerbate the clinical picture of schizophrenic patients suggests that amphetamine intoxication may be a heuristic model for other forms of schizophrenia as well. Not only do modest doses of amphetamines and their analogues such as methylphenidate (Ritalin) create florid symptomatology in schizophrenic patients, but the patients themselves report that the drugged state mimics their natural schizophrenic psychosis (Snyder, 1974); that is, the induced psychosis is perceived as a genuine exacerbation of their endogenous psychosis rather than as a superimposed drug high.

Largely because amphetamine molecules so closely resemble naturally occurring catecholamines, researchers presume that they exert their effects at catecholamine-utilizing synapses. Amphetamines are believed to release catecholamines from presynaptic terminals, although they may also interfere with the uptake process, which would also have the effect of increasing available catecholamines at post-synaptic receptors (Meltzer & Stahl, 1976).

Whether amphetamine has a stronger affinity for dopamine (dopaminergic) or for norepinephrine (noradrenergic) synapses is not completely clear. There is, however, evidence from animal research that both are involved. Amphetamine causes behavioral excitation in animals, which is regarded primarily as a norepinephrine effect. It also induces repetitive, stereotyped behavior such as compulsive grooming and sniffing, an effect probably mediated by dopamine neurons. There is increasing evidence, however, that the major pharmacological action of amphetamines is at dopaminergic synapses. Amphetamines produce euphoria in human volunteers even when norepinephrine release is inhibited by a concurrently administered blocking agent; they also elevate dopamine metabolites, but not norepinephrine metabolites, in spinal fluid (Meltzer & Stahl, 1976). Thus it appears that brain dopamine potentiation is a major pharmacological effect of amphetamine administration.

In light of these various leads, the dopamine hypothesis holds that the schizophrenic psychosis is related to neuronal hyperactivity at dopaminergic synapses. Such hyperactivity could conceivably be due to one or more specific regulatory errors: (1) too much dopamine might be released into the synapse; (2) postsynaptic dopamine receptors might be hypersensitive and react excessively to normal amounts of released dopamine; and (3) there may be errors in the uptake and inactivation of dopamine. These potential errors in effect describe alternative subhypotheses. In any case, the result would be the functional equivalent of too much dopamine at the synapse.

The Evidence. The chief support for the dopamine hypothesis comes from analyses of the mode of action of drugs known to be therapeutic for schizophrenia, in particular the phenothiazines and the butyrophenones. As discussed in Chapter 6, these compounds are no mere tranquilizers for schizophrenic excitement but act specifically on the core symptoms of the disorder. Clinical studies have shown their predominant action to be the relief of Bleuler's fundamental symptoms of thought disorder and affective blunting, with less marked effects on such accessory symptoms as hallucinations and delusions (Cole & Davis, 1969). The striking clinical effects of these agents have earned them the colloquial designation of antipsychotic and/or antischizophrenic drugs.

These agents were used to treat schizophrenic patients for several years before either their precise clinical effects or their pharmacological mode of action were fully appreciated. By the mid-1960s, however, it became increasingly apparent that they were true antipsychotic compounds that exerted their effects by blocking the action of dopamine at postsynaptic receptor sites. In 1963, Carlsson and Lindquist discovered that these drugs *increased* the rate of dopamine synthesis in mouse brain tissue. They reasoned that this effect was due to a blockade of dopamine receptor sites and that the increased synthesis represented a reflexive adjustment by the presynaptic neuron to overcome the block. This speculation has subsequently been supported by numerous further observations. For example, one test relies on the sensitivity to dopamine of an enzyme—adenylate cyclase—localized at postsynaptic cell membranes. Adenylate cyclase activation is thought to be an important mechanism in the process of neural impulse regeneration at postsynaptic dopamine receptors. Studies have shown that antipsychotics inhibit the activation of adenylate cyclase by dopamine. More particularly, the clinical potency of various antipsychotics is strongly correlated with the degree to which they inhibit adenylate cyclase activation (Iverson, 1975). Other work has shown that the affinity of antipsychotics for postsynaptic receptor sites (i.e., the degree to which they become attached to receptors) is also highly correlated with their clinical efficacy (Creese, Burt, & Snyder, 1976). The generalization is therefore warranted that drugs that alleviate fundamental symptoms of schizophrenia also block dopamine receptors in proportion to their clinical potency. It is but a small step to conclude that schizophrenic symptoms are related to hyperactivation of one or more of the dopamine pathways in the brain.

An untoward side effect of antipsychotic drug treatment provides further evidence. Schizophrenic patients on therapeutic regimes of certain of the antipsychotics are often troubled by muscular rigidity, tremors, and the loss of fine skilled movements. These symptoms are also seen in Parkinson's disease, a neurological disorder associated with the depletion of dopamine in nigro-striatal neurons (Fig. 3.7). Thus many antipsychotics produce a functional form of Parkinson's disease, presumably due to their block of nigro-striatal dopamine synapses. Parkinson's disease can be alleviated by increasing brain levels of dopamine through administration of the dopamine precursor, l-dopa. When given to schizophrenic patients, however, l-dopa exacerbates the symptom expression in much the same way as does amphetamine administration. In sum, drugs that are effective in treating schizophrenic symptoms produce side effects associated with dopamine

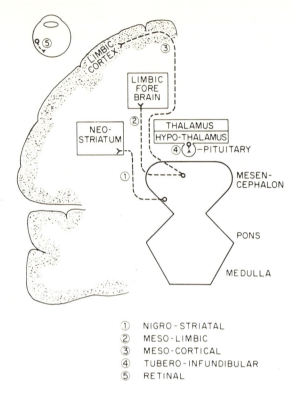

①	NIGRO-STRIATAL
②	MESO-LIMBIC
③	MESO-CORTICAL
④	TUBERO-INFUNDIBULAR
⑤	RETINAL

FIG. 3.7.   Major dopamine pathways. (From Meltzer & Stahl, 1976.)

depletion; drugs that increase available dopamine (and thus alleviate Parkinsonian symptoms) worsen the symptoms of schizophrenia.

The dopamine hypothesis of schizophrenia is primarily inferential; that is, it is a deduction that combines observations on the clinical effects of amphetamines and antipsychotic compounds with a knowledge of the synaptic mechanisms by which they exert their effects. The hypothesis would be immeasurably enhanced if more direct evidence were available, either in the form of altered levels of dopamine metabolites in body fluids or in anomalies of dopamine-synthesizing enzyme activity in brain tissue of schizophrenic patients.

Unfortunately, no such evidence has yet been found. For example, tests have been made for altered levels of homovanillic acid (HVA), a major metabolite of dopamine, in the cerebrospinal fluid of schizophrenic patients. Excessive brain dopamine levels would be expected to lead to elevated HVA levels in undrugged schizophrenic patients. Studies comparing patients to nonschizophrenic controls, however, find no differences in cerebrospinal

HVA levels (Matthysse & Lipinski, 1975). On the other hand, elevated HVA levels are observed in schizophrenic patients for several weeks after initiation of neuroleptic drug treatment, which is consistent with the Carlsson and Lindquist (1963) hypothesis of increased dopamine synthesis following receptor blockade by these drugs (Post & Goodwin, 1975).

Other studies have examined activity levels of enzymes that regulate the synthesis or inactivation of dopamine. The enzyme dopamine-beta-hydroxylase (DBH) is responsible for the conversion of dopamine to norepinephrine in noradrenergic neurons (Fig. 3.3), and therefore diminished DBH activity causes a relative excess of dopamine over norepinephrine at these sites. In an unusual study, Wise and Stein (1973) reported reduced DBH activity in autopsied brains of schizophrenic patients. DBH activity was assayed in brain tissue from 18 patients who had died of natural causes while hospitalized and from 12 controls who had died suddenly in accidents or from heart attacks. The schizophrenic group showed reduced DBH activity in all brain regions examined. However, a subsequent study by Wyatt, Schwartz, Erdelyi, and Barchas (1975) on postmortem tissue from nine schizophrenic and nine control subjects was unable to reproduce these findings. Although there was a tendency toward reduced DBH activity in the schizophrenic sample, the differences were not statistically significant. Nor were Wyatt and his colleagues able to find any differences in DBH activity levels in the blood plasma of schizophrenic patients and controls.

Wyatt's group also reported reduced levels of the enzyme monoamine oxidase (MAO) in the blood platelets of schizophrenic patients. In neuronal tissue, this enzyme regulates the intracellular inactivation of catecholamines, and thus reduced activity would be consistent with heightened dopamine levels. Yet six studies have found no differences between schizophrenic and control subjects in *brain* MAO levels. The observation of reduced blood platelet MAO activity, though robust, thus remains a finding without clear theoretical implications. Because MAO activity is genetically controlled, however, platelet assays do hold promise as a biochemical index of a genetic abnormality in schizophrenia, as discussed in the following chapter (Wyatt & Murphy, 1975).

Although abnormal levels of dopamine metabolites have not been demonstrated in schizophrenic patients, this is not necessarily fatal to the dopamine hypothesis. It may simply mean that the apparent excessive dopamine activity in schizophrenia reflects a heightened sensitivity of postsynaptic receptors rather than abnormal levels of DA synthesis. It is also possible that gross assays of cerebrospinal fluid or brain tissue are not sufficiently sensitive to isolate dopamine abnormalities in specific brain regions. Given the impressive indirect evidence from pharmacological studies, the dopamine hypothesis remains one of the soundest clues to a biochemical characterization of schizophrenia (Matthysse & Lipinski, 1975).

The Orthomolecular Hypothesis

The Model. The orthomolecular hypothesis is not nearly as specific as the transmethylation or the dopamine hypotheses of schizophrenia. It describes a general orientation that views schizophrenic symptoms as secondary to deficiencies of brain nutrients, and it directly implies a treatment that centers on the prescription of an "orthomolecular" diet, including particularly the administration of massive doses of vitamins.

This approach shares a common intellectual origin with the transmethylation hypothesis. In 1952, Osmond and Smythies speculated that schizophrenic symptoms could be accounted for by an abnormal methylation of brain amines to produce an endogenous psychedelic substance akin to mescaline. Shortly thereafter, Osmond and Hoffer (1962) initiated clinical studies on the efficacy of vitamin B_3 (niacin) in the treatment of schizophrenic patients. As noted previously, the rationale for niacin therapy rests on its presumed chemical action as a methyl acceptor: If schizophrenic symptoms are produced by methylated amines, then a substance that competes for methyl groups should act to inhibit the transmethylation of brain amines to psychedelic substances.

This treatment rationale is considered dubious today in light of the continued inability to isolate psychedelic amines or their metabolites in the body fluids of schizophrenic patients and in view of the more recent evidence that niacin probably does not markedly reduce brain pools of available methyl.

Yet niacin continues to play an important role in the orthomolecular treatment of schizophrenia. However, the use of niacin no longer depends on the validity of the transmethylation hypothesis. Schizophrenia is now seen as a vitamin-deficiency disease rather than a disorder of amine metabolism. Linus Pauling, the Nobel Prize winning chemist, outlined this theory in a 1968 paper in which he introduced the term "orthomolecular psychiatry":

> The functioning of the brain is affected by the molecular concentrations of many substances that are normally present in the brain. The optimum concentrations of these substances for a person may differ greatly from the concentrations provided by his normal diet and genetic machinery. Biochemical and genetic arguments support the idea that orthomolecular therapy, the provision for the individual person of the optimal concentrations of important normal constituents of the brain, may be the preferred treatment for many mentally ill patients. Mental symptoms of avitaminosis sometimes are observed long before any physical symptoms appear [pp. 270–271].

The psychosis associated with the niacin-deficiency disease pellagra is most often cited as an appropriate model of schizophrenia by orthomolecular psychiatrists. First described in the eighteenth century, pellagra reached epidemic proportions in the early part of this century among poor and inadequately nourished sharecroppers in the southern United States. Its dietary origin was demonstrated in 1915 and its specific etiology in 1937. The first signs of pellagra are usually a mild degree of anxiety, irritability, restlessness, and fatigue. Later symptoms include a characteristic dermatitis seen as a reddening of the skin followed by a coarse scaling of the extremities and inner surfaces of the thighs. Digestive disturbances and diarrhea are also diagnostic. A certain percentage of untreated cases will progress to the confusion, disorientation, defective memory, and delirium of an organic brain syndrome. As described in Box 3.3, an acute psychosis, including hallucinations, delusions, thought disorder, and severe depression, may also ensue (Noyes & Kolb, 1963).

Orthomolecular psychiatrists point out that the human population can be considered to suffer from as many deficiency diseases as there are vitamins and other "essential" nutrients; that is, man does not have the genetic machinery to manufacture certain nutrients from biochemical precursors but

---

Box 3.3—Pellagral Psychosis

Patient a 30-year-old female.... Complained of recent loss of weight, diarrhea, peculiar skin condition.... Her mouth became very sore and an eruption of the skin developed over the backs of both hands and extended halfway to the elbow.... She began to talk in a very irrelevant fashion, was very apprehensive. She frequently screamed and cried out in the middle of the night. At times during this period, she complained of depression and threatened suicide.... Frequently she was confused, on one occasion wandered for a long time about the city. She became progressively worse....

Her speech was irrelevant and incoherent. For instance, she would call out to her children whom she imagined were in a room downstairs. She often heard her husband talking to her or behaved as if she were at home cooking a meal for her family. Occasionally she had overactive periods when she was very impulsive and resistive. Her mood tended to that of depression. She felt downhearted over her "terrible ailment." She was preoccupied with the feeling that harm would happen to her or to her family. She felt that people were "working against" her. She stated that she was afraid that her food was poisoned or that some injections would be given to her to put her "out of the way."

Hallucinations were present in both the visual and auditory fields. She "saw" patients looking in at her at night, or heard her children downstairs calling her by name. Her odd behavior in the wards frequently was a response to these hallucinations. She was completely disoriented for time, place, and person. She showed marked defects of memory for recent events. She was unable to give the events of her past life with any degree of sequence.

—Adapted from Strecker, Ebaugh, and Ewalt (1951, pp. 197–198)

must absorb them from dietary sources. The dietary absence of any of these essential nutrients is associated with a characteristic deficiency disease, as in the case of pellagra.

Because there is now good evidence that schizophrenia requires a genetic predisposition (see Chapter 4), whereas pellagra may be induced by dietary deficiencies alone, the pellagral model of schizophrenia is inexact. This disparity inclines many orthomolecular psychiatrists to model schizophrenia on a subclass of deficiency diseases—the vitamin-*dependency* diseases, in which the patient requires massive doses of specific vitamins to correct an inherited metabolic disorder. Dependency diseases are associated with abnormal amino acid metabolites in body fluids and clinical symptoms including anemia, convulsions, and mental retardation. Specific disorders have been reported for inherited dependencies of vitamins B_1, B_6, B_{12}, and folic acid. These are rare disorders and are usually manifest early in life (A.P.A. Task Force, 1973). Contemporary orthomolecular thinking therefore regards pellagral psychosis as a model of schizophrenia but sees the nutritional deficiency as an expression of a genetic predisposition analogous to vitamin-dependency diseases (Pauling, 1968).

Orthomolecular therapists treat schizophrenic patients with a straightforward "medical model" approach. At intake, the patient will usually be given a battery of laboratory assessments, including tests for glucose tolerance, thyroid function, and liver function, as well as standard blood count and urine analyses. Symptomatology is generally assessed with the Hoffer–Osmond Diagnostic (HOD) Test, a 145-item true–false scale that probes the perceptual and cognitive changes characteristic of early schizophrenic episodes. All test findings are interpreted to the patient, including a biochemical explanation of his or her schizophrenic phenomenology. The HOD Test is explained as an index of "metabolic disperception" and serves as a bench-mark against which treatment gains may be evaluated (Hawkins, 1973a).

Patients are strongly encouraged to treat their schizophrenic difficulties like "any other illness." They are advised to avoid excessive fatigue and stress and are placed on a hypoglycemic diet to reduce the intake of sugar, starch, and caffeine. Standard antipsychotic drug treatment is prescribed. The dose and type of drug will vary as in any clinical regimen with individual needs and response. The megavitamin aspect of the therapy centers around the administration of niacin (nicotinic acid or nicotinamide). The standard dose is 3 grams/day but may rise to many times this level as indicated. In addition, ascorbic acid (Vitamin C), pyridoxine (Vitamin B_6), and Vitamin E are routinely prescribed as supplements. The inclusion of the supplementary vitamins is based primarily on clinical impressions of their adjunctive therapeutic efficacy (Hawkins, 1973b).

The Evidence. In assessing the orthomolecular approach, a distinction should be made between the orthomolecular *hypothesis*, as set out most clearly in Pauling's 1968 paper, and orthomolecular *treatment*, which may include a variety of therapeutic techniques in addition to the defining use of large doses of Vitamins C, B_3, B_6, and B_{12}. The orthomolecular hypothesis is compatible with a range of nutritional treatments in addition to this currently preferred combination of chemicals. Any failure to demonstrate the efficacy of current megavitamin treatment would not therefore constitute disproof of the general hypothesis. On the other hand, any demonstration of efficacy can only be regarded as consistent with the general hypothesis rather than as conclusive.

Researchers agree that inadequate nutrition can produce deleterious psychological effects. In a famous experimental test (Keys, Brozek, Henschel, Mickelson, & Taylor, 1950), volunteer subjects were placed on a low-caloric diet for 24 weeks, resulting in an average 25% weight loss. The psychological concomitants included depression, apathy, anxiety, and irritability; normal sociability was replaced by tactlessness and explosive tempers; self-esteem gave way to feelings of incompetence and inferiority. These effects were reversed when the subjects were again placed on an adequate diet. More recently, nutritionists have begun to investigate the brain mechanisms underlying these alterations. For example, the manipulation of dietary amino acids can be shown to influence brain concentrations of various transmitter substances in experimental animals. Rats fed a meal high in carbohydrates show an influx of brain tryptophan and proportional increase in serotonin synthesis. Brain tyrosine concentrations may be similarly increased by protein diets rich in its amino acid precursor phenylalanine, and it appears that this in turn influences the rate of catecholamine synthesis (Kolata, 1976). As is the case with natural experiments like pellagra, such experimental evidence is compatible with the orthomolecular hypothesis but does not prove that the specific condition of schizophrenia is secondary to imbalances of brain nutrients. It must still be shown that such imbalances in fact characterize schizophrenic patients.

Many orthomolecular psychiatrists regard the apparent clinical benefits of megavitamin treatment as proof of the orthomolecular hypothesis. But this stance encounters both logical and empirical problems. Logically, megavitamin therapy might work for reasons that have little to do with orthomolecular theory. For example, vitamins in large doses have actions independent and different from their normal enzymatic actions. Niacin causes vasodilation and lowers blood cholesterol at high doses (A.P.A. Task Force, 1973). Thus the mode of action of megavitamin treatment may be quite different from the nutritional supplementation demanded by orthomolecular theory.

The clinical efficacy of megavitamin therapy is even more controversial. The systematic evidence in favor of the treatment rests on two studies carried out by Hoffer and Osmond in the 1950s (Hoffer, 1966, 1969). The subjects of the first study were 30 hospitalized schizophrenic patients placed into three groups: placebo, nicotinic acid, or nicotinamide. The vitamins were given at doses of 3 grams/day for 33 days. In addition, all patients were continued on individually prescribed treatment regimes, which could include other drugs, psychotherapy, and electroconvulsive therapy (ECT). Little difference was noted among the groups during the 33-day hospitalization period, but at a 1-year follow-up, seven of the 10 placebo subjects required further hospitalization, compared to four of the 20 subjects in the combined nicotinic-acid–nicotinamide groups. Hoffer and Osmond's second study involved a total of 82 patients treated for varying lengths of time over a 4-year period. All received individually tailored conventional therapies, in addition to which 43 received a placebo and 39 received nicotinic acid. In this study, the nicotinic-acid group showed significant improvement over the placebo group while in the hospital, but long-term differences in relapse rates were minimal (A.P.A. Task Force, 1973). Hoffer (1969) summarizes results of the two studies by saying that megavitamin therapy works best for cases of early schizophrenia, that it most often must be combined with ECT or antipsychotic drug treatment, and that it is more effective in preventing relapse than in reversing the disorder in the first place.

In the years since these results first became known, thousands of schizophrenic patients have been treated with massive doses of niacin and other vitamins. Many private-practice psychiatrists and, in some cases, entire clinics now regard megavitamin therapy as an effective adjunctive treatment for schizophrenia (e.g., Hawkins, 1973a, b).

In light of the increasing popularity of megavitamin therapy, the American Psychiatric Association in 1973 undertook a review of its rationale and efficacy, including an analysis of more recent attempts to replicate the original Hoffer and Osmond results. The report concluded that "the results and claims of the advocates of megavitamin therapy have not been confirmed by several groups of psychiatrists and psychologists experienced in psychopharmacological research [A.P.A. Task Force, 1973, p. 45]."

This sharp challenge to orthomolecular psychiatry rests primarily on two major investigations. The first studied a group of 75 patients who received 3 grams/day nicotinic acid (47 patients) or placebo (28 patients) for 2 years. Niacin therapy or placebo were in addition to other types of therapy employed at the discretion of the attending psychiatrist. The results showed no differences between the two groups in length of hospitalization, readmission rates, ratings of symptomatic improvement, or home and community adjustment. A post-hoc analysis of the data did indicate, however, that niacin in conjunction with anti-psychotic drugs benefited a subgroup of patients with a good premorbid history [i.e., so-called reactive schizophrenic patients (Wittenborn, Weber, & Brown, 1973)].

The second investigation cited by the A.P.A. consisted of a series of studies sponsored by the Canadian Mental Health Association. In none of these studies was niacin treatment, singly or in combination with other therapies, found to be efficacious. One study found that the therapeutic efficacy of nicotinic acid as the sole medication in newly admitted schizophrenic patients was no greater than an inactive placebo. Another study compared antipsychotic drugs plus niacin with a drug-only condition. The combined therapy was no more effective than antipsychotic drug treatment alone in either newly admitted or in chronically hospitalized schizophrenic patients. A third study found that nicotinic acid was unable to counteract the methionine-induced exacerbation of clinical symptoms (A.P.A. Task Force, 1973).

The promise of niacin treatment heralded by the early investigations of Hoffer and Osmond has not, therefore, been confirmed by subsequent independent investigations, with the possible exception of cases of early schizophrenia. But megavitamin therapists criticize the adequacy of these recent investigations as tests of orthomolecular treatment. Where controlled studies necessarily rely on standard doses of single vitamins for limited durations, clinical treatment may more flexibly employ a variety of vitamins in varying concentrations and for variable lengths of time, depending on patient response. In light of their clinical impressions that megavitamin treatment is a useful adjunct to conventional therapies, practitioners are unlikely to drop a relatively harmless treatment on the basis of what they consider an inadequate experimental test of orthomolecular therapy. As with many other treatments in psychiatry and clinical psychology, megavitamin therapy continues amid controversy regarding its efficacy and with minimal scientific justification.

COMMENTARY

The recent biochemical literature on schizophrenia conveys a strong sense of optimism, a confidence that the road leading to a certain understanding has at last been found. This is in marked contrast to the sense of confusion, if not disillusionment, that characterized biochemical research in years past. The turnabout can be traced to two widely cited review articles by Seymour Kety, an eminent psychiatrist and biochemist (Kety, 1959a, b). Kety took his colleagues to task for diffusing their efforts rather than focusing on promising leads, for pursuing research built on questionable assumptions regarding the nature of schizophrenia, and, especially, for ignoring the dictates of sound experimental methodology. Kety's papers pointed to the transmethylation process and to amphetamine psychosis as leads likely to yield the greatest future payoff. Kety's critique and his prescient suggestions have led rather directly to a now sophisticated and exciting field of scientific endeavor that holds a key position in research on schizophrenia.

The transmethylation, dopamine, and orthomolecular hypotheses do not exhaust biochemical investigations of schizophrenia. Indeed, as increasing knowledge of the structure, function, and disorders of the central nervous system accumulate, new ideas are continually tested against the mystery of schizophrenia. For example, Torrey and Peterson (1976) have recently spelled out an interesting analogy between schizophrenia and several rare degenerative neurological diseases caused by "slow" viruses whose effects are manifested years after the initial infection. This hypothesis is in the tradition of biochemical investigations built on analogies between schizophrenia and other better understood conditions. But it, like other leads that have not been covered here, lacks the voluminous supporting research on schizophrenic patients of the three major hypotheses we have discussed.

Among neuroscientists, the dopamine hypothesis is considered the strongest of the three. It rests on several solid observations. Amphetamines in sustained doses can produce the symptoms of acute paranoid schizophrenia in volunteer subjects and can also exacerbate the symptoms of schizophrenic patients. They act primarily by potentiating the release of dopamine at dopaminergic synapses. In contrast, antipsychotic drugs, known to alleviate Bleuler's fundamental symptoms of schizophrenia, appear to act by blocking the action of dopamine at postsynaptic receptor sites. Strong correlations are found between the clinical potency of various neuroleptics and their dopamine-blocking actions. The inference is that schizophrenic patients suffer from heightened activity in one or more of the several dopaminergic neuronal pathways of the brain. This hypothesis both guides and is consistent with a growing experimental literature (e.g., Meltzer & Stahl, 1976; van Praag, 1977).

The recent empirical success of the dopamine hypothesis has tended to displace the older transmethylation hypothesis from the center of scientific attention. Yet the latter must still be considered viable. It rests on the plausible assumption that a relatively minor enzymatic error transforms naturally occurring brain amines to amines having psychedelic properties. Single methylation of brain amines is a normally occurring process in the metabolic inactivation of many amines, and the transmethylation hypothesis requires but the di- or tri-methylation of amine compounds to produce compounds closely similar in structure to known psychedelic substances. The hypothesis is supported primarily by the ability of methionine, a methyl doner, to exacerbate the symptoms of schizophrenic patients. This effect, replicated in a number of independent investigations, stands as one of the most consistent findings in the biochemistry of schizophrenia and must therefore be taken seriously. It is of course possible that the effects of methionine on schizophrenic patients is mediated by biosynthetic processes other than transmethylation, or that the observed symptomatic exacerbation represents a toxic reaction superimposed on the natural psychosis. These possible qualifications are as yet without substantiation. But even were they to prove valid, they would nonetheless provide important leads to biochemical mechanisms in schizophrenia.

The transmethylation hypothesis suffers from the inability to demonstrate the obverse of methionine loading (i.e., the amelioration of schizophrenic symptoms with the administration of methyl-accepting compounds). The equivocal therapeutic efficacy of niacin is often taken as evidence contrary to the transmethylation hypothesis. But it has been more recently demonstrated that niacin is not in fact a potent methyl acceptor in biological systems (Baldessarini, 1967), so that the transmethylation hypothesis does not depend on niacin's therapeutic effectiveness. Curiously, a well-controlled investigation of the possible ameliorative effects of other more potent methyl-accepting compounds has yet to be undertaken.

The orthomolecular hypothesis stands outside the mainstream of biochemical research in schizophrenia. If the transmethylation and dopamine hypotheses represent currently favored views, then the orthomolecular position is definitely anti-establishment. This is seen nowhere more clearly than in the 1973 American Psychiatric Association Task Force report, *Megavitamin and Orthomolecular Therapy in Psychiatry*, a devastating attack on the orthomolecular movement. The report does provide a systematic survey of the growth of orthomolecular psychiatry and a sophisticated analysis of its theoretical and empirical limitations. But it also proposes scientific standards for evaluating megavitamin therapy that could scarcely be met by the great majority of treatments in the mental health field. And, at points, it descends into vituperative and petty criticisms of published statements of orthomolecular psychiatrists.

The antipathy of the psychiatric establishment contrasts with the testimonials of thousands of patients and their families who have been treated by orthomolecular therapists. By concentrating too narrowly on the admittedly equivocal efficacy of megavitamin therapy, the critics may be missing the larger truth behind such testimonials. The frank medical model approach to schizophrenia taken by orthomolecular therapists, the active enlistment of assistance from patients' families, and the optimistic view of prognosis communicated by therapists to patients are in contrast to more orthodox approaches to the therapy of schizophrenia. It is conceivable that such therapeutic optimism accounts for those successes that do occur while at the same time challenging more conventional approaches and thus raising reactive antagonism.

Because therapeutic outcomes in mental health work are to some extent determined by nonspecific factors, it is poor policy to take therapeutic efficacy (or lack thereof) as evidence for (or against) the theory underlying the treatment in question. The theory must be evaluated in terms other than that provided by therapeutic practice. In this respect, the orthomolecular hypothesis commands little supporting data. Although the assertion that optimal brain functioning depends on adequate molecular concentrations of essential nutrients is eminently plausible, the specifics of the view have yet to be established with regard to schizophrenia. Deficiency diseases like pellagra illustrate the general point, but the biochemical mechanisms by which brain nutrients influence psychological states are only beginning to be explored. In addition, there is no good evidence that schizophrenia or any of its subtypes are associated with nutritionally dependent biochemical imbalances.

In addition to weighing the experimental evidence for these three major biochemical hypotheses, one must also examine the underlying models from which they are derived. At base, the studies reviewed here represent a neurochemical analysis of three induced psychoses taken as metaphors for the schizophrenic psychosis. Biochemical hypotheses are necessarily limited to the extent that the metaphors fail to recapitulate the details of true schizophrenia.

The psychedelic high underlying the transmethylation hypothesis is most apposite to the preclinical subjective changes experienced by many early schizophrenic patients. In both, attention is broadened, perception becomes more acute and vivid, mentation is quickened, and affective experience becomes more labile. This heightened awareness is invested with deep personal meaning in both the early schizophrenic state and the psychedelic high. On the other hand, the psychedelic high is quite removed from the symptoms of later clinical schizophrenia. Although the subjectively dramatic insights and the sense of portentiousness of the psychedelic high suggest schizophrenic delusional formation, the latter is often more bizarre and nihilistic. Psychedelic hallucinations are primarily visual, as opposed to the more typical auditory hallucinations of schizophrenia. The cardinal schizophrenic symptoms of affective blunting and formal thought disorder are absent in the psychedelic state.

The amphetamine psychosis informing the dopamine hypothesis is strikingly similar to acute paranoid schizophrenia. Aggressive feelings and actions, systematized persecutory delusions, and auditory hallucinations are common in both. Yet paranoid schizophrenia is sufficiently unlike other clinical forms of the disorder to the extent that clinicians since Kraepelin have debated the wisdom of combining this condition with other schizophrenic states. As discussed in Chapter 1, distinguishing between paranoid and nonparanoid patients considerably enhances diagnostic validity. Although some observers do report tangential thinking and affective blunting in some cases of amphetamine psychosis, the relatively low incidence of these effects limits the relevance of this state to more classical forms of clinical schizophrenia.

Pellagral psychosis is perhaps the least compelling of the three models of schizophrenia. Although Bleuler's accessory symptoms often appear, affective blunting and formal thought disorder are not typical. Unlike most forms of schizophrenia, the pellagral psychosis is often marked by severe depression, with or without anxiety. The most important distinction between the two states is the presence of an organic brain syndrome of varying extent and severity in pellagral psychosis that clearly separates it from schizophrenic conditions.

It is clear then that none of the three models is an exact analogue of clinical schizophrenia. This may mean simply that a more satisfactory analogue has yet to be found. Or it may reflect a temporal distinction between model psychoses as acute, short-term, and reversible conditions and schizophrenia as a long-term, insidious developmental process. Snyder (1974) argues, for example, that prolonged administration of amphetamines might lead to a more exact recreation of clinical schizophrenia than the acute paranoid state seen with short-term administration. The problem here is that tolerance develops to most psychoactive drugs, so that their effects are usually muted rather than amplified with continued ingestion.

The discrepancy suggests that the biochemistry of schizophrenia is unlikely to be reduced to a single defect, as is implied by available model psychoses. As the clinical condition is heterogeneous, so too must be the underlying biochemical correlates. One possible formulation of this multiple-defect hypothesis is that the individual patient progresses through a series of states, each corresponding more or less to one of the available model psychoses and each associated with a specific biochemical anomaly. In this view, the heightened awareness of early schizophrenia might be seen as correlated with transmethylation errors, and later delusional formation might be correlated with a developing dopamine hyperactivity. The even later stages of schizophrenic affective and thought disorder might be linked to an as yet unknown biochemical imbalance.

An alternative formulation, consistent with Kraepelin's original disease entity approach, would distinguish subclasses of schizophrenic patients on the basis of similar biochemical profiles. Thus it may be possible to link different clinical types to different underlying biochemical imbalances. This approach holds out the hope for more refined diagnostic procedures that would replace symptom syndromes with objective determinations of patients' biochemical profiles.

A third formulation of the multiple-defect hypothesis takes a dynamic view of the biochemical state of the brain at any given time. Even though a discrete defect may in fact exist, the brain will react to the insult by compensatory adjustments, which will ramify through its subsystems and produce secondary biochemical imbalances. For example, Parkinson's disease is associated with a dopamine deficiency in nigro-striatal neurons, and its symptoms can be alleviated by increasing concentrations of brain dopamine through the adminstration of l-dopa. Yet before l-dopa therapy was developed, Parkinsonian symptoms were often controlled by the administration of agents that blocked the activity of the neurotransmitter acetylcholine. Thus a complete biochemical characterization of Parkinson's disease must include both the dopamine deficiency and an apparently compensatory acetylcholine hyperactivity. Treatments that increase available dopamine or decrease available acetylcholine produce similar clinical outcomes.

There can be little question that most schizophrenic patients suffer from heightened activity in one or more of the dopaminergic pathways of the brain. But this does not necessarily indicate that this is the core or only biochemical defect in schizophrenia. It may simply represent an adjustive reaction to biochemical imbalances in neuronal systems that impinge on dopamine tracts. Dopaminergic hyperactivity may correlate directly with paranoid symptomatology (following the amphetamine psychosis model), but other clinical features would be associated with quantitative biochemical aberrations at other levels of neuronal organization. All this implies that no single-defect hypothesis (or associated model psychosis) will ever satisfactorily account for the heterogeneity of schizophrenia. Rather, hypotheses must be constructed on the assumption of a dynamic interaction between multiple neurochemical systems (Antelman & Caggiula, 1977).

good point .

Genetic Factors

It is a common observation, that men born of parents that are sometimes wont to be mad, will be obnoxious to the same disease.

—Thomas Willis (1685)

Thus far we have examined schizophrenia on a variety of descriptive levels: the level of clinical symptoms and syndromes (Chapter 1), the level of subjective experience (Chapter 2), and the level of brain biochemistry (Chapter 3). These are in effect alternate but correlated ways of construing the schizophrenic psychosis. In this chapter and the following one, we turn to more specifically etiological issues by examining evidence concerning genetic and life history precursors of this complex state. This chapter considers evidence supporting a genetic predisposition to schizophrenia, and Chapter 5 assesses the complementary influence of developmental and social–psychological factors.

CONSANGUINITY STUDIES

Genetic studies of schizophrenia are rooted in the "common observation" that schizophrenia tends to run in families, or, less colloquially, that schizophrenia occurs at a higher rate among relatives of schizophrenic patients than in the general population. This has been demonstrated many times over by so-called family or consanguinity studies. In the typical study, relatives are categorized in terms of their degree of genetic relationship to a schizophrenic patient in order to establish whether their risk of also being schizophrenic increases accordingly. Roughly speaking, first-degree relatives—parents, siblings, children—have 50% of their genes in common, whereas second-degree relatives—cousins, aunts and uncles, nephews and nieces, grandparents and grandchildren—have a 25% gene overlap. These differences thus establish a natural experiment in which the degree of genetic relatedness to a schizophrenic patient is the independent variable and the risk of schizophrenia is the dependent variable.

Table 4.1 summarizes the risks for schizophrenia for various types of first- and second-degree relatives of schizophrenic patients. Each figure is a pooled estimate from several independent investigations, the number of investigations being noted in the first column. These figures are usually compared to an estimate of the risk of schizophrenia in the general population of approximately 1% (Slater & Cowie, 1971). (Note that these data derive primarily from European studies employing a relatively restricted definition of schizophrenia and thus are conservative estimates of the prevalence of schizophrenia in the general population and among patients' relatives.)

Second-degree relatives show risks for clinical schizophrenia ranging between about 2% and 3% or between two and three times the general population risk of about 1%. The figures for first-degree relatives are more variable, largely because the reported risk for parents is much lower than that for either sibs or children. The usual explanation for this anomaly is that only the more intact schizophrenic individuals are likely to marry and produce children, so that many potential schizophrenic parents are therefore selected out. When suitable correction is made for this, the parental risk falls between the risks for sibs and for children (Gottesman & Shields, 1972). Most authorities are therefore inclined to accept a figure of 10%, or 10 times the

TABLE 4.1
Risk of Schizophrenia for Relatives of Schizophrenic Patients[a]

Studies	Relationship	Risk
	First-Degree Relatives	
12	Siblings	8.51
5	Children	12.31
14	Parents	4.38
	Second-Degree Relatives	
4	Grandchildren	2.81
4	Uncles and aunts	2.01
5	Nephews and nieces	2.25
4	First cousins	2.91

[a]Adapted from Slater and Cowie (1971).

general population prevalence, as a round estimate of the risk among first-degree relatives in general.

The increasing risk for schizophrenia as a function of one's degree of genetic similarity to a schizophrenic patient may be interpreted as evidence for a genetic precursor to later schizophrenia. However, family members share social environments as well as genes, and environmental similarity will increase within families as the degree of genetic relatedness also increases. It is always possible that living in the same family with a schizophrenic relative, with its attendant stresses and disruptions, increases one's chances of also being schizophrenic for purely environmental reasons. Consanguinity studies are thus classic examples of confounded experiments in that two independent factors—heredity and family environment—vary simultaneously. Thus no clear inference can be drawn as to the determinants of the observed risks. Consanguinity data are compatible with both genetic and social transmission hypotheses of schizophrenic etiology.

TWIN STUDIES

A more satisfactory resolution of this nature–nurture conflict can be achieved by comparing the risk for schizophrenia among identical, or monozygotic, twins of patients with the risk among fraternal, or dizygotic, twins of patients. This method relies on the natural experiment that produces two types of twins differing in their degree of genetic relationship. Monozygotic (MZ) twins arise from the fertilization of a single ovum, which splits several days after conception to produce two genetically identical individuals. Dizygotic (DZ) twins arise from the fertilization of two separate ova, producing twins, who like ordinary siblings, share on the average 50% of their genes in common. If the assumption is made that the co-twins of any MZ or DZ pair are raised in similar environments, then any difference in the risk for schizophrenia between the MZ and DZ co-twins of schizophrenic patients is evidence for the operation of a genetic factor.

The assumption of environmental similarity does not mean that environmental variation is absent *between* pairs of either MZ or DZ twins. Obviously, the range of environments for a sample of twin pairs will be as great as the range in the population from which they are drawn. Twins are born to families of varying ethnic, socioeconomic, and cultural backgrounds, having varying values, family structures, and child-rearing practices. The similarity assumption simply means that the average environmental difference *within* pairs of twins will not differ appreciably for samples of MZ versus DZ twins. In statistical terms, the twin method assumes more or less equal environmental variation, but differing genetic variation, between samples of MZ and DZ twins.

how decide what 'at risk' is.

Some have argued (e.g., Jackson, 1962) that MZ twins tend to be raised differently than DZ twins, so that systematic environmental differences must be present between the two types. For example, MZ twins are necessarily of the same sex, whereas only half of all DZ twins will be same-sexed. To the extent that boys and girls are reared differently, the within-pair environments of a sample of MZ twins will be more similar than those for a sample of DZ twins. For this reason, twin studies often limit comparisons to MZ versus same-sex DZ pairs. Identical twins undoubtedly also elicit more similar reactions from parents, peers, and others than is the case for fraternal twins. On the other hand, the nature and extent of MZ–DZ pair differences are, in principle, open to empirical determination and assessment for their contribution to the etiology of schizophrenia. Thus, although average environmental differences undoubtedly exist between samples of MZ and DZ twins, it is nonetheless true that no differences of etiological significance have ever been demonstrated (Gottesman & Shields, 1972). Although future investigations might conceivably uncover such differences, their absence to date strengthens the inferences that twin studies generate concerning the role of genetic factors in schizophrenia.

More than a dozen major twin studies of schizophrenia have been reported over the last half-century. All have employed essentially the same procedure. First, schizophrenic patients who are also twins are identified. These are known as index cases, or probands. Information is then collected on the co-twins to determine each pair's MZ or DZ status and whether the co-twin is also schizophrenic. Pairs in which both twins are schizophrenic are said to be *concordant*; pairs in which only one twin is schizophrenic are called *discordant*. A co-twin may be discordant for schizophrenia either because he or she suffers from some other psychiatric disability or because he or she is psychiatrically normal.

It is convenient to distinguish twin studies conducted prior to about 1960 from those carried out after that time. The results of a half-dozen early studies, as reanalyzed by Gottesman and Shields (1966a), are presented in Table 4.2. Without exception, each reported higher MZ than DZ concordances. The pooled data showed that 65% of MZ co-twins of schizophrenic patients are also schizophrenic, compared with 12% of DZ co-twins—a figure consistent with the risk for ordinary siblings. Because the concordance for MZ pairs is more than five times that of DZ pairs, the immediate conclusion is that there must be a genetic factor in the etiology of schizophrenia.

Curiously, it has only been in the last decade that the majority of North American mental health professionals has taken this conclusion seriously. As with the results of consanguinity studies, the findings of these early twin investigations were compelling only to those already convinced. Although the concordance figures for both MZ and DZ pairs are quite consistent from

TABLE 4.2
Early Twin Studies of Schizophrenia: MZ Versus Same-Sex DZ
Concordance[a]

Investigator	MZ		DZ	
	Pairs	%	Pairs	%
Luxenburger (1928)	11/19	58	0/13	0
Rosanoff et al. (1934)	25/41	61	7/53	13
Essen-Möller (1941)	7/11	64	4/27	15
Kallmann (1946)	120/174	69	34/296	11
Slater (1953)	24/37	65	8/58	14
Inouye (1963)	33/55	60	2/11	18
Totals	220/337	65	55/458	12

[a]Adapted from Gottesman and Shields (1966a).

study to study, weaknesses in the methods employed to gather the data raised enough doubts to obviate their cumulative impact.

Concordance figures necessarily depend on what we now know to be a fairly unreliable diagnostic system, so that diagnostic errors might have inflated concordance figures. For example, Essen-Möller's case material (Table 4.2) can be interpreted as demonstrating an MZ concordance ranging from zero to 86%, depending on the liberality with which schizophrenia is diagnosed (Gottesman & Shields, 1966a). In Kallmann's widely cited 1946 study (Table 4.2), a pair of twins in which one showed marked schizophrenic deterioration and the other massive neurotic symptoms would be considered concordant (Kringlen, 1967). Clearly, the concordance figures of these studies are softer than would at first appear to be the case.

A second major problem was that zygosity determinations were often made on the basis of judgments of physical similarity, sometimes from second-hand reports, rather than by use of more objective measures such as similarity of blood groups or fingerprints. To the degree that less than objective methods were used in assigning pairs to MZ or DZ categories, a potential source of bias was present, especially in cases where one investigator made both zygosity and diagnostic judgments.

By far the most serious criticism of these early studies (and one that applies with equal force to other areas of research on schizophrenia) is that the methods of identifying schizophrenic twins probably yielded samples that did not represent the entire population of schizophrenic patients. Ideally, a twin study should select its sample by first identifying all twin births in a defined population for a given time period, followed by an identification of those pairs in which one or both members became schizophrenic at some time in their lives. But this strategy demands a refinement in record keeping that is difficult if not impossible to find in most countries, so that early investigators

[handwritten marginal note: sources are already slightly biased]

were often obliged to begin with the material at hand (i.e., schizophrenic patients of twin birth who were residents or former residents of mental hospitals). This method produces an atypical sample of schizophrenic persons to the extent that only the more severe cases are hospitalized. Because we now know that more severely affected twin pairs are more likely to be concordant than less severely affected pairs (Gottesman, 1968), the resulting concordance figures are overestimates of the true concordance in the general population of schizophrenic twins. Indeed, most objections to these early twin studies stemmed less from their support of a genetic factor in schizophrenia than from skepticism concerning its magnitude. The very high MZ concordances implied that hereditary factors largely determined later schizophrenia rather than being one factor in what most clinicians saw as a multiply determined disorder.

As these criticisms took hold among genetic researchers, there emerged a second series of twin studies conducted with a high degree of methodological sophistication (Allen, Cohen, & Pollin, 1972; Fischer, 1973; Gottesman & Shields, 1966b, 1972; Kringlen, 1968; Tienari, 1971). Their cumulative impact has been to resolve methodological disputes and to produce more precise formulations of the role of heredity in the etiology of schizophrenia.

Studies by Kringlen (1968) and Gottesman and Shields (1966b, 1972) are particularly fine examples of this latter series. Both relied on extensive personal investigation, as well as official records, of their twin samples. Zygosity determinations in a majority of cases were made by an analysis of blood groups. Kringlen's Norwegian sample consisted of schizophrenic patients of twin birth hospitalized over a 30-year period. This unusually broad sample was made possible by cross-checking a national file of all persons ever hospitalized with a psychotic disorder against a separate birth register. The Gottesman and Shields English sample was collected in an equally systematic manner: Index cases were identified from a pool of 16 years' consecutive admissions to a short-stay psychiatric hospital, an index case defined as a patient with a diagnosis of schizophrenia having a twin surviving to adulthood.

Although the problem of diagnostic unreliability was not directly attacked, both studies were able to assess diagnostic effects on the concordance data by varying the definition of concordance in the co-twins of index cases. Under a "narrow" criterion, both the index and the co-twin were required to have had an officially recorded hospital diagnosis of schizophrenia, of either the process or reactive form. Under a "broad" criterion, the index twin always bore a hospital diagnosis of schizophrenia, while the co-twin could bear other diagnoses. For Kringlen, these included nonspecific reactive psychoses and borderline schizophrenia, while Gottesman and Shields included co-twins hospitalized with any other psychiatric diagnosis.

TABLE 4.3
MZ Versus Same-Sex DZ Twin Pair Concordance

Concordance Criterion	Kringlen (1968)		Gottesman and Shields (1966b)	
	MZ%	DZ%	MZ%	DZ%
Narrow	25	7	42	9
Broad	38	10	54	18
Number of pairs	55	90	24	33

Major results of both studies are seen in Table 4.3. Clearly, concordance figures increase when a broader concordance criterion is used. Even under the broad criterion, however, the figures in both studies are substantially lower than those reported by early investigators. It is also clear that Gottesman and Shields found systematically higher concordances than did Kringlen. It is not impossible that the true population concordances in fact differ between Norway and England, a phenomenon not unknown in population genetics. On the other hand, Kringlen's national sample was probably more representative than the single hospital sample of Gottesman and Shields, and it is to be expected that concordance figures will decrease with increasingly more representative samples. If one were obliged to choose a best estimate of MZ concordance for schizophrenia, it would be tempting to settle on an average of Kringlen's "broadly" defined 38% and Gottesman and Shields' "narrowly" defined 42%. In both cases, these MZ concordances contrast with DZ concordances of approximately 10%, a figure that we have seen is a good estimate of the risk of schizophrenia among all first-degree relatives of schizophrenic patients (Table 4.1).

Deciding on exact figures to express MZ and DZ concordances is less an issue, however, than the major conclusion these and other recent twin studies allow to be drawn with a great deal of certainty: The risk of schizophrenia increases with the degree of genetic similarity to a schizophrenic person.[1] In other words, a genetic predisposition is a necessary condition for the

---

[1]The risk for schizophrenia of an MZ twin of a schizophrenic patient is somewhat greater than the percentage of concordant pairs. Consider a sample of five MZ pairs of which two are concordant and three are discordant for schizophrenia. The *pairwise concordance* is 2/5 = 40%. But there are four individuals (in the two concordant pairs) who are schizophrenic twins of a schizophrenic case and three individuals (in the discordant pairs) who are nonschizophrenic twins of a schizophrenic case. Thus the *casewise concordance* is 4/(4 + 3) = 57%. In the absence of a single method for computing concordance, it is wise to regard the pairwise concordances in Table 4.3 as conservative estimates of the population concordance (Gottesman & Shields, 1972).

development of clinical schizophrenia. That it is not a sufficient condition is also seen in these data. Because approximately 60% of MZ pairs are discordant for schizophrenia, we can conclude that a substantial fraction of genetically predisposed individuals will not develop clinically relevant symptoms of schizophrenia. The important question then becomes one of determining the environmental events that trigger the expression of schizophrenia in the remaining cases. Twin studies therefore provide some of the best evidence that environmental factors must also be involved in the etiology of schizophrenia.

ADOPTION STUDIES

A powerful demonstration of the role of genetic factors in schizophrenia is provided by studies of children born to schizophrenic parents but raised from infancy in foster or adoptive homes. Few such studies have been conducted, presumably because of the rarity of such adoptions and the difficulty of following up the adoptees into adulthood. Yet their evidential value is great, precisely because they involve a clear separation of hereditary factors from the influence of rearing by schizophrenic parents.

Two important studies in this mold, by Heston (1966) and by Rosenthal, Wender, Kety, Schulsinger, Welner, and Ostergaard (1968), evaluated the psychiatric status of adults who had been raised in foster or adoptive homes and who also had at least one natural parent known to be schizophrenic. Both studies compared such index cases with control groups of children born to psychiatrically normal parents and also raised in adoptive settings. Although the adopting homes could conceivably have contained one or more schizophrenic individuals, there is no reason to believe that this unlikely event would have occurred more frequently for the index than for the control cases. As summarized in Table 4.4 (Wender, 1969), a total of eight cases of schizophrenia were observed among the adopted children in the two studies taken together. Without exception, each was the offspring of a schizophrenic parent. These eight cases represent 9% of the total index group, which is consistent with the risk for schizophrenia among children of schizophrenic parents living in the same family (Table 4.1).

The Heston and the Rosenthal et al. studies also found that an additional 21% of the children of schizophrenic parents, compared with 6% of the control children, showed schizophreniclike behavior diagnosed as "schizoid" or "borderline" schizophrenia. These terms are used to designate features that are not psychotic yet resemble clinical symptoms—minor thought disorder, suspiciousness, rigidity, emotional dullness, and peculiar ideation of a delusional nature. The DSM-II term, *Latent Schizophrenia* (Chapter 1), expresses the same concept. People with such traits are generally neither

TABLE 4.4
Schizophrenic Diagnoses Among Offspring of Schizophrenic
Parents (Index Cases) and Nonschizophrenic Parents (Control
Cases)[a]

	Schizophrenia	Borderline Schizophrenia
Heston (1966)		
Index (N = 47)	5	8
Control (N = 50)	0	0
Rosenthal et al. (1968)		
Index (N = 39)	3	10
Control (N = 47)	0	6
Combined		
Index (N = 86)	8 (9%)	18 (21%)
Control (N = 97)	0 (0%)	6 (6%)

[a]Adapted from Wender (1969).

hospitalized nor treated, although they often show difficulty in assuming conventional adult roles. Many lead the life of social isolates, holding low-status, transitory occupations. The heightened incidence of such cases among the offspring of schizophrenic parents suggests that the genetic pre-disposition—the genotype—for clinical schizophrenia also underlies these borderline conditions.

An important study by Kety and his colleagues (Kety, Rosenthal, Wender, Schulsinger, 1968, 1976a; Kety, Rosenthal, Wender, Schulsinger, & Jacobsen, 1976b) approached the experiment-in-nature provided by adoption somewhat differently from the Heston and the Rosenthal et al. studies but found similar results. Instead of starting with schizophrenic mothers and following up their adult offspring, this project first identified schizophrenic adults who had been adopted in infancy and then followed up both their biological and adopting relatives. From more than 5000 Danish adoptions between 1924 and 1947, Kety and colleagues identified 33 adoptees who had subsequently been hospitalized with a DSM-II diagnosis of chronic, acute, or latent schizophrenia. A control group, matched on such items as age, sex, and social class of the adopting family, was selected from adoptees who had never been psychiatric patients. A search of population records yielded a total of 512 biological and adoptive relatives—parents and siblings—of both groups, and psychiatric interviews were carried out with over 90% of those still living. On the basis of the interview protocols, three raters arrived at a consensus diagnosis for each relative, including the two DSM-II categories of chronic and latent schizophrenia or a diagnosis of possible ("uncertain") schizophrenia. The results are set out in Table 4.5. Of the four groups, only the

TABLE 4.5

Prevalence of Schizophrenia Spectrum Disorders in the Biological and Adoptive Relatives of Schizophrenic Index and Control Subjects, from Consensus Diagnosis on Interview[a]

Type of Relative	Number of Relatives Identified	Diagnosis of Schizophrenia in Relatives							
		Chronic		Latent		Uncertain		Total	
		Number	%	Number	%	Number	%	Number	%
Biological relatives of schizophrenic adoptees	173	5[b]	2.9	6	3.5	13[c]	7.5	24[d]	13.9
Biological relatives of control adoptees	174	0	—	3	1.7	3	1.7	6	3.4
Adoptive relatives of schizophrenic adoptees	74	1	1.4	0	—	1	1.4	2	2.7
Adoptive relatives of control adoptees	91	1	1.1	1	1.1	3	3.3	5	5.5

[a]From Kety et al. (1976b).
[b]$p < 0.05$ (significances apply to differences between biological relatives of schizophrenic adoptees and controls; other differences were not significant).
[c]$p < 0.01$.
[d]$p < 0.001$.

biological relatives of schizophrenic adoptees are genetically related to hospitalized schizophrenic patients. All three of the schizophrenic diagnoses were more highly represented in this group than in any of the other three, among which no statistically reliable differences were found.

These three adoption studies supplement family and twin studies in demonstrating the importance of genetic factors in later schizophrenic conditions. And they do so in a way that successfully separates genetic transmission from rearing by schizophrenic parents. In addition, they strongly suggest that the schizophrenic genotype is not specific to classical forms of schizophrenic psychoses but may also give rise to an allied but nonpsychotic condition referred to as borderline or latent schizophrenia.

THE SCHIZOPHRENIC SPECTRUM

The notion of a spectrum of schizophrenic disorders arising from a common genotype is therefore given a great deal of credence by recent adoption studies. Kety et al. (1968) see the spectrum as defined on one extreme by cases of chronic schizophrenia, on the other extreme by a heterogeneous collection of borderline or latent conditions, and with cases of reactive schizophrenia holding an intermediate position.

The notion of a spectrum of allied impairments takes into account the variability of schizophrenia and thus avoids descriptive difficulties that arise from attempting to break a fundamentally variable phenomenon into discrete types or disease entities. A spectrum implies that different behavioral expressions (phenotypes) of the underlying genotype represent shadings on a continuum rather than discrete syndromes of differing genetic etiology.

Yet by broadening the concept of schizophrenia, the spectrum notion carries along its own problems. It is at least possible that the spectrum does not end with the borderline conditions but may also include nonschizophrenic disorders as well. It will be recalled that twin studies revealed varying degrees of concordance depending on the rigor with which the co-twin of an index case was diagnosed. For example, Kringlen (1968) reported that 31% of the MZ co-twins of process schizophrenic patients were concordant for schizophrenia. However, only 31% of the discordant co-twins could be considered entirely free of psychiatric disorder. Of the remaining co-twins, 9% fell into the schizophrenic spectrum, and a hefty 29% suffered from a variety of other psychiatric conditions such as character disorder, anxiety state, neurotic depression, or neurosis. Likewise, Gottesman and Shields (1966b) found that only 21% of the MZ co-twins in their sample were without signs of psychopathology, although only 42% were strictly concordant for schizophrenia.

The finding of multiple forms of psychological disability among the co-twins of schizophrenic patients is consistent with the tendency among many mental health professionals, especially in North America, to assume a very broad definition of schizophrenia. Such unofficial but popular diagnostic terms as "pseudoneurotic" and "pseudopsychopathic" schizophrenia are often used to indicate clinicians' beliefs that an underlying schizophrenic disorder often masquerades as a neurotic or psychopathic condition (Snyder, 1974).

Yet such a broadening of the definition of schizophrenia creates a theoretical impasse for genetic theorists. If the schizophrenic genotype can lead not only to one of the spectrum disorders or psychiatric normality but also to various other forms of disability, then schizophrenia is a genetic condition in only a trivial sense. Under these conditions, the genetic predisposition would have to be defined as a general tendency to mental illness, which can be unpredictably expressed in manifold phenotypes. One is reminded of Neumann's nineteenth-century dictum: "There is only one kind of mental disorder; we call it insanity."

But scientists are generally uneasy with concepts that explain both too much and nothing in particular, and the notion of a generalized predisposition to mental illness sits poorly with most researchers. The existence of a wide range of nonschizophrenic disability in the MZ co-twins of schizophrenic patients has to be evaluated against population base rates for such disabilities. We would not expect a schizophrenic condition in one person to confer an immunity to other forms of disorder on his relatives, and

TABLE 4.6

Consensus Diagnoses Outside the Schizophrenia Spectrum in Biological and Adoptive Relatives[a]

	Interviewed relatives[b] (%)			
	Index Group		Control Group	
Diagnosis	Biological (N = 81)	Adoptive (N = 31)	Biological (N = 121)	Adoptive (N = 41)
Psychiatrically normal	37	36	41	27
Organic illness	9	16	5	15
Neurotic illness	5	10	5	5
Affective illness	2	3	9	7
Personality disorder	33	26	32	37
All nonschizophrenic diagnoses	49	55	51	63

[a]From Kety et al. (1976b).

[b]The Ns represent interviewed relatives whose consensus diagnoses were outside the schizophrenia spectrum.

there is no evidence that other disorders occur any more or less frequently among schizophrenic patients' relatives than in the population at large. The Kety et al. (1976b) study of biological and adoptive relatives of schizophrenic patients addresses this issue. Although, as we have seen, biological relatives of schizophrenic patients had a higher frequency of spectrum disorders than did their adoptive relatives or the biological and adoptive relatives of controls, this was not accompanied by a higher frequency of other psychiatric conditions (Table 4.6). Thus the soundest conclusion to date is that the presence of other psychiatric disability in the biological relatives of schizophrenic patients is no greater than in the general population. The increased risk of schizophrenic spectrum disorders among biological relatives, however, suggests a specific genotype for schizophrenia that is expressed in varying degrees of severity.

MODE OF INHERITANCE

Given that a genetic contribution to schizophrenia has been established, it is of interest to determine the specific genic mechanism by which the predisposition is transmitted between generations. The importance of knowing the mode of inheritance lies in the inference to be made concerning the biochemical pathway between the genetic code and its phenotypic expression. Since the primary product of most genes is an enzyme or other protein necessary for normal biosynthesis, the biochemical pathway will become more complex as a greater number of genes are involved. For this reason, evidence of transmission via a single aberrant gene would be the most parsimonious case, and theories of the mode of inheritance in schizophrenia will naturally begin by examining various monogenic hypotheses.

But no simple monogenic model appears to fit the empirical risk data. A single gene can be expected to show segregation among generations according to classical Mendelian inheritance. If schizophrenia were inherited as a simple dominant trait, the risks for schizophrenia among patients' relatives would be 100% among MZ co-twins, 50% among first-degree relatives, and 25% among second-degree relatives. If simple recessive inheritance were the rule, the expected risk would remain at 100% for MZ co-twins and would be 25% for DZ co-twins and for ordinary siblings. The risk for children of a schizophrenic parent under recessive inheritance cannot be precisely specified but should be considerably lower than the risk for sibs. Obviously, neither of these simple single-gene models fits the empirical data from family and twin studies (Table 4.1 and 4.3). A particularly critical test of monogenic inheritance is available from marriages between two schizophrenic persons. Of the children of such unions, 75% would be expected to be schizophrenic under simple dominant inheritance and 100% under simple recessive inheritance (Rosenthal, 1971). The empirical risk figures, derived from five studies of such marriages, range from 35% to 44% (Erlenmeyer-Kimling, 1968).

Because risk figures have conventionally been provided only for clinical forms of schizophrenia, it has been suggested that simple dominant inheritance might account for the empirical risks among patients' relatives if the diagnostic category were broadened to include the full spectrum of schizophrenic disorders (Heston, 1970). Although this would indeed move the risks toward those expected under simple dominant-gene theory, they would still fall short of theoretical expectation. For example, about 30% of the children of one schizophrenic parent, as opposed to the theoretically expected 50%, develop any type of schizophrenic spectrum disorder (Table 4.4). In addition, it will be recalled that twin studies find that even if co-twin similarity is defined as *any* psychiatric impairment among the MZ co-twins of schizophrenic patients, concordance reaches only 70% to 80% (Gottesman & Shields, 1966b; Kringlen, 1968). Certainly, MZ co-twin similarity for a spectrum diagnosis will necessarily be less than 70% to 80% and thus fall far short of the theoretically expected 100%.

Because simple monogenic models of inheritance fail to account for the empirical data, genetic theories are obliged to consider multifactor modes of inheritance—models that postulate the combined action of multiple genes in the predisposition to schizophrenia. Of the several multifactor models that have been proposed at one time or another, the most prominent are a modified dominance model and a polygenic model, each of which has its defenders and critics.

Modified Dominant Inheritance

Under this model a single dominant gene is held to be responsible for the core characteristics of schizophrenia, but is phenotypic expression is thought to be altered, or reduced in frequency, by the presence of other modifying genes. In its most general form, the model postulates individual differences in a genetically determined resistance to the major gene (Rosenthal, 1971). In individuals with the defective gene, the phenotype would vary from cases of frank clinical schizophrenia through schizoid personalities to apparent normality, depending on the degree of inherited resistance.

Because the notion of "genetically determined resistance" is extremely vague, attempts have been made to specify the mechanisms involved. Meehl's (1962) theory of the genetic etiology of schizophrenia is perhaps the most ambitious of these. Meehl begins by postulating the genetic inheritance of a major "schizogene" whose chemical products cause an aberration in synaptic transmission, which he dubs "synaptic slippage." The psychological correlate of this neural defect is "cognitive slippage," a concept analogous to Bleuler's fundamental symptom of associative disturbance. All individuals with the schizogene will inevitably develop a degree of cognitive slippage, which in turn will give rise to such secondary traits as social withdrawal, anhedonia, and ambivalence. Thus this tetrad of personality traits is the phenotypic expression of the defective gene. Meehl describes this configuration as "schizotypic." Only a subset of schizotypic persons will eventually develop into cases of frank schizophrenia. In other words, the degree of expression of the defective gene will vary along a spectrum of clinical disorders and allied personality types. Meehl (1962) theorizes that the degree of expression will depend both on the aversiveness of the schizotypic person's early family milieu and the presence or absence of inherited modifying traits.:

> If the interpersonal regime is favorable, and the . . . person also has the good fortune to inherit a low anxiety readiness, physical vigor, general resistance to stress, and the like, he will remain a well-compensated "normal" schizotype, never manifesting symptoms of mental disease. He will be like the gout-prone male whose genes determine him to have an elevated blood uric acid titer, but who never develops clinical gout [p. 830].

Meehl's theory would therefore predict personality differences between borderline schizophrenic conditions—schizotypic personalities—and clinically schizophrenic patients. In the absence of such research, however, modified monogenic models such as Meehl's remain theoretical possibilities only.

A potential problem for any monogenic model is the relatively high and apparently stable frequency of schizophrenia in all populations where prevalence statistics have been systematically collected. Whatever one's view of the social and psychological implications of schizophrenia, it is clearly biologically maladaptive in that schizophrenic patients marry at only about 70% of the general population rate. Under these conditions, a gradual elimination of the schizophrenic gene and a continual decrease in the incidence of schizophrenia would be expected. One intriguing solution to this problem is that schizophrenia is a disorder of relatively recent origin and that insufficient time has elapsed for the defective gene to be eliminated in the general population. As noted in Chapter 1, Kraepelin's *dementia praecox* appears to be anomolous among major psychiatric syndromes in that it is absent from the prenineteenth-century nosologies of psychological disorder. It is not inconceivable therefore that schizophrenia is a product of modern industrialized societies. Although most textbooks hold schizophrenia to be a world-wide phenomenon, there is in fact little evidence that it appears in cultures untouched by the reach of Western industrial civilization (Torrey, 1973).

It is unfortunately difficult to decide on historical and cross-cultural grounds whether schizophrenia is of recent origin or whether the condition simply went unrecognized as a separate clinical entity before the rise of psychiatry and psychology in the nineteenth century. Assuming that it has existed considerably longer than the life of Kraepelin's *dementia praecox,* genetic theory provides a second explanation for its persistence. It is possible that the selective disadvantage of clinical schizophrenia is compensated for by a selective advantage among unaffected gene carriers, resulting in the maintenance of gene frequency in the general population. In this view, we might expect nonschizophrenic relatives of schizophrenic patients to manifest a biologically or socially advantageous trait or traits at a somewhat higher frequency than the population norm. The difference need not be large; it is estimated that a mere 6% reproductive advantage among nonaffected carriers would maintain the population frequency of the hypothetical gene (Slater & Cowie, 1971).

Although no such balancing advantage has been isolated, a speculative possibility is contained in the ancient notion that madness and creative endeavor are both the outcome of an unusual imaginative faculty. Shakespeare linked the lunatic and the poet as being "of imagination all compact," and Dr. Johnson took the classical position that insanity was an object lesson in the excesses of imagination. In more contemporary terms, psychologists have often pointed to the similarity between the loose associative structure in schizophrenic patients and the ability of creative persons to combine disparate ideas to form novel productions. Although the evidence is far from complete, a few genetic studies have in fact reported a high incidence of unusual personalities among the normal relatives of schizophrenic patients (Heston, 1966; Karlsson, 1966). As discussed earlier, Heston's important study found that both clinical schizophrenia and borderline disorders occurred more frequently among the adopted offspring of schizophrenic mothers than among control adoptees. In addition, however, the unaffected index cases contained more "spontaneous," "colorful," and "successful" personalities, who held more creative jobs (e.g., musician, teacher, and home designer) and pursued more imaginative hobbies than did the control adoptees. Although such observations are hardly equivalent to Dryden's famous couplet, "Great wits are sure to madness near allied/ And thin partitions do their bounds divide," they do, at least, direct attention away from an exclusive focus on the pathology of schizophrenia and toward a search for its possibly adaptive features.

Polygenic Model

Because monogenic models must make certain as yet unverified assumptions to account for the observed deviations from Mendelian ratios among relatives of schizophrenic patients, a polygenic model is now preferred by many genetic theorists. It shares a multifactor assumption with the modified monogenic approach but does not require a single major gene as a necessary condition. Instead, the schizophrenic genotype is seen as composed of a number of genes of more or less equal effect that combine in an additive fashion to determine the phenotype. The model derives from the genetics of continuously graded traits like height and I.Q., which do not lend themselves to categorical classifications and in which environmental factors are known to be important in determining the degree of expression of the genotype. Applied to schizophrenia, the polygenic model explicitly assumes an interaction between genetic and environmental effects such that both sources of influence are necessary for a schizophrenic outcome whereas neither is by itself sufficient. The phenotype depends both on the number of predisposing genes and on the severity of the relevant environmental stressors. Thus schizophrenia could result from a large number of genes interacting with less than severe life stress or a smaller number of genes interacting with more severe stress. Given the same degree of genetic predisposition, the phenotype is graded on a continuum of severity according to the amount of imposed life stress. Or given similarly stressful environments, the severity of the phenotypic expression depends on the number of predisposing genes.

Whereas a monogenetic model is consistent with a view of schizophrenia as a discrete disease, polygenic inheritance suggests that the clinical disorder represents an extreme on a continuum of "schizoidness" or "schizophrenicity." Thus the appropriate analogy for schizophrenia would be with psychological traits such as manifest anxiety or extraversion rather than with genetically determined diseases like phenylketonuria (PKU). The polygenic model is consistent with the notion of a schizophrenic spectrum beginning with the extreme of process schizophrenia and shading off in degrees to reactive states, borderline conditions, and psychiatric normality at the opposite extreme.

Unlike monogenic models, whether single or modified, the polygenic model does not carry specific predictions about the risk of schizophrenia in various classes of relatives of affected individuals. It simply predicts that the number of polygenes, and therefore the probability of schizophrenia, will increase as a function of the degree of relationship to a known patient. Likewise, it is known that the risk of schizophrenia increases with the number of relatives already affected, which can be accounted for on the reasonable assumption that the greater the number of affected relatives, the greater the number of inherited polygenes (Rosenthal, 1971). A final observation that lends itself to a polygenic interpretation is the increased probability of concordance for schizophrenia among the MZ co-twins of more severely affected patients (Gottesman, 1968). This can be accounted for by assuming a common number of predisposing genes within twin pairs but differing numbers between pairs.

COMMENTARY

The information generated by genetic studies is among the soundest and most extensive in the entire area of research on schizophrenia. Criticisms directed at consanguinity and twin studies carried out in the half-century prior to about 1960 had the salutary effect of sharpening both concepts and methods, and the sophistication of subsequent investigations has been exemplary. Recent twin investigations have solved earlier problems of sampling and zygosity determination, and they have dealt as effectively as is currently possible with the unavoidable lack of precision of psychiatric diagnosis. Novel studies of the adopted offspring of schizophrenic parents and of the biological and adoptive families of schizophrenic adoptees have provided a means of separating heredity and postnatal environmental factors and in the process have confirmed the major conclusions to be drawn from twin and consanguinity studies.

This cumulative information makes possible several very important generalizations:

1. Clinical schizophrenia requires an inherited predisposition as a necessary condition. Only a subset of the general population is at risk for schizophrenia, and no amount of stressful life experience can conceivably produce schizophrenic outcome in persons lacking the necessary genetic constitution.

2. A genetic predisposition is not a sufficient condition for the emergence of clincial schizophrenia. Medical genetics has discovered an increasing number of genetically determined diseases such as PKU and sickle-cell anemia that are universally expressed in gene carriers. Schizophrenia is not among them. Of persons genetically at risk for schizophrenia, some large portion close to a majority will escape breakdown and hospitalization with a diagnosis of clinical schizophrenia. On the other hand, approximately one-half of gene carriers who escape clinical schizophrenia will show peculiarities of behavior and cognition that are schizophreniclike but not psychotic. The terms *borderline* or *latent schizophrenia* are conventionally used to designate these personality types, which are genetically allied with the more severe forms of clinical schizophrenia.

3. Genetic studies provide the best single source of evidence that environmental factors must play an important role in the etiology of schizophrenia (Gottesman & Shields, 1972). This paradoxical conclusion follows from the variable phenotypic outcome of gene carriers, an outcome that may range from clinical schizophrenia through borderline conditions to apparent normality. To state that genetic factors are necessary but not sufficient also implies that life history factors are necessary but not sufficient, a topic to be pursued in the following chapter.

It is erroneous to speak of the genetic transmission of schizophrenia per se. In a strict sense, the genetic inheritance is some anomaly of the DNA code and thus a potential error or errors in the production of enzymes or other proteins involved in biochemical reactions. Under appropriate environmental circumstances, the potential error will be actualized and, in some as yet unknown manner, will set the person on the road to later schizophrenic breakdown. Therefore, the existence of aberrant biochemical events is predictable from knowledge of a genetic predisposition to schizophrenia. But a proper appreciation of the potential complexity of the biochemical pathway between the schizophrenic genotype and its ultimate phenotypic expression in clinical schizophrenia is called for. As the geneticist H. J. Muller put it:

> Whatever may be the nature of the primary chemical products of genes within the cell, these products must be of thousands of different kinds, corresponding with the thousands of different genes, and these products must interact with one another in innumerable ways to form secondary products, tertiary products and those ever further removed from the genes. It is usually only after a most intricate web of these interactions has been followed through that those end-products are at last found which we become aware of as the characteristics of the organism [quoted in Shields, 1973, p. 541].

The isolation of a biochemical error or even a series of errors in schizophrenia would lead to the development of a biochemical test or tests for schizophrenia to complement, or even supplant, error-prone diagnoses based on overt symptom pictures. Perhaps a step in this direction is the recent discovery that peripheral blood levels of the enzyme monoamine oxydase (MAO) are reduced in schizophrenic patients as a group and that the amount of reduction is correlated with the severity of the clinical picture (Wyatt & Murphy, 1975). Because blood MAO levels are highly similar within pairs of MZ twins *discordant* for schizophrenia, it has been suggested that MAO activity may serve as a biochemical marker for the schizophrenic genotype. This is not to say that reduced MAO activity is *the* or even an important biochemical correlate of schizophrenia. Although MAO is known to be involved in the intraneuronal metabolism of brain amines, there is no evidence that neuronal (as opposed to blood) levels are reduced in schizophrenic patients. This does not, however, detract from its potential use as a correlate—a biochemical marker—of the inherited predisposition.

It is clear that the incidence of schizophrenia among relatives of index cases follows no simple pattern of Mendelian inheritance, but the data are as yet insufficient to choose between modified monogenic and polygenic modes of inheritance. Precisely because the polygenic model implies a highly complex biochemical pathway between the genic code and its phenotypic expression, a modified monogenic model is often preferred as a working hypothesis. This model assumes a single major schizophrenic gene having an incomplete or a graded expression due to the modifying action of other genes. However, the phenotypic correlates of the hypothetical modifying genes have yet to be demonstrated in schizophrenia, so that the model is in search of corroborating evidence.

The polygenic model accounts more easily for certain important facts, such as the increased probability of schizophrenia with greater numbers of affected relatives and the increased probability of concordance in the co-twins of more severely affected MZ index cases. Because polygenic models explicitly acknowledge a genetic–environmental interaction, they also account better for the life history factors we know must be involved in schizophrenia. Because the polygenic model need not postulate a large number of genes in the inherited predisposition, the difference between it and a modified monogenic model is basically a question of the number of polygenes needed to account for the diversity of the phenotypic expressions of the inherited genotype. To the extent that their postulated number is limited, the polygenic model approaches a monogenic model with a limited number of modifying genes. Because genes are only known by their effects, whether biochemical or behavioral, the exact specification of the mode of inheritance must await the development and application in genetic studies of reliable and differentiated measures of the biochemical and psychological correlates of schizophrenia.

5 Life History Factors

> *We are, I believe, justified in directing our attention to the factors which we see at work in the life history of so-called dementia praecox.*
>
> —Adolf Meyer (1910)

In the previous chapter we concluded that a genetic predisposition is a necessary, but not sufficient, condition for the development of clinical schizophrenia. A corollary of this generalization is that only a subset of the general population—carriers of the schizophrenic genotype—is at risk for schizophrenia; no amount of adverse life experience can potentiate schizophrenia in genetically unaffected individuals. A second corollary is that only a portion of those genetically at-risk will in fact become schizophrenic at some time in life. Genetic studies indicate that the schizophrenic genotype underlies a variety of phenotypic manifestations, ranging from classical forms of schizophrenia through borderline conditions to psychiatric normality. Because the determinants of this phenotypic diversity are necessarily environmental, a complete understanding of the etiology of schizophrenia requires the specification of those life history events that interact with the genetic predisposition to produce a schizophrenic outcome.

This chapter considers evidence and associated investigative methods regarding nongenetic precursors of later schizophrenia. It is organized under three main headings. The first, "Developmental Studies," draws a composite picture of the personality and social characteristics of preschizophrenic children as revealed by an analysis of several major life history investigations. The second and third sections, "Obstetrical Complications and Later

Schizophrenia" and "The Families of Schizophrenic Patients," deal with two categories of events widely investigated as possible potentiating life stresses in the etiology of schizophrenia. We shall see that no simple solutions to the problem of environmental potentiators of clinical schizophrenia are forthcoming. A final "Commentary" suggests that this conclusion requires a rethinking of implicit etiological models of schizophrenia.

DEVELOPMENTAL STUDIES

Methodological Considerations

The isolation of etiologically important life history factors ideally requires that preschizophrenic children be monitored from conception and birth onward. But such a program immediately encounters a fundamental difficulty: How is it possible to identify preschizophrenic children before they become schizophrenic in a clinical sense? The very notion of "preschizo-phrenic" requires an adult diagnosis as a criterion. Until recently, this problem was circumvented by reconstructing life histories through interviews with patients and their families following hospitalization for schizophrenia. This so-called *retrospective* method was the basis for the information systematized by Kantor, Wallner, and Winder (1953) in their analysis of differential life history factors associated with process and reactive schizophrenic patients, as discussed in Chapter 1. Although such recon-structive analyses are not without value, they do have serious limitations. Retrospective accounts of past events are by their nature not primary observations but interpretations of events and subject to grave distortion. The distortion may enter at the reporter's original perception of the event in question, at the stage of recall (or lack thereof) from memory, in the process of reporting, or in some combination of all of these. These problems are by now sufficiently well recognized as to require only mention.

In more recent years, research on schizophrenia has benefited from the application of nonretrospective methods of collecting information on children prior to the onset of schizophrenia. The so-called *follow-back method* begins with the identification of a population of patients hospitalized for schizophrenia as adults. Then particular institutions—schools, camps, child guidance clinics, etc.—through which this group has passed as children are identified. Institutional files are then searched for items of information that differentiated this group from appropriate controls before the onset of schizophrenia. A second approach, known as the *follow-up method,* begins with institutional records, usually those in child guidance clinics, kept on children with a presumably higher than average risk for developing later schizophrenia. If enough time has elapsed for the children seen in the clinic to have passed into adulthood, those showing an eventual schizophrenic outcome can be identified. Comparisons are then made between information in their records and information in records of children who passed through the same institution but did not become schizophrenic as adults. A great advantage of both follow-back and follow-up methods is that the raw data are unbiased by the reporter's knowledge of the child's eventual schizophrenic outcome. A major disadvantage is that the childhood records may be either silent or incomplete on items relevant to the etiology of schizophrenia.

A final means of identifying preschizophrenic children for study, and one increasingly favored by researchers, has come to be known as the *high-risk method*. As in the follow-up method, a population of children with a higher than average risk of developing schizophrenia is first identified. Unlike the follow-up method, however, the entire group is followed longitudinally until it separates into schizophrenic and nonschizophrenic groups in later life, the second group providing a comparison for the first. During the longitudinal period, testing and observation are periodically conducted with subjects on whichever items of information the investigator hypothesizes may be relevant to later schizophrenia. In adulthood, the information is analyzed for differences between eventually schizophrenic and eventually nonschizophrenic subgroups. In theory, high-risk groups may be constituted on any criteria (such as visits to child guidance clinics) presumed to be associated with schizophrenia in adulthood. In practice, most investigators choose to monitor children of schizophrenic parents. As genetic family studies show, approximately 10% of children of one schizophrenic parent and 45% of children of two schizophrenic parents will themselves become schizophrenic in later life. This method, which is most precisely described as the longitudinal study of genetically at-risk children, has two major advantages: It allows a fairly precise prediction of the final numbers of schizophrenic adults to be found in any original sample of children, and it allows monitoring to begin at birth. The length of time required to complete such a study, on the order of 20 to 30 years, is a major drawback. Of the numerous on-going high-risk studies of schizophrenia in this mold, none has yet been completed. A second disadvantage, which this method shares with less elaborate follow-up methods, is that the study sample is not necessarily representative of preschizophrenic children in general. If, for example, high risk is defined as having one schizophrenic parent, any resulting sample will not include representatives from the 90% of eventually schizophrenic adults who do not have a schizophrenic parent. Whether such unrepresentativeness in fact biases results from high-risk investigations is a priori unknowable. But the problem is at least recognized and can be assessed by carefully comparing high-risk results for consistency with results derived from follow-back, follow-up, and retrospective methods.

Studies of preschizophrenic children must also come to grips with the problem of choosing appropriate comparison groups. It is by now routine to match preschizophrenic and control subjects on such criteria as age, sex, social class, and area of residence. But more refined matchings should also be made. For example, it may be inappropriate to compare preschizophrenic children to children who show an eventually normal outcome (i.e., any nonpsychiatric adult status). This caveat follows directly from what we know of the genetics of schizophrenia: If schizophrenia arises from an interaction of a genetic predisposition and environmental potentiators, the relevant environmental factors will not necessarily distinguish the life histories of those with eventual schizophrenic outcomes from those with eventual nonschizophrenic outcomes. In other words, equivalent life experiences may be associated with schizophrenic outcomes in predisposed individuals and nonpsychiatric outcomes in those lacking the predisposition. Research comparing the life histories of schizophrenic and nonschizophrenic adults may therefore fail to find any differences between the two groups and erroneously conclude that the particular events compared are without etiological significance for schizophrenia.

If differences *are* found between schizophrenic patients and nonpsychiatric controls, however, there is no guarantee that such differences are specific to schizophrenia. They may simply be precursors of later psychiatric problems in general rather than of schizophrenia in particular. Therefore a more stringent comparison is between the life histories of eventually schizophrenic patients and the life histories of individuals with other psychiatric difficulties. Typically, comparisons will be made with patients suffering from other functional disorders requiring hospitalization, such as psychotic depression, severe neurosis, or psychopathic character disorder.

But even comparisons with other psychiatric conditions may fail to isolate life history differences specific to later schizophrenia, for the same reasons operating in comparisons with nonpsychiatric controls; that is, any phenotypic difference between such groups could be due to experiential factors, genetic factors, or some interaction of the two. The ideal comparison is therefore between life history factors of eventually schizophrenic and eventually nonschizophrenic adults who have equivalent genetic risks for schizophrenia. Any differences found between these groups are necessarily due to life history differences, operating as either main effects or in interaction with the schizophrenic genotype. One means of effecting such a control is through the study of monozygotic twins *discordant* for schizophrenia. Here schizophrenia in the affected twin is evidence for the operation of the schizophrenic genotype, which must also be present in the unaffected twin. But their different adult outcomes must be due to factors other than the genetic predisposition, and these factors are, presumably, capable of being identified through close scrutiny. Cases of MZ twins discordant for schizophrenia are fairly rare, but approximately one hundred cases that have appeared in the world literature over the years provide an important archive (Wahl, 1976). A second method of controlling for genetic risk is through the study of offspring of schizophrenic parents. As already noted, approximately 10% of offspring of one schizophrenic parent and 45% of offspring of two schizophrenic parents will show an eventual schizophrenic outcome. These offspring must necessarily be genetically predisposed. In addition, an unknown proportion of the nonschizophrenic children of such parents will also be carriers of the schizophrenic genotype. Thus comparisons between eventually schizophrenic and eventually nonschizophrenic children of schizophrenic parents will approach a control for genetic factors while allowing life history differences to emerge.

The following exposition deals with four recent inquiries into the life situation and individual characteristics of preschizophrenic children. Each exemplifies a particular combination of data-gathering method and choice of control group. Together, they provide a fairly rich and consistent description of the psychological characteristics of the preschizophrenic child. Curiously, none has isolated specific environmental events that could be said to be potentiators of the schizophrenic genotype. However they do implicate the child's obstetrical history and/or family milieu as possible factors, and the remainder of the chapter is devoted to a detailed consideration of these sources of influence on later schizophrenia.

The NIMH Twin Study

This study (Pollin & Stabenau, 1968; Stabenau & Pollin, 1970) focused on 14 pairs of discordant monozygotic twins and their families. Each family had volunteered to be housed for 2 to 3 weeks at the National Institute of Mental Health while undergoing extensive evaluation. The majority of pairs (10) was female, and they ranged in age from late teens into the thirties. Each family participated as individuals or as a group in as much as 100 hours of interviews and, in addition, underwent extensive psychological and medical testing. Subsequent observations were made during home visits and in interviews with relatives, friends, and teachers. Although the world literature contains case reports appearing over the years on 86 pairs of discordant monozygotic twins, the NIMH study is unrivaled in the size of its sample and the extensiveness of its data collection. Differences between the schizophrenic index twins and their nonschizophrenic co-twins appeared in three areas: (1) birth and neonatal constitutional factors; (2) patterns of parent-twin perceptions and relationships; and (3) personality development.

The NIMH index twins appeared to have been born at a lower state of physiological and biological maturation and competence than their co-twins. Of the 14 index twins, 12 weighed less at birth; in early infancy, the majority also experienced various problems such as respiratory disorders, sleep and eating difficulties, colic, and infectious episodes. Five had well-documented evidence of cyanosis (oxygen deprivation) at birth. Of the two index twins who did not weigh less at birth, one became cyanotic after release from hospital, and the other had a severe case of spotted fever at age 3.

Consistent differences were observed in the way the parents perceived and related to the twins. The preschizophrenic twin was most often seen as the weaker and more vulnerable of the two. The mother became more involved with the weaker twin, but the relationship was characterized by greater anxiety and ambivalence, sometimes reaching conscious rejection.

Personality and developmental differences were consistently found. The index twins from earliest childhood were described as the more dependent, submissive, fearful, and compliant of the two. They also tended to pass through developmental stages (e.g., walking, puberty) later than their co-twins. Friendships with peers were fewer in number and less satisfactory. The preschizophrenic twins themselves recognized their relative incompetence in reporting that from childhood on they saw the world as stressful, unpredictable, and difficult to cope with.

Pollin and Stabenau also compared their findings with the 86 cases previously reported in the world literature. Table 5.1 lists these comparisons for the 14 NIMH pairs, the 86 previously reported pairs, and the total 100 pairs. Items characterizing the preschizophrenic twins by a two-to-one ratio or better included nine behavioral characteristics (neurotic as a child, submissive, sensitive, serious–worrier, obedient–gentler, dependent, well-behaved, quiet–shy, and stubborn) and six physical characteristics (central-nervous-system illness as a child, birth complication, neonatal asphyxia, weaker, shorter, and lighter at birth). Items favoring the nonschizophrenic co-twins by a two-to-one ratio or better included: more intelligent, better at school, the spokesman, outgoing, lively, the leader, and becoming married.

Pollin and Stabenau (1968) outlined two models of the life course of the preschizophrenic child compatible with these findings. The first emphasizes constitutional factors: The preschizophrenic child may begin life with a relative neurological deficiency as a result of adverse intrauterine experiences or early postnatal insults such as cyanosis or debilitating diseases. This deficiency would then serve as a constitutional basis for subsequent psychological vulnerability in coping with normal developmental tasks and environmental stresses. Opportunities for personality growth and differentiation would be correspondingly restricted. Ultimate schizophrenic breakdown would occur when the increasing relative vulnerability engaged the genetic predisposition. An alternative, but not incompatible model, emphasizes the transactions between the vulnerable child and the family, especially the parents: An original judgment of weakness and dependency is made in comparison with the more viable co-twin. As the comparison is repeatedly

TABLE 5.1
Monozygotic Twins Discordant for Schizophrenia (100 Pairs)
Early Characteristics[a,b]

Item	Other Studies		NIMH Study		Total		Ratio (I/C)
	I[c]	C[d]	I	C	I	C	
Neurotic as child	11	1	5	0	16	1	16.0
Submissive	27	2	10	2	37	4	9.3
Sensitive	26	3	12	2	38	5	7.6
Serious-worrier	10	2	12	2	22	4	5.5
Obedient-gentler	21	2	10	4	31	6	5.2
CNS illness as child	12	2	5	2	17	4	4.3
Birth complication (any)	18	5	6	1	24	6	4.0
Asphyxia at birth	8	3	4	0	12	3	4.0
Dependent	2	0	10	3	12	3	4.0
Well behaved	9	0	7	5	16	5	3.2
Quiet-shy	16	4	9	4	25	8	3.1
Stubborn	14	4	6	3	20	7	2.9
Weaker	16	10	11	1	27	11	2.5
Shorter	27	16	13	1	40	17	2.4
Lighter at birth	29	18	12	2	41	20	2.1
Slower development (walking)	3	1	6	4	9	5	1.8
Somatic illness as child	9	9	9	5	18	14	1.3
Second born	27	29	10	4	37	33	1.1
Fiery	9	5	5	9	14	14	1.0
Athletic	0	4	5	3	5	7	–1.4
Leader	9	—	5	9	14	30	–2.1
Outgoing-lively	8	26	5	9	13	35	–2.7
Spokesman	4	11	3	11	7	22	–3.1
Better at school	6	18	2	11	8	29	–3.6
More intelligent	2	7	2	9	—	16	–4.0
Married, co-twin not married	1	21	0	5	1	26	–26.0

[a]From Pollin and Staubenau (1968).

[b]Number of twins where item clearly differentiated one twin by intrapair co-twin comparison.

[c]Schizophrenic index twin (I).

[d]Nonschizophrenic monozygotic co-twin (C).

made and confirmed, it becomes an essential component of the preschizo-phrenic child's identity and self-image. This role and self-image are incompatible with normative expectations for independence and competence, so that the child is in a state of continual conflict. The conflict is only exacerbated by a corresponding ambivalence on the part of the parents, who are both impelled to protect a sickly child and angered by the extraordinary demands placed on them. A schizophrenic outcome is the result of this chronic, unresolved, psychological and interpersonal conflict.

The Watt School Records Study

This painstaking follow-back study (Watt & Lubensky, 1976; Watt, Stolorow, Lubensky, & McClelland, 1970) examined teachers' comments concerning the social and emotional adjustment of adolescents before they had been hospitalized for schizophrenia. The starting point was a list of every patient, 15–34 years old, who was first admitted to any Massachusetts mental hospital over a given 6-year period. This list was checked against the files of the public high school in a large industrial and residential suburb of Boston. Records were found for 54 students, 27 males and 27 females, who had been later hospitalized for schizophrenia. The investigators estimate that few of the to-be-schizophrenic patients were missed in their search and that the 54 subjects reflected the socioeconomic mix of the community. Each index case record was matched with records of school peers on the basis of sex, age, race, and parental social class.

The basic data were derived from ad lib comments written annually by tenth-grade homeroom teachers (e.g., "Jimmy is quiet and well-behaved. He is well-liked by his classmates but lacks self-confidence and seldom participates in class discussion. He works hard at his studies but has a short attention span."). These evaluations were coded into 23 bipolar dimensions, which were grouped into five broad categories. Table 5.2 shows the defining dimensions for each of the five major categories and indicates those ratings on which the preschizophrenic students differed from their controls. Boys were slightly lower than their controls on self-control and dependability and were significantly less achieving, cheerful, adjusted, pleasant, cooperative, considerate, and well-behaved. In terms of broader categories, boys could be described as less conscientious, less emotionally stable, and less agreeable than their controls. No differences were found for boys on the extraversion and assertiveness categories.

In contrast, preschizophrenic girls were described as slightly less secure and sociable but significantly more immature, maladjusted, quiet, and egocentric than their controls. They also tended to be seen by teachers as *less* nervous than their controls, which the authors interpret as complementary to their generally introverted pattern. In terms of broad categories, the girls, like the boys, were less emotionally stable than their controls. But this was associated with a social introversion in girls as compared with disagreeableness and unconscientiousness among the boys. These sex differences seemed to demonstrate that preschizophrenic boys are negativistic, unpleasant, and *actively* maladjusted, whereas preschizophrenic girls are calm, immature, and *quietly* maladjusted. This suggests important sex differences in the predictors

TABLE 5.2
Summary of Category Difference Scores that Significantly
Distinguished Preschizophrenics From Controls[a]

	Significance Level Schizophrenics vs. Controls	
Scale	Boys	Girls
Factor 1: Conscientiousness		
1. careful–careless		
2. attentive–distractible		
3. achieving–underachieving	.05	
4. organized–disorganized		
5. motivated–unmotivated		
6. dependable–undependable	.10	
Factor 2: Emotional Stability		
7. self-controlled–emotional	.10	
8. calm–nervous		.005
9. secure–insecure		.10
10. cheerful–depressed	.025	
11. mature–immature		.05
12. adjusted–maladjusted	.001	.025
Factor 3: Extraversion		
13. group participation–little		
14. popular–unpopular		
15. sociable–unsociable		.10
16. talkative–quiet		.025
Factor 4: Assertiveness		
17. assertive–passive		
18. leader–follower		
19. independent–dependent		
Factor 5: Agreeableness		
20. pleasant–unpleasant	.025	
21. cooperative–negativistic	.001	
22. considerate–egocentric	.05	.01
23. well-behaved–antisocial	.025	

[a]Adapted from Watt and Lubensky (1976).
Note: Preschizophrenic girls were less nervous than their controls.
Preschizophrenics were more maladjusted in all other comparisons.

of later schizophrenia among adolescents. But Watt and Lubensky (1976)
also find a common theme across the two sexes:

If a single expression can capture the essence of a pattern of results so complex
as this one, it is *emotional immaturity*. Immature emotional development is the
description, more often implied than stated explicitly, that more often

characterizes the preschizophrenic children of both sexes. There were frequent references to "crying with slight provocation," being overshadowed by older siblings, insensitivity to the feelings of others, late development of physical and scholastic skills, temper outbursts, and self-consciousness. The introversion of the girls and the extreme alienation of the boys, especially in later childhood, seem like natural outgrowths of a history of retarded emotional development [p. 372].

The Judge Baker Schizophrenia Research Project

This follow-up study (Fleming & Ricks, 1970; Ricks & Berry, 1970) was based on an analysis of therapists' notes from the files of Boston's Judge Baker Guidance Clinic. Files were available for over 15,000 children who had been seen at the center and had reached adulthood by 1965. A cross-check of these files against the Mental Health Department files of the state of Massachusetts for 1965 disclosed a sizable number of former guidance clinic patients who had been subsequently hospitalized with a diagnosis of schizophrenia. Adequate guidance clinic records were found for 30 later *chronic* schizophrenic patients—those who were continuously in the hospital during the course of the study—and 38 later *released* schizophrenic patients—those whose hospitalizations had been terminated by return to some degree of participation in community life. All of the subjects were male, most were from lower class and lower middle-class homes, and all had been seen at the guidance center between the ages of 11 and 16. The files of these children were paired with records from a control group of 37 children also seen at the clinic but who had achieved satisfactory work and social adjustment as adults.

The childhood records of the *chronic* schizophrenic sample fell into two major patterns, labeled "withdrawn" and "delinquent." Children with the withdrawn pattern suffered from poor social adjustment and exhibited a variety of serious psychiatric symptoms. Adjustment in school and in the community was very poor, and friendships were rare. Acting-out behavior in the home, such as defiance of parents, tantrums, and disorganized destructive activity was frequent, although acting out in the community was rare. Early evidences of psychoticlike behavior, low self-esteem, and obsessive thinking were frequent. In addition, frequent mention was made in the records of symptoms suggestive of neurological impairment. These included hypo-activity, rigidity, abnormalities of speech, abnormal gait, poor coordination, and impaired attention span. In contrast, the delinquent pattern among these later *chronic* patients was characterized by extensive acting out in the community—stealing, lying, truancy, and destructive activity—as well as in the home. Although this group had few childhood and adolescent friendships, those that did exist showed a degree of sociability absent among the withdrawn children. Like the withdrawn children, these children showed low self-esteem and symptoms consistent with neurological impairment: hyperactivity, incorrigibility, short attention span, and overreaction to frustration.

The *released* schizophrenic group showed three major modal patterns of childhood and adolescent adjustment. One large group showed no unusual difficulties to distinguish them from the control children. A second group showed a withdrawal pattern similar to that seen in the *chronic* group but with the absence of obsessive thinking, psychoticlike symptoms, and symptoms associated with neurological impairment. The third group showed an acting-out pattern similar to that seen in the delinquent *chronic* schizophrenic sample, including deviant sexual behavior and sadistic, aggressive behavior toward peers, but symptoms suggesting neurological impairment were infrequent. The *released* schizophrenic group, then, showed either no destructive pattern or patterns of behavioral adjustment similar to those seen in the *chronic* cases, although in a somewhat muted form. The chief factor that distinguished *chronic* from *released* cases was the presence of signs of neurological impairment. In fact, the files of the later *chronic* group often contained formal diagnoses of brain damage or possible brain damage based on neurological examination.

A second analysis of these records (Fleming & Ricks, 1970) examined the phenomenological correlates of preschizophrenic breakdown as noted in therapists' records. The sample consisted of 24 to-be *chronic* schizophrenic patients, 25 to-be *released* schizophrenic patients, and a control group of 25 children who subsequently showed adequate adult adjustment. The median age of the sample when seen at the guidance clinic was 13, and the median age of first hospitalization for the schizophrenic groups was 19.5 years. The records were systematically coded into 81 items derived from published accounts of prepsychotic experience. The items were grouped into four more general categories: Anxiety, Vulnerability, Unreality, and Isolation–Alienation. Comparisons showed relatively minor differences in the subjective experiences of *chronic* versus *released* groups but showed marked contrasts between them and the nonschizophrenic controls. Table 5.3 presents a selection of the many items Fleming and Ricks found to differentiate the later schizophrenic and control children. Many of these items are highly reminiscent of the altered state of consciousness in the schizophrenic psychosis described in Chapter 2. Interestingly, the typical child in this study was an early adolescent almost 7 years away from first hospitalization for schizophrenia.

The first group of items describes elevated levels of *Anxiety* in preschizophrenic children, as seen in a generalized oversensitivity and overreactivity as well as in disturbances of speech. The heading of *Vulnerability* contains items reflecting passivity experiences (i.e., feelings that one's behavior or thoughts are uncontrollable or actually being influenced by others to one's detriment).

TABLE 5.3

Percentage of Subjects in Chronic Schizophrenic, Released Schizophrenic, and Socially Adequate Control Groups Experiencing Particular Types of Anxiety, Vulnerability, Unreality, or Isolation and Alienation[a]

Item	Chronic	Released	Control
Anxiety			
Nervousness, agitation, trembling, jumpiness; overreaction to noises.	73	76	36
Speech disturbances or difficulties associated with anxiety; stuttering, stammering, hesitation, blocking in speech, rise in voice.	79	72	46
Vulnerability			
Vulnerability, defenselessness; unprotected in a world that seems no good, hostile, unfair; feels deserted, betrayed.	88	88	60
Loss of self-control, not knowing when or how to stop: press of sudden urges, impulses, or thoughts racing without control.	62	60	28
Feelings of aimlessness, random, meaningless activity; pressured compliance with the demands of others.	70	76	32
Feels that other people can read his thoughts or see through him; experiences "ideas of reference."	46	40	8

Unreality			
Unreality, unfamiliarity of own experiences; inconsistency, discontinuity, lack of sameness.	52	35	8
Senses blurred or disfunctional so that things look, feel, taste wrong or different; perception disturbed in quality or intensity.	42	40	8
Feelings of a delirious nature—illusions, visions, hallucinations, delusions.	46	24	8
Feelings of self-estrangement, detachment, depersonalization, dissociation, sense of being incomplete, unreal, dead.	42	48	12
Feelings of disintegration, personal dissolution, internal fragmentation; inner disorganization felt in physical, mental, or emotional terms.	46	28	8
Isolation and Alienation			
Feelings of being turned inward, timid, withdrawn; self-protective apathy and indifference; solitary, insulated, isolated.	83	72	52
Desire to withdraw from others; avoids people and wants to crawl into self; tries to hide feelings, uses unresponsiveness, evasiveness.	92	72	56
Feels apart from others; like a stranger, outsider, on-looker; cut off from everyday life; friendless and forlorn.	96	84	48
Feels less developed than other children, not keeping up with his class, age group, group of friends.	96	92	56
Feels insignificant, unimportant to others, feelings of being looked upon as small or of no account.	83	92	64

[a] Adapted from Fleming and Ricks (1970).

Unreality feelings are highly similar to the dissociative experiences definitive of adult schizophrenic psychosis. These include derealization, depersonalization, perceptual illusions, hallucinatory experiences, and various forms of identity dissolution. Unlike experiences in the other three categories, experiences in this category are particularly preschizophrenic in that they occur very infrequently among control children. Finally, items defining *Isolation-Alienation* seem to describe the subjective aspect of the social maladjustment described in the Ricks and Berry study. Feelings of social estrangement, insignificance, and personal failure are correlated with a tendency to withdraw from others behind a facade of apathy and indifference. Obviously, the prodromal signs of schizophrenic psychosis extend downward in time for a considerable period prior to first hospitalization.

In summarizing these two studies, Ricks and Berry (1970) see the vulnerable preschizophrenic child as lacking components of integrated, competent adjustment, or at least having these components seriously underdeveloped. The child generally knows that he is vulnerable, alienated and isolated, and unable to establish satisfactory relationships with his peers. Intense anxiety and various forms of dissociative experience are accompaniments. Low self-esteem and a more or less total sense of rejection and worthlessness are also common. Angry confrontation, temper tantrums, and other forms of acting-out that test the limits and toleration of peers and family members appear to be episodic attempts to reestablish contact and to ward off increasing feelings of incompetence and isolation. These elements are common in the histories of both later *chronic* and later *released* schizophrenic patients. The distinction between the two adult outcomes appears to hinge on signs of possible neurological impairment in the later *chronic* group. Ricks and Berry suggest that a neurological deficiency may act to set an upper limit on the degree to which some schizophrenic patients can marshal resources— social, vocational, or personal—to overcome the schizophrenic breakdown and achieve a satisfactory degree of personality integration.

The Mednick–Schulsinger High-Risk Study

This long-term longitudinal study (Mednick, 1970; Mednick & Schulsinger, 1968, 1970) of preschizophrenic children began in Denmark in 1962 with the selection and testing of 207 offspring of severely schizophrenic mothers and 104 children of psychiatrically normal mothers. The object was not to study children of schizophrenic mothers per se but to maximize the probability that a sizable number of the original index group would eventually become schizophrenic as adults. As we saw in the previous chapter, approximately 10% of the children of one schizophrenic parent will themselves become schizophrenic in later life, and an additional 20% or so will show milder forms of borderline or latent schizophrenia. In a group of 200 such children, then, we can expect a frank schizophrenic outcome in approximately 20 children and a total incidence of schizophrenic spectrum disorders in approximately 60 children.

The Mednick–Schulsinger project is thus an ambitious attempt to isolate childhood precursors of later schizophrenic breakdown by following their 207 high-risk children into adulthood. As this group becomes differentiated, observations made in 1962 can then be compared among the subset that develops clinical schizophrenia, the subset that develops associated schizophrenic spectrum disorders, and the subset that remains psychiatrically normal. Additional comparisons can be made between each of these groups and the 104 low-risk children of psychiatrically normal mothers.

Mednick and Schulsinger estimate that it will take 20 to 25 years for the 1962 sample, whose mean age was then 15 years, to pass through the major risk period of schizophrenia. Therefore, final results will not be available until well into the 1980s. However, preliminary findings have been reported on 20 high-risk subjects, 15 males and 5 females, who developed various forms of psychiatric disability by 1968 (Mednick, 1970; Mednick & Schulsinger, 1968). Of these, 13 had been admitted to psychiatric hospitals with a variety of diagnoses including schizophrenia. The remaining seven had not been hospitalized but were diagnosed by the authors as showing schizophrenic, borderline, psychopathic, or alcoholic conditions. This total group of 20 is most accurately described as disturbed children of schizophrenic mothers. The final tally of schizophrenic cases among them must await the end of the risk period. This so-called "Sick Group" was then matched on age, sex, social, class, and rated level of adjustment in 1962 and compared with 20 symptom-free high-risk children of schizophrenic mothers (the "Well Group") and 20 low-risk children of psychiatrically normal mothers (the "Control Group").

The 1962 assessment included a diagnostic interview, a parent interview, a school teacher's report, the legally required form prepared by the midwife attending the subject's birth, personality and intelligence testing, a word association test, and an electrodermal (GSR) conditioning procedure. This latter was included to test Mednick's (1958) hypothesis that preschizophrenic individuals have low thresholds for stress arousal and will therefore show rapid conditioning and heightened generalization of autonomic stress responses. The procedure included nine pairings of a tone as the conditioned stimulus (CS) with an aversive noise as the unconditioned stimulus (UCS). Following the final conditioning trial, tests were made for the amplitude of the conditioned GSR to the tone CS and to two generalization stimuli (GSI and GSII), which were tones of higher frequencies than the CS.

Comparisons between the Sick, Well, and Control Groups revealed the following:

1. Children in the Sick Group tended to lose their mothers to a mental hospital quite early and permanently. By 13 years of age, for example, 81% of

the Sick Group, compared with 40% of the Well Group and 35% of the Control Group, had mothers completely absent from the home. This was attributed to the greater severity of schizophrenia among the Sick-Group mothers.

2. Teachers' reports indicated that 53% of the Sick Group, compared with 18% of the Well Group and 11% of the Control Group, were disturbing to their classes in terms of being disciplinary problems, domineering, aggressive, creating conflict, or disrupting the class with talking.

3. On the word association test, in which the subject was asked to give as many one-word associations as possible to a stimulus word, the Sick-Group children tended to show associative drift. Contrary to instructions and cautions, they often began responding to their own responses; for example, to the stimulus word "table," they might respond "chair, top, leg, girl, pretty, sky...." Those in the Sick Group, who did not show drifting did so by restricting themselves to one or two responses per stimulus word.

4. Electrodermal conditioning showed a number of differences suggesting heightened autonomic reactivity in the Sick Group. Figure 5.1 shows the differences among the three groups to the postconditioning test stimuli. GSR amplitudes are displayed for two presentations of the CS and each of the two conditioned generalization stimuli. The conditioned GSR is considerably greater in the Sick Group, as is the response to each of the generalization

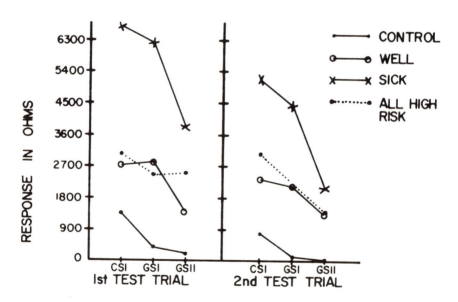

FIG. 5.1.   Electrodermal response amplitudes for Sick, Well, Control, and total High-Risk Groups. (From Mednick & Schulsinger, 1968.)

stimuli. Levels in the Well Group parallel those for the total 207 high-risk children as a whole but are, in turn, higher than levels in the Control Group.

5. Midwife reports showed the Sick Group to have had a greater number of obstetrical complications (OC's) during gestation and birth, including mother's illness during pregnancy, placental difficulty, prolonged labor, anoxia at birth, prematurity, and umbilical cord complication. No single item differentiated the three groups, but 70% of the Sick Group had suffered one or more complications, compared with 15% of the Well Group and 33% of the Control Group.

Mednick and Schulsinger discuss these observations in terms of low stress tolerance among the Sick-Group children. The electrodermal findings provide a direct measure of heightened stress reactivity; disruptive classroom behavior may be interpreted as a behavioral index of a poorly modulated response to social stressors. Obstetrical complications and early maternal loss may, in turn, be possible precursors of low stress tolerance. A further analysis showed that the severity of OC's was correlated with heightened electrodermal reactivity among Sick-Group members but not among Well- or Control-Group members. In other words, OC's are associated with later hyperresponsiveness in high-risk children who ultimately become psychiatric cases. Since these children also tended to lose their mothers to mental hospitalization at an early age—a finding suggesting greater severity of schizophrenia in these mothers—there appears to be a dual influence of high genetic risk and OC's on later stress tolerance. In Mednick's (1970) words, OC's "seem to damage the modulatory control of the body's stress-response mechanisms" in genetically predisposed children.

Summary

Despite marked differences in investigative method and in the selection of subject samples, these four major studies arrive at similar descriptions of the preschizophrenic child. Pollin and Stabenau (1968) characterize their index twins as viewing the world as more stressful and less predictable, and themselves as less competent in dealing with its demands, then their co-twins. Watt and Lubensky (1976) describe preschizophrenic tenth-graders as "emotionally immature," in the sense of being outpaced by peers, insensitive to the feelings of others, overly self-conscious, and prone to upset and temper outbursts with slight provocation. The early adolescent guidance clinic children studied by Ricks and Berry (1970) appeared to lack components of integrated, competent adjustment and saw themselves as incompetent, alienated, and isolated. Mednick and Schulsinger (1968, 1970) present psychophysiological observations consistent with their view of the preschizophrenic child as having a low threshold for stress onset and impaired ability to adapt to stressful situations over time.

The Fleming and Ricks (1970) study indicates that at least some preschizophrenic children see themselves in much the same way as do independent observers. About 90% of disturbed preschizophrenic adolescents felt helplessly inadequate and defenseless in a world they saw as hostile, rejecting, and unfair. Feelings of nervousness, agitation, and jumpiness are common, as are attempts to withdraw from others and assume a passive, unemotional outward appearance. They also feel friendless, unliked, and insignificant. Precursors of their later psychotic symptoms are not uncommon. Many report distortions of sensation and perception, as well as more severe symptoms of depersonalization, identity fragmentation, and delusions of control by outside forces.

The combined data of these studies suggest two major forms in which the preschizophrenic child attempts to adjust to his or her personal difficulties. The first is an extropunitive, delinquent pattern marked by acting-out in the classroom, community, or home. Truancy, stealing, lying, aggression toward peers, destructive activity, and disruption of school classes are particular signs (Mednick & Schulsinger, 1968, 1970; Ricks & Berry, 1970). These children are seen by their teachers as emotionally unstable, disagreeable, inconsiderate, and uncooperative (Watt & Lubensky, 1976). A second group becomes introversive and withdrawn. They are described by parents as dependent, sensitive, and fearful (Pollin & Stabenau, 1968; Stabenau & Pollin, 1970) and by teachers as insecure, unsociable, quiet, and egocentric (Watt & Lubensky, 1976). These contrasting modes of adaptation may be sex-linked. Watt and Lubensky differentiated the sexes in terms of "actively maladjusted" boys and "quietly maladjusted" girls. Active maladjustment characterized teachers' reports in the mostly male sample of Mednick and Schulsinger, and quiet maladjustment serves to describe Pollin and Stabenau's mostly female sample. Ricks and Berry do contrast a "withdrawn" pattern with the predominent "delinquent" pattern in their all-male sample, but the former includes acting-out and destructive activity in the home.

Preschizophrenic children are also often described as developmentally retarded. Parents of discordant MZ twins report that the affected twins passed more slowly through normal developmental stages (Pollin & Stabenau, 1968; Stabenau & Pollin, 1970), and teachers often mention retardation in physical and scholastic skills (Watt & Lubensky, 1976). Especially noteworthy are deficiencies in social skills. Most studies noted the poor peer relationships of these children. They tend to be either completely friendless or to have stormy, tenuous relationships. There is some suggestion that their social isolation arises from an inability to understand, care for, or empathize with peers or, in some cases, from their own aggressive acting-out behavior toward peers (Ricks & Berry, 1970; Watt & Lubensky, 1976).

An important high-risk study by Fish (1975) suggests that retarded development from birth is typical of preschizophrenic children. Fish's subjects were 12 infants of schizophrenic mothers. By 10 years of age, two had been diagnosed as childhood schizophrenics, three as showing severe personality disorder, and five as showing moderate personality disorder. Severe personality disorder was defined (Fish, 1975) as "pathologic disorders of thinking, identification, and personality organization resembling schizophrenia, but without gross psychotic disruption [p. 60]." During the first 2 years of life, seven of the 12 children showed what Fish terms "pandevelopmental retardation," in terms of physical growth lags, delayed postural and motor skill development, poor visual-motor coordination, and deficient language development. In general, the more severe and enduring the developmental retardation, the more severe was the psychiatric disturbance at age 10. Assuming that Fish's more severe cases will show adult schizophrenic outcomes, her data complement the foregoing studies in isolating retardation in physical, sensorimotor, emotional, and social development as precursors of adult schizophrenia.

Fish also joins Pollin–Stabenau (1968, 1970) and Ricks and Berry (1970) in associating this developmental retardation with the possibility of underlying brain impairment. Each of these studies reports a high incidence of "soft" neurological signs among preschizophrenic children. (Such signs are "soft" in that they do not point to any localizable brain damage but are common accompaniments of diffuse, relative neurological inefficency.) Four of Fish's 12 children showed a quiescent postnatal state characterized by decreased nystagmus, decreased spontaneous motor activity, crying, and flaccid muscle tone. A majority showed delays in visual fixation on grasped objects, delays in reaching and manipulating in the first year, and retarded form perception in the second year. According to Ricks and Berry, "soft" neurological signs are correlated with the severity of adult outcome. Among later *chronic*, but not *released*, patients, frequent mentions were made in childhood records of such signs as abnormalities of speech and gait, poor coordination, hypo- or hyperactivity, and impaired attention span. Many had in childhood been referred for neurological examination for possible specific brain damage. Parents' reports in the Pollin–Stabenau (1968, 1970) study are less detailed, but early "biologic" differences were noted between the index and control twins, which the authors interpret as signs of relative neurological incompetence.

The prodromal signs of schizophrenia may thus be described on many levels. At least a subset of preschizophrenic children—that which tends to be more severely schizophrenic in later life—shows a variety of soft neurological signs. Developmental retardation subsequently appears in the form of deficits in sensory and motor skills. In later life, retarded development is seen in social and emotional spheres. These lags relative to peers are accompanied by low thresholds for stress reactions, as seen in heightened autonomic reactivity and in a propensity toward emotional outburts with slight provocation. The preschizophrenic child's estrangement from peers is especially notable and appears to be due both to poor impulse control and to an inability to empathize with others. Finally, such children rather correctly see themselves as incompetent and socially isolated, and they often complain of living in an anxiety-provoking, hostile, and rejecting environment. By early adolescence, many begin to experience prodromal signs of schizophrenic breakdown, including perceptual anomalies, dissociative experiences, and delusions of control by outside agents. By late adolescence, many of these children have been hospitalized with a frank schizophrenic psychosis.

OBSTETRICAL COMPLICATIONS AND
LATER SCHIZOPHRENIA

The material so far discussed is primarily descriptive. It paints a rather dramatic picture of the development of the preschizophrenic child, but it fails to isolate any specific stressors that could be said to be responsible for the observed developmental anomalies. We turn now to a consideration of one heavily researched etiological possibility—that of obstetrical trauma. The source of this hypothesis is the association of developmental retardation with soft neurological signs in at least some preschizophrenic children.

Pregnancy and birth complications are known to be linked in infancy to such signs of neurological inefficiency as hypo- or hyperactivity, distractability, poor coordination, and asymmetrical muscle tonus, on the one hand, and to such psychological deficiencies as impaired IQ, conceptual ability, social development, and emotional stability, on the other hand. The degree of neurological and psychological impairment varies with the severity of the obstetrical complication (Werner, Simonian, Bierman, & French, 1967). In the general population of infants, these traumatic impairments tend to dissipate or to be overcome in later development, so that few residues are observed in later childhood. This is not universally true, however, and some children will continue to show the effects of early obstetrical complications in the form of such disorders as epilepsy, cerebral palsy, mental deficiency, reading disabilities, tics, and speech impairments (Pasamanick & Knobloch, 1960). It is therefore possible that obstetrical complications (OC's) are also correlated with the observed developmental retardation among preschizophrenic children.

Because any etiological formulation of schizophrenia must take into account the known genetic predisposition, there are three major hypotheses relating OC's to later schizophrenia:

1. Children genetically at risk for schizophrenia experience a higher than normal incidence of OC's and are thus doubly at risk. Both the OC's and the

genetic loading may be parallel, but etiologically independent, factors. The OC's create a state of neurological inadequacy that interacts with normal life experiences to trigger the genetic predisposition to schizophrenic psychosis.

2. Children genetically at risk for schizophrenia experience no greater than normal rates of OC's. However, that subset of genetically at-risk children that later becomes schizophrenic will be found to have experienced a higher frequency of OC's than their nonaffected at-risk cohorts. The OC's are thus the environmental trigger for the expression of the genotype.

3. Children genetically at risk for schizophrenia experience no greater than normal rate of OC's, nor is there any difference in OC's between at-risk children who do and who do not become schizophrenic in later life. There is thus no specific etiological relationship between OC's and schizophrenia. Early childhood vulnerability and subsequent psychosis may represent an unfolding of the genetic predisposition in an average expectable environment.

The first possibility has been rather decisively disconfirmed by carefully controlled studies of pregnancy and delivery complications among children of schizophrenic parents. Following up their finding that the disturbed children of schizophrenic mothers suffered more OC's than comparison groups, Mednick, Mura, Schulsinger, and Mednick (1971) studied hospital records of 83 children born to a schizophrenic mother or father, 83 children born to a mother or father with a history of hospitalization for character disorder, and 83 children whose parents were free of psychiatric difficulties. No differences were found among the three groups in recorded frequencies of either pregnancy difficulties (e.g., staining during fourth–ninth month, severe eclampsia) or delivery complications (e.g., induced labor, long labor duration). Children of schizophrenic parents were more frequently of low-normal birthweight, however.

A similar obstetrical-record study of 20 process and 22 reactive schizophrenic women, each matched demographically with nonpsychiatric control women, was reported by McNeil and Kaij (1973). Again, no differences were found in the frequency of pregnancy complications, labor and birth complications, placental complications, or predischarge neonatal disturbances. There was, however, a tendency for children of process schizophrenic mothers to be somewhat lighter in weight than normally expected for their gestational age.

Finally, Zax, Sameroff, and Babigian (1977) reported on the course of pregnancy and delivery, as well as the child's neonatal status among demographically matched schizophrenic women, neurotic depressive women, character disorder women, and nonpsychiatric control women. Depressive mothers showed the highest incidence of OC's; schizophrenic mothers fell between depressive mothers and the other two groups but were not significantly different from either. Schizophrenic women did tend to produce infants having low birthweight (under 2500 grams). A secondary analysis showed that the risk of OC's was more strongly related to the severity of the mother's psychiatric problem than to the specific diagnosis.

Sufficient grounds exist, then, for rejecting the first hypothesis—that OC's occur more frequently in children genetically at-risk for schizophrenia and thus account directly for the childhood antecedents of schizophrenia. There is consistent evidence of slightly lower than average birthweight among offspring of schizophrenic parents, but this is better interpreted as an early sign of developmental retardation than as a cause of later developmental lags. The two remaining hypotheses must therefore be considered: Either OC's interact with genetic predisposition to trigger the prodromal signs of later schizophrenia, or these signs occur independently of OC's. In the first case, we would expect to find a higher incidence of OC's among genetically at-risk children who later become schizophrenic than in their nonschizophrenic but equally at-risk peers or siblings. In the second case, we should expect to find no obstetrical differences between these two high-risk groups with differing outcomes, nor between them and the population at large.

The available data are as yet insufficient to allow for a choice between these two alternatives. The best support for the former is the previously cited Mednick–Schulsinger (1968, 1970) observation of higher OC's among high-risk children who later suffer psychiatric disturbance (the Sick Group) as compared with nondisturbed high-risk children (the Well Group) and with low-risk children (the Control Group). Yet these data are only preliminary. Schizophrenic outcome was not a necessary criterion for inclusions in the Sick Group, and the Well subjects were still in young adulthood and so remain at risk for ultimate schizophrenia. Bolstering the Mednick–Schulsinger findings are the retrospective Pollin–Stabenau (1968, 1970) reports of parents of discordant monozygotic twins, in which birth complications and anoxia at birth more frequently characterized the preschizophrenic twin. Like the Mednick and Schulsinger data, these findings are consistent with the second hypothesis, yet they too are less firm than could be wished. Not only were the data collected retrospectively, and therefore subject to error, but the obstetrical histories of MZ twins discordant for schizophrenia may not be typical of the histories of most preschizophrenic children, who are born as singletons. Because twin pregnancies and births are generally more problematic and complicated than is the case for singletons, it is possible that the Pollin and Stabenau findings hold for MZ twins discordant for schizophrenia but not for schizophrenic births in general.

These findings also need to be balanced against data consistent with the third hypothesis, suggesting that early vulnerability and later schizophrenic outcome are independent of any adverse obstetrical history. Fish (1975) reports that psychiatric disturbance among genetically at-risk children does not require earlier obstetrical complications. Of the 10 (of 12) high-risk children in her series who showed childhood schizophrenic or personality disorder by age 10, seven had shown developmental retardation in infancy, but only one had a history of OC's. Fish suggests that the soft neurological signs and developmental lags seen in preschizophrenic children are not of the quality seen after intrauterine or perinatal trauma but are, rather, early expressions of the genetic predispositon. She further suggests that abnormal pregnancy or birth may add an organic defect or a degree of mental retardation in genetically at-risk children but that such traumas are not necessary for early vulnerability and later schizophrenia.

The often reported finding of slightly lower than average birthweights in genetically at-risk neonates is consistent with this third alternative. Since the birthweight deviation is relatively minor, it is unlikely to be the cause of later developmental retardation. It may, however, be an early sign of a life-long relative immaturity and retardation among preschizophrenic children. Some evidence for this is provided in the previously cited obstetrical study by Mednick et al. (1971), which found a positive correlation between birthweight and developmental retardation at 1 year for offspring of schizophrenic parents.

Two further studies strongly suggest that the vulnerability of the preschizophrenic child extends downward from birth into the prenatal period. In 1961, Sobel reported double the frequency of infant mortality and congenital malformation in the children of hospitalized schizophrenic women than would be expected from general population norms. These findings have recently been replicated and refined as part of a nation-wide study of obstetrical history and early development sponsored by The National Institute of Neurological Diseases and Strokes (Rieder, Rosenthal, Wender, & Blumenthal, 1975). From among a sample of 10,000 pregnant women, approximately 200 cases were found in which either the mother or father had a history of psychiatric hospitalization. These cases were broken down into cases of certain schizophrenia, possible schizophrenia, and other psychiatric disability; each of these groups was matched with pregnant women with no psychiatric history. The certain schizophrenic group experienced about twice the frequency (7.5%) of adverse pregnancy outcomes than did their controls (3.8%). In addition, deaths among control offspring were generally associated with specific complications of pregnancy such as infection or placental difficulty, whereas the deaths among schizophrenic parents' offspring were in each case attributed to "unknown" causes. The deaths appeared to be correlated with more severe forms of schizophrenia in the parents: Of the seven deaths among the 93 offspring of schizophrenic parents, five were offspring of chronic cases.

In overview, there is no evidence that childhood precursors of later schizophrenia—early development lags, later social maladjustment and poor emotional modulation, and, in some cases, signs of poor neurological integration—are due in any direct manner to obstetrical trauma. Three recent and highly credible studies have found the incidence of OC's among the high-risk children of schizophrenic parents to be no greater than that of psychiatric and nonpsychiatric comparison groups. This leaves two possibilities for the role of OC's in the etiology of preschizophrenic childhood problems. In the first case, they may act as specific environmental stressors that potentiate the genetic predisposition. Data from the Mednick–Schulsinger high-risk project and the Pollin–Stabenau twin study support this possibility in finding that genetically at-risk children who show prodromal signs of later schizophrenia are more likely to have a positive history for OC's than equally at-risk children with more benign life history outcomes. Yet, for the reasons discussed, these data are not strong enough to support the generalization that OC's are a necessary etiological factor in all cases. This raises the final alternative, in which OC's are neither necessary nor sufficient etiological factors. That is, although OC's may be a contributing factor in some cases of later schizophrenia, the same outcomes may occur without such trauma. This case is argued most persuasively by Fish (1975), who finds that early sensory-motor retardation and childhood psychiatric disturbance among genetically at-risk children occurs without a positive history of OC's.

This last possibility is somewhat unsatisfactory in that it leaves unanswered the question of environmental factors responsible for developmental retardation in genetically at-risk children. That intrauterine factors may be operating is suggested by the higher than normal frequency of fetal deaths of "unknown" origin among chronic schizophrenic women. An adverse intrauterine environment may also account for the slightly lower than normal birthweights among surviving offspring of schizophrenic women. This last hypothesis, then, extends the notion of developmental retardation downward in time to encompass the genetically at-risk fetus, while widening the search for precipitating factors of etiological significance (Rieder et al., 1975).

THE FAMILIES OF SCHIZOPHRENIC PATIENTS

As Fish (1975) emphasizes in her discussion of neurological and developmental anomalies among infants of schizophrenic parents, it would be "the height of naivete" to assume that rates of neurological and psychological maturation are fixed at birth and unfold independently of the quality of the rearing environment: "A biologic vulnerability is just that—it can be exaggerated by a destructive or impoverished environment and can be compensated for by a constructive environment [p. 71]." Among unselected children, for example, the relationship between OC's and later childhood developmental deviations is mediated by various socioeconomic conditions. By the age of 7, children raised in middle-class homes with a stable family structure and educated parents show few adverse effects of neonatal retardation due to obstetrical trauma. Children with similar obstetrical histories reared in lower socioeconomic status homes, or in an unstable family structure, or with poorly educated parents, are more likely to show behavioral, intellectual, and psychiatric problems by the same age (Sameroff & Zax, 1973; Werner et al., 1967).

Prediction of developmental outcome therefore requires at a minimum information concerning both the child's biologic and temperamental characteristics and the nature and quality of the rearing environment. In terms of the etiology of schizophrenia, it is important to isolate those rearing factors, at different stages of development, that distinguish genetically at-risk children who succumb to later breakdown from similarly at-risk children who escape breakdown.

There is an unfortunate dearth of information on this specific problem, even though a large amount of information has been collected on families with schizophrenic offspring. Past studies in this vein fall into two major classes: (1) uncontrolled clinical investigations of families with schizophrenic children; and (2) controlled laboratory observations comparing interaction in families with schizophrenic offspring to families with either normal or otherwise disturbed offspring. A major problem is that in both cases, families have usually been selected for study *after* the child has become schizophrenic rather than on what we now know to be the more pertinent basis of high genetic risk and/or early developmental anomalies *prior* to hospitalization for schizophrenia. Not only is critical information lost on these at-risk cases who do not succumb to later schizophrenia, but any deviant interaction patterns observed may reflect no more than the family's adjustment to the particulars of the child's schizophrenic psychosis and treatment history. Thus neither method is appropriate for isolating rearing factors of etiological significance, which requires a demonstration that the rearing factors antedate schizophrenia in the child and, also, that they differentiate such cases from similarly at-risk cases without a schizophrenic outcome.

The reasons for the methodological inadequacies of past family research are primarily historical. The beginning of family studies of schizophrenia in the 1950s predated the accumulation of overwhelming evidence for a genetic factor in schizophrenia, as well as detailed neurological and psychological evidence for developmental retardation in infancy and childhood. Thus a purely environmental hypothesis of the origin of schizophrenia, centering on the social transmission of irrationality from parents to child, was tenable in the absence of firm evidence of a biological vulnerability. That such is no longer the case helps to explain the recent decline in the popularity of family studies in favor of more methodologically appropriate longitudinal studies of at-risk children (Goldstein & Rodnick, 1975). A second reason for the decline of such studies, over and above their limitations in addressing etiological issues, is that they have been empirically disappointing. That is to say, hypotheses derived from observational studies of selected families have not been supported by more stringent laboratory investigations. Whereas the former often present a picture of families with schizophrenic offspring as deviant in the extreme, the latter have isolated few if any atypical interaction patterns. This point is elaborated in the following discussion, which begins with an exposition of some well-known hypotheses based on clinical observations, then details important criticisms of this approach, and finally reviews the results of a large number of controlled laboratory investigations. The related question of possible personality abnormalities among parents of schizophrenic patients is also considered.

Clinical Case History Studies

According to Chodoff and Carpenter (1975), clinical investigators tend to share a two-part hypothesis of the family background of schizophrenic patients. First, schizophrenia, or at least its more severe forms, is held to develop in a seriously disturbed famliy milieu. And second, the elements of schizophrenic psychosis are said to be transmitted from parents to child through characteristically "schizophrenogenic" patterns of communication. The second proposition thus defines the mechanism by which family disturbance is translated into the child's ultimate schizophrenic breakdown.

This view is presented most clearly in the several reports of Lidz and his colleagues on 17 families with an adolescent or young adult hospitalized for schizophrenia (Lidz, 1973; Lidz, Fleck, & Cornelison, 1965). Each family was intensively observed for at least 1 year by means of repeated interviews, family therapy, psychological testing, and home visits. This information was combined into a series of descriptive reports, which were summarized as follows (Lidz, Fleck, Alanen, & Cornelison, 1963):

> All of the families were seriously disturbed. The difficulties pervaded the entire family interaction and could not be encompassed by focusing upon isolated segments of the data alone, even though in a series of papers we have sought to focus on differing aspects of the family milieu and to analyze the family transactions from various perspectives. We have noted the severe psychopathology of the fathers as well as of the mothers, and we have found that these families were either "schismatic"—that is, divided into two antagonistic and competing factions—or were "skewed" in that the serious personality disturbances of one parent set the pattern of family interaction. We have described the irrational and paralogical modes of thinking and communicating that prevail in these families, suggesting that the children received a very faulty training in reality testing. . . . To summarize, we do not consider it likely that any single factor such as a faulty mother–infant relationship will prove to be responsible in itself for causing schizophrenia, but we have found that the

structure and interaction of these families are highly detrimental to the ego development of children raised in them [pp. 2–3].

Lidz and his colleagues conjectured that schizophrenia is the inevitable result of the family's failure to provide the essentials requisite for reasonably integrated personality development in the child. Caught up in their own problems and marital conflicts, the parents are said to fail to provide the nurturance necessary for the child's development of personal autonomy; to fail properly to convey to the child the basic skills, values, and knowledge of the external culture; and to fail to provide the stability necessary for normal ego development.

Other investigators have described the transmission of irrationality from parents to child by such well-known concepts as "the double bind" (Bateson, Jackson, Haley, & Weakland, 1956) and "mystification" (Laing & Esterson, 1964). The former is a special kind of conflict situation in which the child is subjected to incongruent parental messages from which he can escape only by denying important aspects of his experience. The similar concept of mystification describes a process by which parents are said to distort or deny the child's experience of the world.

In the most typical case, the double bind is said to occur between the child and his "schizophrenogenic mother," whose own psychological disturbance leads her to control her interpersonal anxiety by controlling the psychological distance between herself and the child. A double bind requires several sequential elements: (1) a primary negative injunction, which may take the form of "do not do such and such or I will punish you," or the form "if you do not do such and such I will punish you"; (2) a secondary injunction conflicting with the first at a more abstract level usually communicated by nonverbal means, and also enforced by implied punishment; and (3) a tertiary negative injunction, again often implicit, prohibiting the child from escaping from the field. Bateson et al. (1956) give the following example:

A young man who had fairly well recovered from an acute schizophrenic episode was visited in the hospital by his mother. He was glad to see her and impulsively put his arm around her shoulders, whereupon she stiffened. He withdrew his arm and she asked, "Don't you love me anymore?" He then blushed, and she said, "Dear, you must not be so easily embarrassed and afraid of your feelings." The patient was able to stay with her only a few minutes more [p. 259].

The interpretation of this sequence begins with the assumption that the mother both wishes to affirm her lovability while avoiding anxiety produced by true closeness. The child is enjoined to display affection under the vague suggestion that being "embarrassed" and "afraid" is abnormal. But when an affectionate response is made, she punishes it by a stiffening gesture. The child is thus in an inescapable conflict: When he accepts her primary injunction, she will withdraw; yet if he then also withdraws she will chastise him for not "expressing his feelings." The only apparent solution, which Bateson et al. see as the prototype of later schizophrenic pathology, is for the child to deny his experience by distorting the mother's secondary message that she does not love him. Over time, the child will become increasingly unskilled in reading others' messages and unable to express what he is currently feeling. Schizophrenic withdrawal from a perplexing world is seen as the ultimate outcome.

In *Sanity, Madness, and the Family*, Laing and Esterson (1964) present a dramatic series of case studies of schizophrenic patients and their families illustrating the process of obfuscation and denial of the child's experience that defines "mystification." For example, in the case of the "Abbots," the daughter is a 28-year-old woman, Maya, hospitalized for 9 years with a diagnosis of paranoid schizophrenia. Maya's parents are clearly domineering and threatened by any signs of autonomy or independence on her part. Yet they continually fail to recognize that this is the case, instead viewing her struggles for independent selfhood as symptoms of her "illness." In Maya's case, mystification extended into innumerable facets of her public and private existence (Laing & Esterson, 1964):

> Not only did both her parents contradict Maya's memory, feelings, and perceptions, motives, intentions, but they made attributions that were themselves curiously self-contradictory, and, while they spoke and acted as though they knew better than Maya what she remembered, what she did, what she imagined, what she wanted, what she felt, whether she was enjoying herself or whether she was tired, this control was often maintained in a way which was further mystifying [p. 42].

Critique

These examples provide a sense of the devastating assessment of patients' families emerging from the clinical case-history tradition. The families are seen as rife with psychopathology, both in terms of the parents as individuals, and in terms of the interaction between parents and the preschizophrenic child. Specific forms of interaction such as double-binding and mystification are described as the mechanism by which parental irrationality is transmitted to the child, for whom a schizophrenic breakdown is the ultimate outcome. Because these descriptions provide a language for conceptualizing a complex area and because they attempt to address important questions of etiology, they have exercised a profound influence on both researchers and clinicians involved in the study and treatment of schizophrenia.

Yet, this approach has been severely criticized for drawing a grossly distorted picture of the family background of the typical schizophrenic patient and thereby doing a disservice to families already burdened with a disturbed, vulnerable child (e.g., Schopler, 1969; Torrey, 1977). Critics point to a series of both acknowledged and likely sources of bias that limit the validity of such studies on even a purely descriptive level (Hirsch & Leff, 1975; Kety et al., 1976a; Wing, 1964). A critical problem, often ignored in such studies, concerns the representativeness of the family selected for observation. For example, the Lidz group accepted only intact families who agreed to intensive interviewing and long-term observation. This may explain the skewing of their sample toward upper-class families when in fact most schizophrenic patients are of lower socioeconomic status. Laing and Esterson (1964) fail to mention at all the criteria by which their cases were selected. Such studies have also been challenged for failing to specify the criteria and the method used to diagnose schizophrenia in the offspring; Kety et al. (1976a) in fact reject a diagnosis of schizophrenia in some of the children described by Lidz et al. (1965).

The most important failing of the case-history approach is the absence of any built-in comparison with families with nonschizophrenic offspring subjected to the same detailed scrutiny. Disturbed family backgrounds are often found in the life histories of even highly effective and psychiatrically normal individuals, so that the mere presence of a poor rearing environment cannot be taken as an adequate explanation for later psychiatric difficulty. Many years ago, Renaud and Estess (1961) applied the standard psychiatric case-history method to a large sample of men selected for the absence of psychiatric disability and discovered a level of childhood deprivation and family disturbance not different in quality from that generally elicited from the general run of patients in treatment. Similarly, Kidd (1974) reported that almost half of the autobiographies written by students coping effectively with the demands of an academically rigorous college revealed such parental inadequacies as over-anxiety and over-protectiveness, alcoholism, neurotic and psychotic disorders, violent outbursts, absence from home, indifference to child-rearing, and overt preference for the respondent's siblings.

In sum, case studies of families of schizophrenic patients yield information of dubious validity to the extent that cases are not randomly selected, diagnostic procedures are left unspecified, and comparisons are not made with control families scrutinized with the same degree of intensity. It is true that authors of such studies often take pains to introduce their reports as sources of hypotheses for more systematic investigations of fact. Yet it is also the case that such disclaimers are often later forgotten or ignored by both authors and other commentators, so that the reports take on the status of verified findings regarding the family etiology of schizophrenia (Hirsch & Leff, 1975).

Laboratory Interaction Studies

Like clinical case studies, laboratory investigations of interaction in schizophrenic families have conventionally selected families following the child's hospitalization for schizophrenia and so are also incapable of yielding information of an etiological nature. On the other hand, they represent a methodological advance to the extent that explicit procedures are employed for generating and analyzing data and comparisons are made between families with and without schizophrenic offspring (henceforth: schizophrenic and control families). Investigators in this area have also tended to be more cognizant of the need for careful diagnosis of schizophrenia in the offspring, unbiased sampling of schizophrenic families, and matching of control families on such demographic factors as parental age, social class, and family composition.

Jacob (1975) and Hirsh and Leff (1975) have recently reviewed 30 major studies in this vein. About half have compared families with schizophrenic and psychiatrically normal offspring; the remainder have also attempted to control for the effects of mental illness per se by including families with disturbed but nonschizophrenic offspring. Jacob (1975) describes these as "direct observation studies," in which current patterns of interaction among parents and children are directly assessed and systematically recorded. The method, derived from small group research in social psychology, relies on either the direct coding or the recording and later coding of interaction as the family performs a task set by the experimenter. For example, the family might be presented with a mildly ambiguous and controversial statement such as "children should obey their parents," with the instruction to debate its merits. Observations are made of the ensuing patterns of interaction as the family attempts to reach a consensus as to the interpretation and validity of the statement.

Studies of this sort generate an enormous amount of data, depending on the number of interaction dimensions coded for, the configuration of the family group (e.g., patient alone, with parents, sibling alone, all siblings included, etc.), and the number and types of comparison families observed. In addition, specific techniques will differ from study to study, as do the hypotheses tested. Fortunately these studies have been the subject of detailed integrative reviews over the last decade and a half (Fontana, 1966; Frank, 1965; Hirsch and Leff, 1975; Jacob, 1975). A fair generalization is that these reviewers find little evidence from interaction studies for characterizing schizophrenic families as pathological or markedly deviant from the norm. A possible qualification is that Fontana (1966) and Hirsch and Leff (1975) find some evidence for greater disharmony in those families with severely disturbed process schizophrenic offspring. But even qualified statements of this sort are highly tenuous, as reported in Jacob's (1975) comprehensive review.

Jacob addressed his evaluation to the four dimensions of interaction most frequently assessed over the group of 30 relevant studies: (1) conflict; (2) dominance; (3) affect; and (4) communication clarity.

For the conflict domain, nine of 16 comparisons yielded no reliable differences between schizophrenic and control families, four comparisons found more frequent interruptions or disagreement in control families, and three comparisons found more conflict and disagreement in schizophrenic families.

For the dominance dimension, seven of 17 comparisons yielded no reliable differences. Of the remaining 10 comparisons, one found schizophrenic fathers to be more dominant than normal fathers, four found normal fathers and schizophrenic mothers to be more dominant than schizophrenic fathers and normal mothers, and the remaining four were inconsistent and inconclusive.

For the dimension of affect, four of 28 comparisons did not differentiate schizophrenic from control families in terms of amount or quality of affective expression. Five studies found normal families to be generally more expressive or to express more positive affect. The remaining comparisons were inconsistent, finding either schizophrenic or control families to express greater amounts of negative affect.

Only in the area of communication clarity was there a tendency toward consistent results: Schizophrenic families were often found to communicate less clearly and effectively than control families. Only five of 24 comparisons reported no differences between the two types of families. However, the majority of significant comparisons were derived from only one study, and the remainder are based on comparisons between schizophrenic and psychiatrically normal families rather than the more stringent comparison of families with nonschizophrenic but disturbed offspring.

Jacob summarizes this mass of information by first noting the considerable variability and inconsistency among the results across studies. Second, results within particular studies have often been tenuous at best and inconclusive at worst. Of the four interaction dimensions generally assessed in such studies, only that of communication clarity (i.e., linguistic precision) tended to differentiate schizophrenic and control families. But even here Jacob questions whether the phenomenon characterizes schizophrenic families per se rather than families with psychiatrically disturbed offspring in general. He concludes that laboratory investigations have yet to isolate family patterns that can be said to be specifically schizophrenic.

The benign picture of schizophrenic families arising from interaction studies could scarcely be more contrary to that developed by the case-history approach. The two viewed in apposition defeat attempts at comparative generalization; it is as if each were addressing a different subject rather than the same phenomenon. The only practicable basis of comparison is in terms of methodology, which indicates increasingly fewer distinctions between schizophrenic and control families as efforts are made to sample broadly, to subject comparison groups to identical observational procedures, and to guard investigators against observational bias. A reading of Jacob's review suggests at most that some schizophrenic families at some times and on some dimensions can be differentiated from control families. But this hardly qualifies as an empirical foundation for any generalization regarding the distinctiveness of schizophrenic families.

Ironically, there is an element of truth in attempts to relate schizophrenic outcome to family processes. As previously noted, there is good evidence that a biological vulnerability may be either exacerbated or ameliorated depending on the quality of the rearing environment. This must also be true for children genetically at risk for schizophrenia, only a subset of whom become psychotic as adults. Yet attempts to demonstrate that schizophrenic psychosis is associated with markedly deviant patterns of family interaction have not been fruitful. It may be the case, then, that average expectable family environments provide insufficient means for ameliorating the biological vulnerability. In other words, the rearing milieu of the preschizophrenic child needs to be better than average when it in fact appears to be no worse than average. But the precise meaning of "better than average" in terms of specific rearing practices must await longitudinal studies of genetically at-risk children who escape a schizophrenic outcome.

Parental Communication Disorder

If laboratory studies provide little support for the notion of grossly distorted interaction patterns in schizophrenic families, they do raise a question of a somewhat different nature. Jacob (1975) notes that the strongest trend emerging from this literature is the suggestion of less accurate and effective verbal communication among members of schizophrenic families. This is an intriguing suggestion, because linguistic deficiencies among parents of schizophrenic patients might be expected on purely genetic grounds. Linguistic anomalies are a cardinal characteristic of severe schizophrenic psychosis, so that communication difficulties would be expected in some fraction of the offspring of schizophrenic families. In addition, frank schizophrenia (and the possible presence of language disorder) is more frequent among parents of schizophrenic patients than in the general population. As noted in the previous chapter, the risk of schizophrenia among patients' parents is about 4%, as compared with a population prevalence of about 1%. Parents also appear to have higher than average risks for other diagnoses in the so-called schizophrenic spectrum. Kety et al. (1976b) diagnosed "latent" (borderline) schizophrenia in 3.5% and "uncertain" (possible) schizophrenia in 7.5% of the first-degree biological relatives of schizophrenic adoptees, as compared with rates of about 2% for each of these categories in control adoptees. Data from the Judge Baker Schizophrenia Research Project revealed that mothers of children who later became chronically schizophrenic were more often described as suffering from borderline schizophrenia than mothers of remitting schizophrenic patients or mothers of nonschizophrenic controls (Hirsch & Leff, 1975). It is possible, therefore, that the interaction study results reviewed by Jacob reflect a higher incidence of thought disorder associated with schizophrenic spectrum diagnoses in both the offspring and parents within schizophrenic families. The less than perfect reliability of findings of impaired communication in such families may reflect sampling variation; that is, the schizophrenic offspring in interaction studies will not universally show thought disorder, nor will the majority of their parents fall into the schizophrenic spectrum.

As noted in the previous chapter, studies of the genetic transmission of schizophrenia would be facilitated by the discovery of a genetic "marker"—a test for the presence of the schizophrenic genotype in the unaffected relatives of schizophrenic patients. Although some promising work on blood assays of the enzyme monamine oxidase is in progress, potential genetic markers are not limited to biochemical compounds. Genotypic correlates at other levels of functioning—neurological, psychological, or behavioral—are also conceivable.

In fact, a number of attempts have been made to develop psychological tests of the characteristically schizophrenic language disorder that would differentiate patients and their unaffected relatives from other groups. Most work in this vein has centered on attempts to isolate mild disorder, in the form of impaired concept formation or speech anomalies, among patients' parents. But either because the hypothetical defect is highly subtle or because the tests so far developed are insensitive, this effort has been plagued by inconsistencies and contradictions (Hirsch & Leff, 1975). The best example of this generalization is the development, by Wynne and Singer (Singer & Wynne, 1966; Wynne, 1968, 1970a, b), of a test for "communication deviance" among patients' parents and the more recent failure to replicate reported by Hirsch and Leff (1975).

Wynne and Singer suggested that parents of schizophrenic patients will exhibit deviant communication styles during interpersonal interaction because of a genetically determined deficiency in focusing and maintaining attention to external stimuli. According to Wynne and Singer, this attentional dysfunction gives rise to vague, disruptive, and irrelevant verbal behavior during the performance of tasks demanding cooperation and "shared attention" with others. This formulation thus brings together theories of attentional deficit in schizophrenia and the observation of inaccurate communication in laboratory interaction studies. Wynne and Singer's test rests on the analysis of the verbal behavior of patients' parents in a projective testing situation, which is considered a prototype of a joint task demanding a shared focus of attention between subject and examiner for its successful completion. Verbatim transcripts of such testing sessions are scored for about 40 types of communication deviance, such as incomplete phraseology, disqualifications of previous answers, intrusions and disruptions, peculiar word usages, and illogical trains of thought (Singer & Wynne, 1966). The object of analysis is, therefore, the form in which the parent expresses ideas and concepts rather than the content of the parents' projective responses per se. In two separate studies, Wynne and Singer found that communication deviance scores sharply separated parents of schizophrenic offspring from parents of nonpsychiatric control offspring. The separation was such that almost no overlap was found in the distribution of scores for the two groups; schizophrenic parents could be distinguished from controls in 85–95% of the cases on the basis of their communication deviance scores alone (Wynne, 1970b).

These striking results have not, however, stood up to attempts at independent replication. Hirsch and Leff (1975) compared 20 sets of parents of acute schizophrenic patients with an equal number of parents of neurotic or neurotic depressive patients. The first 20 consecutive admissions to three London mental hospitals with a primary diagnosis of acute schizophrenic episode who also showed evidence of schizophrenic psychosis on the Present State Examination (Wing, Cooper, & Sartorius, 1974) comprised the offspring of the experimental group; controls were similarly consecutively selected. This careful study also took pains to make sure that the two sets of parents were equivalent in terms of education, occupation, and tested intelligence; in addition, all testing was performed by examiners blind to the offspring's diagnosis. Although the resulting communication deviance scores showed a great deal more overlap than found by Wynne and Singer, the schizophrenic parents' mean score was in fact reliably higher than that of the control parents. However, a more detailed analysis showed that the frequency of communication deviance was highly correlated with the number of words spoken and that parents of schizophrenic patients (specifically, the fathers) emitted a greater number of words during the testing session. When the two groups' scores were adjusted for the number of words spoken, no differences were found in amount of communication deviance. Therefore, the only difference between parents of schizophrenic and neurotic offspring detected in this carefully designed and analyzed study was the apparently trivial propensity of schizophrenic patients' fathers to be somewhat more loquacious.

Hirsch and Leff (1975) note that the discrepancy between their results and those of Singer and Wynne is most likely due to sampling factors. Because the clinical definition of schizophrenia is much broader in the United States than in Europe, Singer and Wynne's samples may have contained parents whose children would not be given a schizophrenic diagnosis in Great Britain. Furthermore, Wynne and Singer's selection procedure was not systematic, depending to some extent on the referral of cases by colleagues aware of the general hypothesis being investigated. Although it is impossible to be certain, such a referral procedure could have yielded: (1) a disproportionate number of cases in which parents and schizophrenic child were concordant for anomalies of thought and language; and (2) a corresponding underrepresentation of discordant cases.

The question of subclinical forms of thought disorder among parents of schizophrenic patients, whether measured as imprecise communication in interaction studies, as communication deviance during psychological testing, or by other direct testing methods, remains open. Although such anomalies undoubtedly characterize some parents of schizophrenic patients, there as yet exists no entirely convincing evidence that it is characteristic of all such parents or that it clearly distinguishes such parents from those of nonschizophrenic but otherwise psychiatrically disturbed offspring. At this point, the only factor clearly distinguishing parents of schizophrenic offspring is their higher than average rate of schizophrenia and allied spectrum diagnoses. However, these diagnoses are far from universal among such parents. Since one or both parents necessarily transmit the schizophrenic genotype to their affected child, the search for a psychological marker of the genotype in unaffected parents is eminently reasonable. But whether any such marker will be found in anomalies of thought and verbal communication is yet to be decided.

COMMENTARY

Hypotheses emphasizing a genetic–environmental interaction in the etiology of schizophrenia are often subsumed under the more general rubric of "diathesis–stress" models. The first term—*diathesis*—refers generally to constitutional factors predisposing to illness, in this case the schizophrenic genotype. The second term—*stress*—is a proxy for any and all environmental factors responsible for the manifestation of the predisposition. Implicit in this model is the corollary proposition of benign environments in which the predisposition is not actualized. Although the application of the diathesis–stress model to schizophrenia is correct in pointing to genetic factors as necessary but not sufficient for the development of schizophrenic psychosis, it has an unfortunate tendency to oversimplify the etiological issue. The major problem is that the model implies a degree of specificity in both the diathesis and stress terms difficult to reconcile with our knowledge of schizophrenia. There is good evidence, for example, that the diathesis is nonspecific; that is, the same genetic constitution that gives rise to clinical schizophrenia in some individuals may also predispose to other disorders along the so-called schizophrenic spectrum. This implies, in turn, that a simple dichotomy of the stress term into benign and actualizing environments is inaccurate; rather, a graded series of actualizing environments, corresponding to different ultimate conditions along the schizophrenic spectrum, needs to be postulated.

In addition, it is probably a mistake to imbue the stress term in this model with any degree of specificity. Present evidence strongly suggests that there is no specific developmental or life history event that universally characterizes preschizophrenic children and that can be isolated as a necessary condition for later schizophrenic psychosis. The search for a specifically "schizophrenogenic" stressor as a potentiator of the genotype has centered on two candidates, obstetrical complications and disturbed processes of intrafamilial communication. The first tends to be preferred by biologically oriented investigators; the second is a hypothesis widely held by investigators in the clinical case-history tradition. But our review of the available evidence gives little basis for postulating either factor as a necessary precursor of later schizophrenia. Whereas the Mednick–Schulsinger (1968, 1970) high-risk study found a higher than average frequency of OC's among the psychiatrically disturbed children of schizophrenic mothers, Fish's (1975) similar high-risk study found that psychiatric disturbance in such children may appear with a benign obstetrical history. In neither of these investigations have the offspring passed through the adult risk period for schizophrenia, so any conclusion must remain tentative. Yet a reasonable generalization is that OC's may add a degree of impairment to genetically predisposed children but that the occurrence of later schizophrenia does not require an adverse obstetrical history. And similarly for family dynamics: Although many dramatic cases of schizophrenia arising against a background of parental disturbance and destructive interaction patterns have been reported, there is no convincing evidence of the generality of adverse rearing environments in the history of schizophrenic patients. Indeed, few if any differences in the interaction patterns of families with and without schizophrenic offspring can be detected when detailed observations are made in laboratory-based studies. Whereas such studies cannot be considered investigation of child-rearing practices *prior* to the onset of the child's schizophrenia, the very absence of marked family pathology at the point of the child's hospitalization strongly suggests that schizophrenia may arise in unremarkable family milieux.

To put the point slightly differently: The preschizophrenic child appears to find it difficult to cope adequately under typical child-rearing regimes and/or patterns of family interaction, and the ultimate outcome of this difficulty is schizophrenic psychosis. This formulation suggests that the search for etiologically significant deficiencies in schizophrenic family patterns is misplaced; rather, information leading to preventive interventions with preschizophrenic children may derive from more intensive study of atypical outcomes (i.e., children genetically at-risk for schizophrenia who do not succumb to later schizophrenic psychosis). Studies of such "invulnerable" children could conceivably yield important information on individual coping devices, family rearing practices, or social support systems that protect the genetically at-risk child from the decompensation that appears to occur in average expectable milieux. Wahl (1976) concludes a discussion of existing findings on monozygotic twins discordant for schizophrenia with a similar suggestion:

> Once again, however, little attention has been paid to positive factors to which the nonschizophrenic co-twins may have been exposed which facilitated their favorable psychological adjustment and buffered against schizophrenic development.... One could go so far as to explain the findings of premorbid personality differences and the concomitant failure to isolate specific negative environmental causes for these or for schizophrenia by arguing that such specific negative influences can never be found—that premorbid personality differences simply represent the gradual unfolding of a schizophrenic genotype, with the intervention of positive factors permitting some predisposed individuals (e.g., nonindexed co-twins) to make a reasonable adjustment. Such a formulation, no doubt, overstates the case, but investigation of positive factors based on similar formulations is certainly warranted [p. 101].

In light of the difficulty in isolating a specific environmental potentiator or potentiators of the schizophrenic genotype specified by the diathesis–stress model, a more dynamic transactional model of the development of schizophrenia over time may be closer to the truth. Sameroff and Zax (1973) remind us that neither constitutions nor environments are necessarily constant over time; rather, both the child and his or her environment change in important ways. These changes are interdependent, developing as a function of their mutual influence on one another. The child responds to the environment in terms of individual dispositions and is in turn altered by the changed environment that has been created.

This more dynamic view of person–environment transaction suggests a reading of the research on the vulnerable preschizophrenic child in terms of an upward spiraling of psychological incompetence with increasing age. Fairly unremarkable differences in birthweight become detectable soft neurology in early childhood, which leads to slowness in meeting major developmental milestones in later childhood, and thence to the appearance of diffuse psychiatric disturbance in later childhood and early adolescence. And as the preschizophrenic child falls further and further behind his or her age mates in the development of coping resources, the age-graded demands for autonomy and competence inexorably increase. If appropriate skills are not fully acquired at age-specific periods, further developmental challenges will be poorly met and resolved, so that over time normal developmental tasks will become increasingly stressful for the preschizophrenic child.

Although it is convenient to speak of the "typical" preschizophrenic child, it is important to note the variability among preschizophrenic children in various developmental deficits. In addition, the degree of deviation at one stage appears to predict deviation at subsequent levels of development. Thus birthweight, at least among offspring of schizophrenic parents, is correlated with lags in motor development at 1 year of age (Mednick et al., 1971). The degree of developmental retardation—whether defined in terms of neurological indices as in Fish's (1975) work or in terms of conventional indices such as age of crawling, walking, talking, etc., as in the Pollin–Stabenau (1968) MZ twin sample—is in turn correlated with the probability of psychiatric difficulties in childhood and the probability of overt schizophrenia in adulthood. Ricks and Berry (1970) further suggest that among those who suffer schizophrenic breakdown, the degree of chronicity is correlated with the degree of neurological deficiency in childhood.

Remarkably, the preschizophrenic child shows few if any academic deficiencies. School failure is rarely noted in the histories of schizophrenic adults; at most, there may be some minor achievement lags in mathematics, but this does not generalize to verbal skills (Watt & Lubensky, 1976). Yet by mid-adolescence, preschizophrenic turmoil spills over into the school situation. Teachers see such children as emotionally unstable, undependable, and socially isolated. Boys tend to show a delinquent acting-out pattern that reflects a more general adjustment difficulty in the home and community; girls tend to show a more introversive pattern of quiet maladjustment. The pattern of impaired stress tolerance and poor modulation of emotional response noted by teachers and child guidance clinic therapists is paralleled by laboratory observations of autonomic over-reactivity and slowed habituation to stressful stimuli. The phenomenology of preschizophrenic children is of a piece with these external observations. They tend to see themselves as driven by uncontrollable impulses and urges, as friendless in a rejecting and hostile world, as increasingly retarded vis-à-vis peers in social–emotional development. Low self-esteem begins to merge with the harbingers of psychotic breakdown: hallucinatory experience, depersonalization, delusions of control by others, and experiences of derealization. It is but a small step to a full-blown schizophrenic psychosis requiring professional intervention.

6 Patienthood

> *One could say that mental patients* distinctively *suffer not from mental illness, but from contingencies.*
>
> —Erving Goffman (1959)

In the foregoing chapters, we have examined schizophrenia as a clinical and psychological entity and as a scientific conundrum. In this chapter, we address schizophrenia as it articulates with the role of psychiatric patient and with social and professional attitudes regarding appropriate care and treatment. The first section of the chapter considers the social impact of schizophrenia in terms of the number of affected individuals, both treated and untreated, enumerated by epidemiological investigations. The second section considers the reasons for the declining fortunes of the mental hospital as a primary locus of treatment. It focuses on several highly influential accounts of the deleterious effects of this institution on both patients and staff. The third and final section deals with the evolution and current status of the contemporary reform movement in the treatment of severe mental illness known as *deinstitutionalization*. This development holds great promise as a humane and effective approach to the care and treatment of schizophrenic patients, even if the promise remains as yet unrealized.

THE PREVALENCE OF SCHIZOPHRENIA

Over the past fifty years, numerous epidemiological studies of schizophrenia have been conducted in North America, Europe, and the Far East, and it is clear that no single figure can be adduced to express a universal prevalence of

147

the disorder. Differences in reported figures are in part due to methodological variations among studies. National differences in the psychiatric definition of schizophrenia are a prime source of such variation. For example, European psychiatrists tend to adopt a classical Kraepelinian approach to diagnoses and look askance at the North American propensity to include short duration reactive psychoses with good recovery under the same rubric. The very definition of a "case" is also unstandardized. Some investigators prefer to assess only those cases currently in treatment (period prevalence); others include both active cases and former, or inactive, cases (lifetime prevalence). Investigators also differ in the extent to which they attempt to assess the number of never-treated schizophrenic individuals in the population. Although there is some professional dispute as to whether such people may even be legitimately defined as "cases," a small number of studies has made ad-hoc diagnostic assessments through interviews based on household surveys or the use of community informants (Gruenberg, 1974; Yolles & Kramer, 1969).

Even beyond such methodological differences, however, there are probably true underlying differences in the rate of occurrence of schizophrenia across cultures. As we have seen, schizophrenia is the outcome of some complex interaction between genetic endowment and environmental potentiators, and neither factor is likely to be a fixed quantity across distinct population groups. It is often claimed that schizophrenia occurs in all human societies. But in fact no adequate data are available to support any such assertion. Torrey's (1973) review of the cross-cultural literature on this subject showed that schizophrenia has only been proved to occur in Westernized and industrialized nations. Similarly, as noted in Chapter 1, there is little evidence that schizophrenia occurred at any appreciable frequency even in the West before it was first described by nineteenth-century European psychiatrists. But even were schizophrenia to be found in all cultures and epochs, there is no a priori reason to expect similar *frequencies* of occurrence across cultures. Unfortunately, the available epidemiological data confound any true cultural differences with methodological variation among studies, so the issue is at present unresolvable.

In order to avoid the pitfalls of overgeneralization, the following exposition deals only with data collected in the United States since 1950. These figures probably reflect maximum cross-cultural rates, due both to the relatively wide concept of schizophrenia prevailing and to the multiplicity of mental health services available to the U.S. population relative to other areas of the world.

Treated Cases

In 1971, schizophrenia accounted for 22.5% of all patient care episodes (continuing cases plus new admissions) in all U.S. mental health facilities.

These facilities included both in-patient and out-patient services of public and private mental hospitals, Veterans Administration hospitals, community mental health centers, general hospitals, and psychiatric clinics. Schizophrenic episodes amounted to slightly over 900,000 cases, or a rate of 4.39 cases per 1000 population (NIMH, 1977b). This rate does not appear to vary appreciably from region to region. A psychiatric register established in Monroe County, N.Y., reported a treated prevalence rate of 4.78 per 1000 population during 1970 (NIMH, 1977b), and a survey of all cases under treatment in New Haven, Connecticut, including those seen by private psychotherapists, reported a rate of 3.60 per 1000 during a half-year observation period in 1950 (Hollingshead & Redlich, 1958). A round estimate for the yearly prevalence of cases of schizophrenia in treatment in the United States would therefore be approximately .5% of the population. This may slightly overestimate the actual number of schizophrenic individuals, because a given person might experience more than one treatment episode in the course of a year.

Prevalence figures indiscriminately combine new cases appearing during the observation period with old cases continuing into the period. Two different disorders may show similar prevalences even though one occurs rarely but is a chronic condition while the other occurs relatively frequently but with rapid recovery. To distinguish between these two factors, epidemiologists often prefer to measure the incidence of a disorder (i.e., the rate of occurrence of new cases in a population during a specified time period).

The incidence of treated cases of schizophrenia in the United States appears to have increased somewhat over the past quarter-century. Yolles and Kramer (1969) computed an annual rate of .30 new cases of schizophrenia per 1000 population for the Hollingshead and Redlich (1958) survey of treatment facilities in New Haven in 1950. They also reported annual incidences of .48 and .50 per 1000 population for two separate and exhaustive treatment surveys in the state of Maryland in the early 1960s. In 1970, the Monroe County, N.Y., psychiatric register reported an annual incidence of .72 per 1000 population (NIMH, 1977b). In the absence of corresponding population surveys of the untreated incidence of schizophrenia, it is impossible to determine if this apparent upward trend in treated cases represents a true increase or whether it reflects such factors as the relative increase in the percentage of young adults particularly at risk for schizophrenia or an increase in treatment facilities available to the U.S. population. Nevertheless, a rate of .50 per 1000 population, or .05%, may be taken as a fair estimate of the annual treated incidence of schizophrenia in the United States.

A randomly selected individual therefore has about a one-twentieth of one percent chance of becoming schizophrenic in any year. Although this statistic is not particularly ominous, its true significance becomes clearer when this probability is multiplied by life-expectancy figures. Applying the annual .05%

risk to the U.S. mortality figures obtaining in 1960, Yolles and Kramer (1969) estimated that about 3% of the population surviving to age 15 would become schizophrenic at some time in life.

Untreated Cases

Beyond treated cases of schizophrenia lie an unknown number of untreated schizophrenic persons. These include those in the early stages of a schizophrenic psychosis who will eventually find their way into treatement; discharged cases who choose not to seek further treatment for recurrent episodes; and those who never have nor ever will be in treatment. The frequency of untreated cases is extremely difficult to ascertain. To do so would require a systematic household population survey coupled with case study and diagnostic refinement comparable to that available in the best mental health facilities. No study of schizophrenia meeting these requirements has as yet been undertaken. Indeed, the opportunity for only limited observation during a household survey convinces many epidemiologists that the problem is insurmountable. Nevertheless, the question has important implications. A large number of untreated cases surviving in the community would imply that schizophrenia is less catastrophic than most mental health professionals believe and, also, that our knowledge of schizophrenia, which derives from treated cases, is based on biased sampling of the universe of schizophrenic persons.

The famous Midtown Study—a systematic household survey carried out in the mid-1950s in New York City—provides some basis for an approximate estimate of the untreated prevalence of schizophrenia (Srole, Langner, Michael, Opler, & Rennie, 1962). The survey sample consisted of 1660 randomly selected adults living in a residential area of Manhattan. Information gathered from a structured interview was reduced by two psychiatrists into a four-category mental health rating and, where appropriate, into a probable diagnosis. Almost 25% of the sample fell into the lowest of the four mental health categories. These individuals were considered in immediate need of psychiatric help and highly likely to be accepted as cases were they to seek such assistance. About a quarter of this group, or 6% of the entire sample, were judged to be probably psychotic. On the basis of other evidence (Yolles & Kramer, 1969, table 1), we may conservatively estimate that schizophrenia represents about one-third of all cases of psychosis. The Midtown data therefore suggest a 2% prevalence of schizophrenia in the survey population. There is no reason to assume that this figure is specific to New York City or to urban areas or that it is markedly higher than rates found in similarly conducted population surveys (e.g., Dohrenwend & Dohrenwend, 1969, 1974).

Although the Midtown findings excluded cases under in-patient treatment in area mental health facilities, it did include out-patients currently in treatment, as well as individuals who had previously received some form of psychiatric assistance. But, of the 25% of the sample judged to be in need of psychiatric help, fully three-fourths had never been in any form of treatment. Assuming that this fraction also characterizes the treatment history of the schizophrenic individuals in the survey, we may estimate that 1.5% of Midtown residents were untreated cases of schizophrenia. Comparing this to the .5% annual prevalence of treated schizophrenia previously estimated, we arrive at the remarkable conclusion that for every case of schizophrenia in treatment, there are three schizophrenic individuals, judged to be impaired by mental health professionals, who have never been in treatment and, ostensibly, have little interest in seeking such treatment. Even more striking are the results of applying this 3-to-1 ratio to the life-time expectancy for a schizophrenic breakdown: to the 3% of the population that will find its way into treatment at some time in life for schizophrenia, we must add another 9% of the population that will go untreated.

Although our estimate of untreated cases is based on the results from the Midtown study alone, there is no reason to believe its findings are atypical. Other recent community surveys of psychological disability, although less extensive than the Midtown study, vary both above and below Midtown's finding of a 25% rate of potential cases (Dohrenwend & Dohrenwend, 1969). In addition, the 1.5% rate of untreated schizophrenia estimated here is considerably more conservative than the estimate provided by the Midtown study itself (see Langner & Michael, 1963, p. 407).

Some epidemiologists suggest that all schizophrenic individuals will sooner or later find their way into treatment (Gruenberg, 1974). But this view assumes that schizophrenic persons are necessarily socially debilitated and require more than the minimal support available from friends, family, and employers. Yet social competence and vulnerability to schizophrenic episodes may be quite independent. Zubin and Spring (1977) cite evidence that two-thirds of schizophrenic patients are employed immmediately before entering treatment and that even those vulnerable to repeated hospitalization because of symptom recurrence are employed at a level commensurate with former schizophrenic patients who do not relapse. Indeed, the aggressive treatment and rapid discharge policies characteristic today of the management of acute schizophrenic episodes argues against any necessary association between schizophrenia and incompetence to manage one's affairs in the community (Klerman, 1977). It may be true, of course, that cases in treatment are more seriously disturbed than those untreated cases found by community surveys. But this seems unlikely to the extent that diagnostic criteria used in community surveys are the same as those employed for cases in treatment. Community surveys strongly suggest that the universe of schizophrenic persons divides into a large group of socially competent individuals who survive more or less adequately in the community and a smaller group of less socially competent individuals who find their way into treatment.

Demographic Correlates

Schizophrenia is not randomly distributed within the population but occurs with disproportionate frequency in lower socioeconomic strata, young adults, and nonwhites.

Social Class. Social-class differences within communities reflect the varying levels of prestige accorded individuals by other members of the community. Because prestige rankings of occupations differ minimally among respondents of varying social backgrounds (Jencks, 1972), social class is most reliably indexed by scales of the occupational hierarchy. For example, the Hollingshead and Redlich (1958) index of social position uses the following seven occupational categories: (1) executives or proprietors of large concerns and major professionals; (2) managers and proprietors of medium-sized businesses and lesser professionals; (3) administrative personnel of large concerns, owners of small, independent business, and semiprofessionals; (4) owners of small businesses, clerical and sales workers, and technicians; (5) skilled workers; (6) semiskilled workers; and (7) unskilled workers. Because occupational level tends to be correlated with income and amount of education, these factors are also frequently used to index social-class position.

Of the innumerable facts about schizophrenia collected over the past century, few are as consistently reported as the association between schizophrenia and social class. This association is often generally described as an inverse relationship between rates of schizophrenia and social-class position. But it is more precisely described as a disproportionate accumulation of cases in the lowest social-class grouping used in any given study. This holds with few exceptions for both treated cases and untreated cases revealed by community surveys (Dohrenwend & Dohrenwend, 1969; Eaton, 1974; Mishler & Scotch, 1963). Representative findings appear in Table 6.1, which is derived from the Hollingshead and Redlich (1958) survey of treated cases in New Haven, Connecticut, during a half-year observation interval. The data

TABLE 6.1
Incidence and Prevalence Rates per 100,000 Population for
Scizophrenia by Social Class[a]

| | Class | | | |
	I II	*III*	*IV*	*V*
Incidence	6	8	10	20
Prevalence	111	168	300	895

[a]From Hollingshead and Redlich (1958, p. 236).

are expressed as incidence and prevalence rates per 100,000 as a function of a five-category index of social class. The incidence of new cases shows only minor variations between Classes I–II and Class IV; however, the rate in Class V is double that of adjacent Class IV. Although the prevalence rate shows a more orderly increase as a function of class, there is a high accumulation of cases in Class V, which has a rate three times as great as adjacent Class IV. These data are typical of those reported in 20 similar investigations (Eaton, 1974).

The accumulation of schizophrenia in the lowest socioeconomic stratum is not simply a reflection of overall higher rates of psychopathology in this group. Of the major forms of psychiatric disability, personality disorders do show a distribution similar to schizophrenia as a function of class status, but no such relationship appears for either the affective disorders or for the neuroses (Dohrenwend & Dohrenwend, 1969). Thus the class–schizophrenia relationship cannot simply be attributed to a propensity of lower-class environments to generate psychological disturbance of all types. The explanation for the association must be specific to schizophrenia.

Two hypotheses have been debated for a number of years. The *social causation* hypothesis holds that the conditions of life in the lowest social class are conducive to the emergence of schizophrenia in genetically predisposed individuals; that is, either schizophrenia-specific environmental potentiators or schizophrenia-specific coping disabilities, or both, occur more frequently at the lowest socioeconomic levels. The contrary *social-selection* hypothesis proposes that psychosocial impairments secondary to the schizophrenic disorder result in less upward or greater downward social mobility relative to nonschizophrenic individuals. The first hypothesis proposes an etiological relationship between social class and schizophrenia; the second considers the association an epiphenomenon of the disorder.

It is, of course, possible that both social causation and social selection may be operating in any given case. Thus the stress of lower-class existence might contribute to the emergence of schizophrenia, while the presence of schizophrenia operates to limit upward social mobility. But explanations invoking social causation can at best account for only a minority of the cases found at the lowest socioeconomic level, because the great majority of schizophrenic patients are not born into this level; that is, the distribution of the occupational levels of patients' fathers approximates that of the general population. Most lowest-class schizophrenic patients migrate into this class from the relatively higher socioeconomic status of their families of origin (Dunham, 1965; Turner & Wagenfeld, 1967). Therefore the conditions of existence in lowest-class environments cannot be etiologically linked to the emergence of most cases of schizophrenia.

Turner and Wagenfeld (1967) analyzed the social mobility patterns of a large sample of first-admission schizophrenic patients identified by the

TABLE 6.2
Social Mobility Patterns of Schizophrenic and
General Population Groups[a]

Direction	Schizophrenic	General Population
Upward	34.8%	45.6%
None	28.8%	28.9%
Downward	36.4%	25.5%

[a]From Turner and Wagenfeld (1967).

Monroe County, N.Y., psychiatric register. As in other studies, cases of schizophrenia were found to be distributed over a seven-position social-class index based on occupation but over-represented by a factor of three in the lowest category. Turner and Wagenfeld compared patients' current occupations with those of their fathers and contrasted these data to national norms. They found that a smaller number of schizophrenic patients were upwardly mobile and a substantially greater number downwardly mobile than was true for the general population. Nearly identical numbers were nonmobile in both populations (Table 6.2). A more specific examination of lowest-class individuals showed that comparatively fewer schizophrenic patients than controls born into this stratum succeeded in moving out of it, whereas more patients than controls moved downward into it from higher levels.

Schizophrenic patients do not experience any great degree of downward social mobility within *their own* occupational careers. Fully 80% of the Turner and Wagenfeld sample had either remained at the same occupational level over the 10-year period preceding first hospitalization or had in fact moved from lower- to higher-prestige jobs. Social mobility patterns among schizophrenic patients are therefore largely due to their failure to achieve the social-class levels that could be anticipated given their families of origin. Turner and Wagenfeld (1967) concluded that the over-representation of schizophrenic patients in the lowest social class is primarily due to intergenerational social selection rather than to social causation or to downward social drift during patients' own lifetimes.

Age and Race. In addition to social class, age and race are also consistently associated with rates of schizophrenia (Yolles & Kramer, 1969). The figures in Table 6.3, from the Monroe County, N.Y., psychiatric register, are typical of these findings. As seen in the table, the treated prevalence of schizophrenia is minimal before 15 and after 65 years of age. Rates begin to increase at adolescence and peak in the 35–44-year-old group. Corresponding *incidence* data from Monroe County show similar increasing and decreasing trends over the life span, but the peak incidence occurs in the 15–24 and 25–34 age groups (NIMH, 1977b). The disparity in the incidence and prevalence

TABLE 6.3
Treated Prevalence of Schizophrenic by Age and Color: Annual Rates per 1000
Population, Monroe County, N.Y., 1970[a]

Age	Total	<15	15–24	25–34	35–44	45–54	55–64	65+
Total	4.78	.36	5.35	9.13	10.78	7.25	3.77	.96
White	4.53	.34	5.34	8.94	10.39	6.88	3.65	.93
Nonwhite	6.94	.51	5.47	11.18	15.90	15.31	7.55	2.07

[a]From NIMH (1977b)

peaks is a function of the relatively long duration of schizophrenic disorders.

The association of schizophrenia with age allows us to predict an increasing absolute frequency of schizophrenia for the remainder of the century. Because of the postwar "baby-boom," adolescents and young adults are currently the largest single age group in the U.S. population. As this relatively large cohort moves through the age span, it will carry along with it larger numbers of schizophrenic patients until the cohort passes through the high age-risk period (i.e., early middle age) (NIMH, 1977b).

Although most schizophrenic patients are white, nonwhites account for a disproportionate number of cases of schizophrenia at all ages (Table 6.3). This is probably due to the relative social disadvantage and lower social-class status of nonwhites in the U.S. population, which in turn leads to higher utilization rates of public mental health facilities (Yolles & Kramer, 1969). When socioeconomic status is held constant, overall rates of psychopathology do not differ appreciably between whites and nonwhites (Dohrenwend & Dohrenwend, 1969).

THE MENTAL HOSPITAL AND ITS CRITICS

The one in four schizophrenic individuals who find their way into treatment in any given year confront a rapidly changing program of services. One could expect 20 years ago to find the majority of schizophrenic patients as long-term residents in state, county, or V.A. mental hospitals. Once admitted, the patient was likely to remain hospitalized for about 12 years (Yolles & Kramer, 1969). Today the number of schizophrenic residents of such institutions has been cut by more than one-half, and the average length of stay is on the order of 6 months to 1 year (Klerman, 1977; NIMH, 1977b). As of 1971, about 40% of all schizophrenic patients were being treated by the in-patient services of state, county or V.A. mental hospitals; another 20% were in-patients of general hospital psychiatric units or community mental health centers. And close to 40% were treated as out-patients of community mental health centers or hospital psychiatric clinics (NIMH, 1977b).

The trends over the past two decades show a shift from in-patient to out-patient care, from institutional to community settings, and from the public to the private sector (Klerman, 1977). There is every reason to believe that these trends will continue into the future. This development is no less than revolutionary. It foretells the end of the mental hospital as it has been known since its invention in the early nineteenth century as a humane response to the dire straits of the mentally ill. Indeed, it derives from a profound disenchantment with the mental hospital as a treatment medium rather than from any demonstrated superiority of alternative treatment locales.

Seen in historical perspective, the contemporary disrepute of the mental hospital is ironic. The first public mental hospital in the United States, the Worcester (Massachusetts) State Lunatic Hospital, was founded in 1833 as a center for the application of the Moral Treatment precepts introduced by Pinel and Tuke at the end of the eighteenth century. The Friends who established the York Retreat in England under Tuke's guidance envisaged "a place in which the unhappy might obtain a refuge; a quiet haven in which the shattered bark might find the means of reparation and safety" (quoted by Deutsch, 1949, p. 93). The hopes seem to have been justified. At Worcester State Hospital, as at other public and private moral treatment facilities springing up in the same era, patients lived dignified lives under the tutelage of reform-minded physicians, continued to work at their occupations while in the institution, and looked forward to eventual recovery. Close to 60% of newly admitted patients in the early years were eventually discharged as recovered and suffered no subsequent relapses (Grob, 1966).

But the early vitality of the American mental hospital was short-lived. By the end of the nineteenth century, mental hospitals had become merely custodial institutions—holding places for homeless and indigent patients suffering from a variety of chronic maladies. The decline was due to many factors. Rapid industrialization and massive immigration created a large urban underclass, which placed an increasingly severe burden on the public mental hospital. Small patient-centered facilities were replaced by large bureaucratic institutions in which primary care was relegated to poorly paid, poorly trained ward attendants. The optimism of moral treatment gradually eroded and was replaced by more pessimistic theories of the inevitable progress of mental illness into irreversible dementia.

By the twentieth century, the appellation "snake pit" was in common parlance, and the abuses of mental hospitalization became the subject of sporadic exposés by journalists, writers, and former patients. Academic critics joined the clamor for reform more recently. This work usually combined scholarly analysis with moral indignation to produce a devastating critique of the mental hospital as a dehumanizing place of confinement that created more psychopathology than it cured. The following exposition considers three prime examples of this genre: Goffman's "The Moral Career of the Mental Patient" (1959); Rosenhan's "On Being Sane in Insane Places" (1973); and Braginsky, Braginsky, and Ring's *Methods of Madness* (1969).

The Moral Career of the Mental Patient (Goffman, 1959)

For Goffman, admission to the mental hospital is the end point of a series of social contingencies by which altered states of consciousness spill over into bizarre and socially deviant acts, which in turn are interpreted by family, friends, employers, or police as exemplars of mental illness requiring treatment. Few individuals define themselves as mentally ill or as in need of professional assistance; rather, most are brought to the institution under varying degrees of protest. Once incarcerated, the newly admitted patient will often develop a self-justifying rationale to explain how he or she came to be placed in a madhouse (Goffman, 1959):

> The others here are sick mentally but I'm suffering from a bad nervous system and that is what is giving me these phobias.

> My trouble is that I can't work. That's what I'm in for. I had two jobs with a good home and all the money I wanted.

> I got here by mistake because of a diabetes diagnosis, and I'll leave in a couple of days. (The patient had been in seven weeks.) [p. 134].

Yet the staff has its own needs for self-justification, and its construal of the patient's career will be quite different. Because the individual is a patient in a hospital for the mentally ill, case-history reconstructions will emphasize incidents from the previous life course that have "symptomatic significance." This retrospective search for justification for present difficulties is one from which few people, psychotic or not, incarcerated or not, can hope to emerge unscathed. Suspected hereditary taints, childhood excesses, and even the known or suspected misadventures of parents or siblings become grist for the etiological mill. With a perversity that distinguishes psychiatric case histories from other forms of biography, the most embarrassing aspects of the patient's life—actual or suspected—become central (Goffman, 1959):

> Contrary to the reports from the personnel, he says he no longer bangs on the floor or cries in the morning.

> ...conceals the fact that she had her organs removed, claims she is still menstruating.

The patient denied any heterosexual experiences nor could one trick her into admitting that she had ever been pregnant or into any kind of sexual indulgence, denying masturbation as well.

No psychotic content could be elicited at this time [p. 136].

The intimate details of the patient's past and present life are generally known, even available, to staff at all levels. And they may be used to puncture the patient's contrary "line" or other attempts to maintain self-esteem. The least deflating of such staff-to-patient challenges is, perhaps, some form of the common retort "If you are not crazy, what are you doing here?". In general, the mental hospital provides the kind of information to the staff that the patient is most likely to want to hide.

In the transition from "civilian" to "mental patient," the person also undergoes other forms of what Goffman aptly terms "mortification." Patients have little or no social power to influence the dispensation of such privileges as ward assignments, freedom of movement around the hospital, recreational opportunities, and so forth; rather, privileges are unilaterally assigned or withdrawn by staff in terms of their criteria of appropriate progress toward recovery. The potential for abuse is great because power between staff and inmates is so unevenly distributed. Even in the 1970s, an Alabama lawyer found a patient who had been in a straightjacket for 9 years because she would otherwise suck her hands and fingers, another who had been locked in seclusion for 6 years, and frequent instances of attendant beatings of patients with fists and broom handles (Offir, 1974).

But rank cruelty is not, nor has it ever been, the norm in mental hospitals, and a critique of mental hospitalization cannot depend on the selection of extreme examples. In Goffman's view, the process of mortification is more subtle; that is, staff attitudes allow for no distinction between the patient's presumed mental illness and his person. Unlike the case with physical disorders, the staff fails to dissociate the disorder per se from the day-to-day details of living, so that all aspects of patient behavior and belief are taken as signs of the course of the mental illness. All facets of the patient's functioning are thus potential targets for therapeutic modification. Under these conditions, the patient may conform his beliefs and behavior to staff expectations at the cost of relinquishing his former sense of self. Or he may rebel and refuse to change at the cost of loss of privileges and the imposition of sanctions. Or he may learn to manipulate by temporarily adopting the persona that meets the therapeutic requirements of the moment. This third alternative is probably modal, and Goffman's (1959) description is unsurpassed:

He learns that a defensible picture of self can be seen as something outside one's self that can be constructed, lost, and rebuilt, all with great speed and some equanimity. He learns about the viability of taking up a standpoint—and hence a self—that is outside the one which the hospital can give and take away from him. The setting, then, seems to engender a kind of cosmopolitan sophistication, a kind of civic apathy. In this unserious yet oddly exaggerated moral context, building up a self or having it destroyed becomes something of a shameless game, and learning to view this process as a game seems to make for some demoralization, the game being such a fundamental one [p. 140].

For Goffman, then, the central fact of mental hospitalization is the patient's struggle to maintain a sense of selfhood against the staff's destructive incursions. The game is played against a Kafkaesque background of conflicting interests. The staff must attempt to change the patient in order to justify its ostensible therapeutic role. The patient must deny psychopathology in order to maintain self-esteem. The conflict is resolved when the patient learns that selfhood can be maintained by adopting or sloughing off persona as the occasion demands. But this "shameless game" must ultimately demoralize and dehumanize both parties.

On Being Sane in Insane Places
(Rosenhan, 1973)

This study is best known for the ease with which Rosenhan and seven other "pseudopatients" gained entry into 12 different mental hospitals throughout the United States, most with a diagnosis of schizophrenia, by alleging that they had been hearing voices that said, "empty, hollow, thud." But this should not be too surprising. Few people attempt to feign their way into mental hospitals—at least on first admission—and so admitting officers have no particular reason to suspect prepatients' motives. And although the report of a bizarre auditory hallucination hardly justifies a diagnosis of schizophrenia, it is nonetheless true that the a priori probability of schizophrenia given auditory hallucinations is quite high. The study's real significance lies in its firsthand confirmation by disinterested observers of Goffman's earlier analysis. And, in this case, the common experiences of eight pseudopatients in 12 different installations could hardly be dismissed as either limited or idiosyncratic.

The pseudopatients spent from seven to 52 days of incarceration, each finally being discharged with a diagnosis of "schizophrenia in remission." The psychological stresses associated with hospitalization were considerable, and all but one of the pseudopatients would have preferred to have been discharged almost immediately after having been admitted. Rosenhan's description of this experience centers around three major themes: the presumption of illness, staff denigration of patients, and the loss of self-esteem.

Presumption of Illness.   The pseudopatients found that although their admissions diagnosis derived from one alleged symptom, the diagnosis soon came to color all their past and present behavior. It actively biased staff interpretation of patient behavior in ways at once humorous and disquieting. Some instances were trivial: When one pseudopatient took to pacing the corridors out of boredom, the behavior was interpreted by a staff member as nervousness. Note-taking for the purposes of the study was translated in nursing records by the ominous phrase, "patient engages in writing behavior." At other times, the distortions were massive. Complying with the study ground rules to give factual responses to any staff inquiries, one pseudopatient related an unexceptional life history: rather closer to his mother than to his father during early childhood, his relationship with his father grew closer during adolescence. His marriage was warm and stable, with minimal friction and exchanges of anger. His children had rarely been spanked. But because the pseudopatient was ostensibly schizophrenic, this not atypical picture of middle-class family life became distorted as follows in his case study (Rosenhan, 1973):

> This white 39-year-old . . . manifests a long history of considerable ambivalence in close relationships, which begins in early childhood. A warm relationship with his mother cools during his adolescence. A distant relationship to his father is described as becoming very intense. Affective stability is absent. His attempts to control emotionality with his wife and children are punctuated by angry outbursts and, in the case of the children, spankings. And while he says that he has several good friends, one senses considerable ambivalence embedded in those relationships also [p. 253].

Denigration.   Although a student of the mental hospital, Rosenhan was nevertheless abashed by the rejecting attitudes of staff toward patients. To measure this disparagement, the pseudopatients recorded the amount of time various levels of staff were willing to interact with them. On the average, ward attendants spent only 11.3% of their time mingling with patients; day nurses left their stations 11.5 times per shift, including instances of leaving the ward entirely. Psychiatrists emerged on the ward 6.7 times per day, but the time spent mingling was too brief to be recorded. In fact, daily contact of the pseudopatients with psychiatrists, psychologists, and physicians—for whatever reason—averaged less than ½ hour.

The pseudopatients also recorded the range of staff reactions to simple patient requests. For comparative purposes, another colleague approached faculty members on the campus of a university with an extensive series of requests for information and direction. Whereas university professors took time to answer all questions from the complete stranger, a negligible number of mental hospital psychiatrists and nurses answered a single question posed by pseudopatients. The typical reaction was a brief greeting or no response at all, offered without stopping and with eyes averted.

Loss of Self-Esteem. The pseudopatients found the experience of hospitalization overwhelmingly destructive of their sense of personal worth and efficacy. Not only did staff tend to avoid interaction with patients, but those contracts that did occur where often marked by verbal, and in some cases physical, abuse. Patient quarters and possessions could be entered and examined at any time for whatever reason. The details of patients' past and present difficulties were routinely open to examination by any staff member, including volunteer workers, who chose to read their case files. Staff were often noted to confer about patients in their presence as if the patient were invisible or inert. Some pseudopatients came close to blowing their covers in an effort to assert their self-worth. One, a graduate student in psychology, asked his wife to bring his textbooks to the hospital. A second began to engage in psychotherapy with other patients. Yet by the logic that patient behavior is necessarily symptomatic or discreditable, these and other instances were either misinterpreted as pathology or simply ignored.

"Methods of Madness"
(Braginsky, Braginsky, & Ring, 1969)

For all its dramatic impact, the Rosenhan experiment does not yield a complete picture of the career of the mental patient. The average length of each pseudopatient visit was a bit less than 3 weeks, during which time they found themselves caught up in and protesting institutional mortifications. This reaction is not untypical of most first-admission patients. They naturally find the mental hospital unsettling and wish not to be there. Yet most mental patients do adjust to the situation over the long term. And, curious as it may first appear, this adjustment is accompanied by a marked shift in life goals. Rather than wishing to leave, most long-term patients wish to stay. By a process that has come to be known as "institutionalism," longer periods of incarceration are matched by a declining desire to leave the hospital (Wing & Brown, 1970).

The transition from the status of a civilian with a mental health problem to that of a more or less permanently ostracized mental patient is not a simple process of continual victimization and final capitulation; rather, as Goffman first noted, patients learn to manage their self-presentation and their daily activities so as to avoid staff imposition of sanctions and to acquire such perquisites as the hospital offers. The process of adjustment through self-management has been most clearly limned in a series of studies reported in Braginsky et al.'s *Methods of Madness* (1969).

In one of several demonstrations of patients' skill at self-management, Braginsky et al. tape-recorded mental-status examinations of a group of long-term schizophrenic patients. The experimenters explained to one subgroup that the purpose of the interview was to determine if they were ready for discharge. The explanation given to a second subgroup was that the purpose was to determine whether they should be on an open or closed ward. The interviews were subsequently rated by staff psychiatrists for both the patients' degree of manifest psychopathology and their degree of need for hospital control. The experimental question was whether patients could manage staff impressions so as to produce the best possible outcome under the circumstances. We may assume that long-term patients wish to remain in the hospital, and would thus appear "sick" when faced with discharge, but have no desire to have their freedom of movement restricted and would thus appear "well" when faced with a closed ward assignment. The results showed that patients were indeed adept at manipulating staff judgments. Psychiatrists judged the group given "discharge" instructions as showing more psychopathology and as being in need of greater hospital control than was the case for the group given "closed ward" instructions. In brief, when patients' self-interest is at stake, they can present themselves as convincingly "sick" or "well" depending on which self-presentation will increase the probability of a desirable outcome.

The authors also found that long-term schizophrenic patients, rather than succumbing to a stereotyped mental patient role, adopted a variety of different lifestyles in the hospital. Some preferred to spend a majority of their working hours on the wards and in the day room; others passed their days working in kitchens, laundries, and other hospital facilities; a third group spent most of its time pursuing recreational activities in game rooms, gymnasiums, and canteens. These contrasting styles were unrelated to either length of stay in the hospital or to the degree of rated psychopathology; rather, they reflected analogous modes of filling time preferred by the same individuals in their former extra-hospital lives. In other words, patients learned to use the hospital in ways that met their everyday interests as persons quite independently of their psychiatric status.

Braginsky et al. also discovered that most patient–staff contacts were initiated by patients, so that the latter could in effect determine the degree to which their freedom of action was constrained by the staff. A group of "invisible" patients tended not to be known to the psychiatrists ostensibly responsible for their care, had few therapeutic contacts of any kind, and adopted a lifestyle that removed them from staff scrutiny. In addition, "invisible" patients tended to be discharged at a lower rate than more visible patients. Again, we see that the chronic mental patient determines to a significant degree his or her therapeutic involvement and length of stay in the hospital. As Braginsky et al. (1969) summarize:

Mental patients, for all their pathology, are in most respects, most of the time, just like the rest of us; they want to live in a mental hospital in the same way that ordinary persons want to live in their own community—that is, they can be expected to try to satisfy their needs and, to a considerable extent, to be able to do so. But because a mental hospital, while a community of persons, is not just any community but one of a very special and potentially restrictive kind, the patient's attempts to control his own fate will often have to involve devious and indirect tactics [p. 73].

Given the Kafkaesque nature of the mental hospital, its attendant psychological stresses, and the social ostracism implied in the role of chronic mental patient, why would anyone choose to manipulate his or her self-presentations in order to remain in such an environment? The answer is most likely found in the demographics of schizophrenia. As we have seen, most schizophrenic patients are socially downward mobile and tend to aggregate in lower socioeconomic strata. Life outside the hospital thus offers indigence, unsatisfying or no employment, powerlessness, or dereliction. Life inside the hospital, for all its shortcomings, is often preferable. As Braginsky et al. stress, the hospital provides a simpler, more predictable, and protected world in which one may exercise a great deal of fate determination.

The picture of the mental hospital painted by contemporary academic critics is far from the original intention of late eighteenth-century reformers to provide "a place in which the unhappy might obtain a refuge"; rather, one sees an impersonal, bureaucratic holding place for those whose behavior is offensive to the broader society and who have no other place to go. Staff and patients work at cross purposes in a bizarre ritual of mutual self-justification. The staff diagnoses pathology and worthlessness in most aspects of patient behavior and belief. Patients meet staff attitudes with manipulative tactics aimed at preserving a vestige of self-esteem and freedom of action. The system works to transform a citizen with a mental health problem into a member of the deviant subculture of chronic mental patients. In the process, the ideals of mental health, treatment, and cure are made a mockery.

It is worth noting that this view of the mental hospital is not necessarily that of mental patients themselves. Former patients, at least those who write of their experiences, tend to focus their criticism elsewhere. They generally complain of endlessly boring days, bureaucratic routine, their doctors' impuissant and tangential attempts to understand their maladies, and the erratic nature of the treatment provided (e.g., Sutherland, 1976; Vonnegut, 1976). But with the exception of Clifford Beers' *A Mind That Found Itself* (1908), this critical genre has had little influence on either public or professional attitudes toward mental hospital practices, undoubtedly because of the unfortunate tendency of both audiences to discount mental patients' productions. On the other hand, the presumably disinterested analyses by academic critics like Goffman, Rosenhan, and Braginsky et al. have taken hold with state and federal mental health administrators, legislators, public interest lawyers, mental health professionals, and others in a position to influence public policy. It has supplied the theoretical basis for a reform movement as extensive and significant as that which produced the mental hospital 150 years previously.

DEINSTITUTIONALIZATION AND COMMUNITY CARE

Deinstitutionalization is the unwieldy term used to describe the contemporary reform movement in mental health care in North America, Europe, and, to a lesser extent, other industrialized nations. Deinstitutionalization means somewhat different things to different commentators, but a common denominator includes two elements: the eschewal of the traditional mental hospital as the primary treatment locus for mental illness, and the concomitant substitution of community-based services for the mentally ill (NIMH, 1976). Both legislated reform, especially on the federal level, and litigation, in both state and federal courts, have been the agents of change.

Legislation

The countertherapeutic nature of the traditional mental hospital was first acknowledged as a public policy issue in a 1961 report to Congress published under the title, *Action for Mental Health.* The study group that issued the report, the Joint Commission on Mental Illness and Health, was composed primarily of psychiatrists with some representation from psychology, social work, nursing, and interested nonprofessionals. The report predictably called for more funding for research, education, and training. Surprisingly, however, it expressly recommended that "no further state hospitals of more than 1,000 beds should be built, and not one patient should be added to any existing mental hospital already having 1,000 or more patients [p. xvi]." The report (JCMIH, 1961) continued:

> The objective of modern treatment of persons with major mental illness is to enable the patient to maintain himself in the community in a normal manner. To do so, it is necessary (1) to save the patient from the debilitating effects of institutionalization as much as possible, (2) if the patient requires hospitalization, to return him to home and community life as soon as possible, and (3) thereafter to maintain him in the community as long as possible. Therefore, after-care and rehabilitation are essential parts of all service to mental patients, and the various methods of achieving rehabilitation should be integrated in all

forms of services, among them day hospitals, night hospitals, aftercare clinics, public health nursing services, foster family care, convalescent nursing homes, rahabilitation centers, work services, and ex-patient groups [p. xvii].

Action for Mental Health found a receptive auditor in President Kennedy, who had known mental retardation in his own family. In 1963, he delivered to Congress the only presidential message in history on the subject of mental disabilities. Citing overcrowding and the debilitating features of custodial institutions, Kennedy called for a "bold new approach" based on the development and use of community-based treatment facilities. The goal was to keep the mentally disabled in the community and to restore and revitalize their lives through better health programs and strengthened rehabilitation services. The President estimated that resident patients in mental hospitals could be reduced by at least 50% within one or two decades, a goal that was in fact surpassed by the mid-1970s (General Accounting Office, 1977).

The resulting Community Mental Health Centers Act of 1963, amended in 1965, authorized funds for the planning, construction, and staffing of historically novel community mental health centers (CMHCs). States were encouraged to establish CMHCs for catchment areas of 75,000 to 200,000 population. About 2000 catchment areas were created on paper; by the mid-1970s, approximately 600 had been established to serve 87 million people in high priority areas. Under the original legislation, each CMHC was to provide in-patient and out-patient services; partial hospitalization alternatives to full-time hospitalization; emergency care; and consultation to other community agencies such as schools, courts, and welfare services. In 1975, Congress reaffirmed the importance of community care as the "most effective and humane form of care for a majority of mentally ill individuals." At that time, CMHCs were further required to provide follow-up care and transitional services for discharged mental hospital patients as well as intensified services for such target groups as children, the elderly, alcoholics, and drug addicts (NIMH, 1977a).

Although the CMHC is the keystone of the national commitment to deinstitutionalization, it is only one of 135 separate federal programs, administered by 11 major departments and agencies that directly or indirectly promote and support community care for the mentally ill and retarded. For example, in the mid-1960s, Medicare and Medicaid were made available to discharged mental patients; in 1972, supplemental Social Security Income funds were allocated to support the mentally ill living in community placements. In the 1970s, the Department of Housing and Urban Development began to support community residences and to provide rent subsidies for formerly institutionalized patients, and the Rehabilitation Services Administration was directed by Congress to more actively pursue vocational rehabilitation programs for persons with severe physical and mental disabilities (General Accounting Office, 1977). By the end of the

1970s, deinstitutionalization had become the watchword for massive shifts in federal and state programs for the mentally ill.

Litigation

In the last two decades, state and federal courts have become increasingly involved in constitutional issues regarding the proper balance between individual rights and societal interests in the disposition of the mentally ill. If in past eras courts recognized the mentally ill as social wards first and citizens secondarily, the opposite obtains today: Patients are regarded as citizens only coincidentally in need of treatment to remediate their psychological and social difficulties. Judicial doctrine at the highest level now holds that the mere presence of mental illness is not a sufficient justification for abridging or denying a person's constitutional rights. In at least 100 precedent-building cases, the courts have broadly applied constitutional protections to mental patients. Cases have been adjudicated on the Fifth and Fourteenth Amendment guarantees that no person shall be deprived of life, liberty, or property without due process of law, the Fourteenth Amendment guarantee of equal protection of the laws, and the Thirteenth Amendment prohibition against involuntary servitude. Although the goal of most of these actions was the amelioration of abuses against specific patients, they have served to further discredit the mental hospital as a therapeutic institution and thus to reinforce the developing public policy of deinstitutionalization.

Right to Treatment.   The notion that mental patients have a constitutionally guaranteed right to treatment was first broached by Morton Birnbaum, a forensic psychiatrist who argued that states' powers of civil commitment implied a corresponding obligation to provide adequate treatment as opposed to mere custodial care (Birnbaum, 1960). This argument was first applied in the 1966 case of *Rouse* v. *Cameron*, argued before a federal appeals court presided over by Justice David Bazelon. Rouse had been committed to a mental hospital after having been found not guilty by reason of insanity of carrying a dangerous weapon. After 3 years of confinement, he petitioned for a release on the grounds of having received no psychiatric treatment. In its decision, the court held that "The purpose of involuntary hospitalization is treatment, not punishment.... Absent treatment, the hospital is transform[ed]...into a penitentiary where one could be held indefinitely for no convicted offense" (Golann & Fremouw, 1976).

Whereas the *Rouse* case dealt with the right to treatment of an ostensibly mentally ill criminal, the landmark decision in the 1972 case of *Wyatt* v. *Stickney* unequivocally extended this right to civilly committed patients. The *Wyatt* case was the first class action suit successfully brought against a state's entire mental health system. Wyatt and co-plaintiffs—patients and staff of Alabama's Bryce State Hospital—alleged that the rights of involuntarily committed patients were abridged by the inadequate treatment they received. Federal district court Judge Frank Johnson found that patients possessed "the constitutional right to receive such institutional treatment as will give each of them a reasonable opportunity to be cured or to improve his or her mental condition." Because the court found that this right did not prevail in Alabama institutions, it imposed minimal treatment standards, including a provision against institutional peonage, protections to ensure a humane psychological environment, provision for a human rights committee at each institution, physical plant standards, minimum nutritional requirements, individualized evaluations and treatment plans, and minimal staff-to-patient ratios (Golann & Fremouw, 1976; NIMH, 1975).

The right to treatment issue reached the Supreme Court in 1975 in the case of *O'Connor* v. *Donaldson*, the high courts' first consideration of the rights of involuntarily committed mental patients. Donaldson's 15-year confinement in a Florida mental hospital is a study of the abuses of institutional psychiatry; his ultimate vindication was a no less than heroic achievement. Donaldson tells his story in the autobiographical *Insanity Inside Out* (1976). Committed in 1956 at the age of 48 following a less than adequate hearing, Donaldson spent most of his confinement on locked wards without receiving treatment. As a Christian Scientist, he refused drugs and ECT but was denied requests for ground privileges, occupational training, or opportunities to discuss his case with staff. Repeated requests for release made to O'Connor, the hospital superintendent, and other staff were dismissed on the grounds that Donaldson was a "paranoid schizophrenic" unable to make an adjustment outside the hospital. But during the lower court trial preceding the Supreme Court decision, O'Connor was unable to specify the grounds for this negative prognosis. Requests from responsible friends for Donaldson's release to their care were also denied without justification. Donaldson's petitions to numerous state and federal courts and to his state and congressional representatives also came to naught. He was finally discharged in 1971, but only after the intervention of Morton Birnbaum and the American Civil Liberties Union.

Donaldson and his advocates sued O'Connor and another psychiatrist in federal court for monetary damages on the grounds of malicious confinement without treatment for his presumed mental illness. The trial jury found that: (1) he had received no treatment; (2) he was not dangerous, nor was he considered dangerous by anyone at the hospital, including his own doctors; (3) acceptable community alternatives were available to him; and (4) the doctors named in the suit, knowing all this, maliciously refused to release him (NIMH, 1975).

The Supreme Court affirmed this judgment upon appeal by O'Connor and his colleague. In its ruling, the Court chose not to address the issue of a constitutional right to treatment, which nevertheless remains law in lower federal courts. It did hold, however, that a state does not have the authority to confine mentally ill persons simply in order to improve their living standard over that available in the community or to shield the community from encountering them. Even more importantly, the Court held that states cannot confine a nondangerous mentally ill person for mere custodial care:

> A finding of "mental illness" alone cannot justify a State's locking a person up against his will and keeping him indefinitely in simple custodial confinement. Assuming that the term can be given a reasonably precise content and that the "mentally ill" can be identified with reasonable accuracy, there is still no constitutional basis for confining such persons involuntarily if they are dangerous to no one and can live safely in freedom [cited in Golann & Fremouw, 1976, p. 221].

Fast on the heels of the Supreme Court's *Donaldson* decision, a federal district court enunciated a significant extension of the right-to-treatment doctrine in *Dixon* v. *Weinburger* (1975). The suit was filed against the National Institute of Mental Health on behalf of several patients at the federally supported St. Elizabeth's Hospital in Washington, D.C. It alleged that although the patients required continuing care and treatment, they did not require total hospitalization and that in fact the hospital environment was countertherapeutic. As was the case with about one-half of all St. Elizabeth patients, each of the plaintiffs had in fact been screened for outplacement by the hospital but continued to be held for lack of suitable community alternatives. The court agreed that the plaintiffs had a legal right to treatment in less restrictive alternative settings and ordered the District of Columbia and NIMH to provide intermediate care facilities such as foster care homes, nursing homes, and halfway houses. *Dixon* v. *Weinburger* was significant in aligning judicial decision with community mental health ideology concerning the countertherapeutic nature of mental hospitals and the desirability of community treatment for most hospitalized patients. A right to treatment in the least restrictive alternative is now routinely included in most state and federal legislation affecting the mentally ill and retarded.

Commitment Procedures.   Right-to-treatment cases challenge the mostly custodial care prevailing in traditional mental hospitals. Only by indirection, as in the *Donaldson* case, do they address the constitutionality of the legal procedures by which patients are committed to institutions in the first place. This is an area in which due process has generally been observed more in the breach than in the execution. But it is also an area in which constitutional guarantees are unambiguous: Both the Fifth and Fourteenth Amendments guarantee that no person shall be deprived of liberty without due process of law; the Fourteenth Amendment further guarantees that no person shall be denied equal protection of the laws. The constitutional adequacy of commitment statutes varies tremendously from state to state, to say nothing of the procedural variations obtaining among courts. Thus reform requires a laborious process of challenging statutes or their application, coupled with the equally lengthy process of legislative enactment of more adequate laws.

The federal courts have indicated that such reform is required. The case of *Jackson* v. *Indiana* (1972) concerned a 27-year-old mentally retarded deaf mute arrested for stealing $9. He was found incompetent to stand trial and summarily confined in a mental hospital without a hearing. After 3½ years of confinement without any change in his condition, he petitioned for release. The Supreme Court found that confinement absent a due process hearing was unconstitutional and ordered his release. Although this case was specific to procedures arising under the criminal law, the case of *Lessard* v. *Schmidt* (1972) dealt directly with civil commitment. In this case, a three-judge federal district court held Wisconsin statutes to violate due process on several grounds: (1) failure to give the patient timely notice of the charges justifying detention; (2) failure to require notice of the right of a jury trial; (3) permitting hearings in which the person was not represented by counsel; and (4) permitting confinement without proof of mental illness and dangerousness beyond a reasonable doubt (NIMH, 1975). Similar decisions have struck down or challenged civil commitment statutes in Michigan, South Dakota, and West Virginia. By the mid-1970s, at least a half-dozen courts had ruled that involuntary commitment can rest only on a criterion of dangerousness to self or others, as opposed to the mere presence of mental illness or the need for treatment (Klein, 1976).

Under prodding from the courts and against the background of the deinstitutionalization movement, many states moved in the 1970s to revamp civil commitment statutes. The Massachusetts Mental Health Code, enacted in 1970, is typical of this more progressive legislation. Under the Code, only the superintendent of a mental health facility may apply for a commitment order. The petition must be initiated within 3 days of any notice given a voluntarily admitted patient or within the 10-day expiration period of an involuntary emergency admission. The hearing itself must be held within 2 weeks of the superintendent's application. The patient has the right to be present at the hearing and to be represented by counsel. A commitment order may be issued only upon the petitioner's demonstration beyond a reasonable doubt that the patient is indeed mentally ill and is likely to inflict serious harm upon himself or others. The likelihood-of-serious-harm criterion requires evidence of a substantial risk of physical harm to others, as indicated by assaultive or violent behavior, or of a substantial risk of physical injury to the patient himself because of impaired judgment or inability to protect himself in the community. In addition, the petitioner must establish that hospitalization is the least restrictive alternative available to the patient. A first commitment order is valid for a maximum of 6 months, at which time the hospital may initiate a second hearing for a commitment for up to 1 year. The lower court's decision may be appealed to a higher state court, and the patient may petition the Superior Court for immediate release under a *habeus-corpus*-like writ (Massachusettes General Laws, Chapter 123).

Needless to say, such statutes severely limit the proportion of mental patients at risk of involuntary confinement. The application of stringent due-process safeguards generally results in a marked reduction in yearly commitments. Thus, in 1977, only 480 patients were involuntarily confined in West Virginia, compared with more than 1200 in 1974. Involuntary commitments in Michigan fell from 5800 in 1973 to 3900 in 1976. The legal status of numerous involuntarily confined patients has also been upgraded. Following the *Lessard* v. *Schmidt* (1972) decision, Wisconsin mental health officials reviewed the histories of all previously committed patients in state institutions. As a result, about 800 were discharged to community care, 2400 were readmitted as voluntary patients, and the cases of 3300 were sent back to the courts for rehearings. By mid-1976, only 331 involuntarily committed patients were in Wisconsin institutions, a 90% decline (*Wall Street Journal*, 1978).

The Role of Antipsychotic Drugs

The deinstitutionalization movement would not have been possible without the development of antipsychotic drugs in the 1950s. As has been frequently noted, resident mental hospital populations began to decline in the mid-1950s just as these drugs were introduced on a large scale. Because of this conjunction of events, many commentators credit deinstitutionalization almost entirely to antipsychotics. But as we have seen, this is to oversimplify the course of events. Disenchantment with the traditional mental hospital was rife by the mid-1950s. This disenchantment was given theoretical coherence by Goffman and other academic critics, whose work began to appear at this time. The JCMIH 1961 *Action for Mental Health* report had its origins in a 1955 act of Congress calling for a thorough assessment of the mental health needs of the nation. At the same time, certain state governments, notably California's, had projected the intolerable future financial burdens of a steadily increasing chronic hospital population and were taking steps to establish intensive, community-based treatment programs for the mentally ill (Bloom, 1973). The notion of a constitutionally based right to adequate treatment had its origins in the same period (Birnbaum, 1960).

It is thus extremely difficult to disentangle the independent contributions of antipsychotic drugs and more general reformist ferment to deinstitutionalization. Several European studies suggest that the decline in resident mental hospital populations in fact began before the widespread introduction of antipsychotic agents (Klerman, 1977). But it would be foolish to doubt the massive independent contribution of drugs or their reinforcing effect on reformist sentiment.

Classification of Antipsychotics. Chlorpromazine, the prototype of many subsequent antipsychotic compounds, was developed shortly after World War II as a sedative and antihistiminic agent for use in preparing patients for surgery. The French surgeon H. Laborit noted, however, that chlorpromazine induced a tranquil, indifferent state without loss of consciousness in surgical patients and suggested its possible benefit to excited and agitated psychiatric patients. Soon thereafter, French psychiatrists reported successful therapeutic trials with psychotic patients, and by the mid-1950s the drug was in widespread use in both Europe and North America (Baldessarini, 1977; Snyder, 1974).

Chlorpromazine is one of several commonly employed phenothiazine derivatives having antipsychotic properties (Table 6.4). The phenothiazine nucleus is a tricyclic structure consisting of two benzene rings joined through a central ring containing a sulfur and a nitrogen atom. The many

TABLE 6.4
Chemical Classification of Commonly Used Antipsychotic
Agents[a]

Class	Examples	Trade Names
Tricyclics		
Phenothiazines	Chlorpromazine	Thorazine, etc.
	Thioridazine	Mellaril
	Trifluoperazine	Stelazine
	Fluphenazine	Prolixin
Thioxanthenes	Chlorprothixene	Taractan
	Thiothixene	Navane
Dibenzazepines	Clozapine	Leponex
	Loxapine	Loxitane
Butyrophenones	Haloperidol	Haldol
Diarylbutylamines	Pimozide	Orap
Miscellaneous	Molindone	Moban
	Reserpine	Serpasil, etc.

[a]From Baldessarini (1977) and Pletscher and Kyburz (1976).

phenothiazine antipsychotics differ primarily in the nature of the side chain adjacent to the central ring:

Chlorpromazine

Trifluoperazine

A second class of tricyclic antipsychotics—the thioxanthenes—was subsequently developed from phenothiazine compounds by replacing the central nitrogen atom with a carbon atom, as in chlorprothixene. More recently, the dibenzazepine tricyclics, such as clozapine, were developed via further modification of the central ring:

Chlorprothixene   Clozapine

In addition to the tricyclic compounds, a number of structurally dissimilar agents are also widely used as antipsychotics. These include the butyrophenones, such as haloperidol, and the related diarylbutylamines, such as pimozide. Haloperidol and pimozide are in fact two of the most potent antipsychotic agents yet developed:

Haloperidol   Pimozide

In addition to the tricyclics and the butyrophenones and related compounds, a number of miscellaneous agents of varying molecular structure also have antipsychotic properties. These include molindone, an indole derivative, and reserpine, a natural antipsychotic derived from the Indian snakeroot plant *Rauwolfia serpentina* (Baldessarini, 1977; Pletscher & Kyburz, 1976).

Molindone

Reserpine

Clinical Efficacy. A sizable number of sophisticated clinical trials of antipsychotic agents were completed by the end of the 1960s. This led to some winnowing of compounds found not to be superior to placebos or to be consistently less effective than chlorpromazine. The remainder are approximately equally efficacious. This is in spite of their varying chemical structure and differing potencies (i.e., the dose necessary to produce clinical effects). Provided that adequate doses are employed, commonly used antipsychotics produce better results than placebos in 80% to 90% of all comparisons; approximately 75% of schizophrenic patients improve within 6 weeks compared with approximately one-quarter of placebo controls (Baldessarini, 1977; Cole & Davis, 1969).

As the term implies, *antipsychotic* agents are effective in the management of a number of conditions in addition to schizophrenic psychosis, particularly drug-induced psychoses, some forms of mania, and, occasionally, psychotic reactions associated with acute organic brain syndromes. Yet they also have a remarkable specificity for key symptoms of the schizophrenic psychosis. Cole and Davis (1969) collated the results of several studies reporting the comparative efficacy of phenothiazine and placebos on specific schizophrenic symptoms. Because the separate studies used somewhat different symptom definitions and rating methods, Cole and Davis assessed the separate results under common rubrics adopted from Bleuler's distinction between fundamental and accessory symptoms (Table 6.5). Marked differences between drug and placebo occur consistently for the fundamental symptoms and for the accessory symptom of "resistiveness–uncooperativeness." Less striking but clinically significant effects are also seen on such accessory symptoms as hallucinations and paranoid delusions. Interestingly, uncontrolled clinical trials usually show a greater absolute reduction over time in accessory as opposed to fundamental symptoms with antipsychotic drug treatment. But as Cole and Davis (1969) point out, this is because accessory symptoms tend to improve over time in the absence of drug treatment, so drug effects are added to "spontaneous" improvements. Phenothiazines have little superiority over placebos for such nonschizophrenic symptoms as anxiety, depression, and disorientation. In short, phenothiazines and allied agents deserve the appellation "antipsychotic" when clinical change over time is considered and the appellation "antischizophrenic" when symptom amelioration compared to placebo is considered.

TABLE 6.5
Analysis of Symptom Sensitivity to Phenothiazines[a]

Bleuler's Classification of Schizophrenic Symptoms	Study 1	Study 2	Study 3	Study 4	Study 5
Fundamental Symptoms:					
Thought disorder	++	++	++	++	++
Blunted affect–indifference				++	+
Withdrawal–retardation	++	++	0	++	++
Autistic behavior– mannerisms	++	++	0	++	0
Accessory Symptoms:					
Hallucinations	++	++	+	+	0
Paranoid ideation	0	++	0	+	+
Grandiosity	0	0	0	0	+
Hostility–belligerence	++	++	?	+	+
Resistiveness– uncooperativeness	++	++	?	++	++
Nonschizophrenic Symptoms:					
Anxiety–tension–agitation	0	0	?	+	0
Guilt–depression	++	0	0	0	0
Disorientation				0	
Somatization					0

[a]Adapted from Cole and Davis (1969).
++ = Symptom areas showing marked differences between drug and control groups.
 + = Symptom areas showing significant but less striking differences.
 0 = Areas not showing differential drug superiority.
 ? = Inadequate data for analysis.

Antipsychotics also moderate the schizophrenic attention dysfunction revealed in the performance of various laboratory tasks (see Chapter 2). Spohn, Lacoursiere, Thompson, and Coyne (1977) examined the performance of chronic schizophrenic patients divided into chlorpromazine or placebo groups on tasks requiring the ability to maintain focused attention, or set, and on tasks requiring selective attention to relevant as opposed to irrelevant aspects of a task. Both forms of attention improved gradually over an 8-week treatment period with chlorpromazine but not with placebo. Because individual differences in the amount of improvement on attentional tasks correlated with clinical judgments of symptom amelioration, Spohn et al. (1977) concluded that the normalization of attentional mechanisms is a significant component of the antipsychotic action of phenothiazine treatment.

Other specific forms of therapy appear to add little to the therapeutic effects of antipsychotic agents for hospitalized schizophrenic patients. An important study reported by May (1968) compared the clinical outcomes of phenothiazine drug treatment alone, drug treatment plus psychotherapy, psychotherapy alone, and electroconvulsive therapy alone. A control condition consisted of standard ward care in a good-to-superior public mental hospital. The patients were first-admission schizophrenics who fell into the middle third of a prognostic continuum (i.e., neither very good nor very poor treatment risks). Each treatment condition continued for up to 1 year or until the patient was released as a treatment success or judged to be a treatment failure. Of the phenothiazine-alone patients, 96% were released after an average stay of 130 days. The comparable figures for psychotherapy plus drug treatment were also 96% released and an average stay of 139 days. Psychotherapy alone (65% and 185 days) was not significantly different than milieu (ward) treatment alone (58% and 163 days). Surprisingly, ECT, which is not usually considered an antipsychotic therapy, fell into a middling position between drug and milieu treatments (79% released after a mean of 135 days).

A 2-year trial of psychotherapy with or without phenothiazine treatment reported by Grinspoon, Ewalt, and Shader (1967) found little clinical change in chronic schizophrenic patients with psychotherapy alone but significant clinical improvement with psychotherapy plus phenothiazine treatment. In light of these results, conventional psychotherapy without concomitant antipsychotic drug therapy cannot be considered an efficacious treatment for schizophrenia. Even more pointedly, there is no good evidence that long-term psychotherapy adds to the considerable clinical affects of drug therapy alone.

Complicating Side-Effects. The therapeutic power of antipsychotic agents is not without its costs in terms of untoward side-effects. The major problems include sedation, acute neurological symptoms, and a long-term movement disorder known as *tardive dyskinesia.* The first two problems are reversible; the third may be irreversible and thus a potentially serious limitation of antipsychotic drug therapy.

Sedation.   Drowiness and somnolence may occur within the first few days of antipsychotic drug treatment, sometimes lasting as long as a week or two. Most patients develop a tolerance to this effect after the first few days of treatment (Cole & Davis, 1969). The marked sedative actions of the phenothiazines, especially chlorpromazine, led to the early designation of antipsychotics as "major tranquilizers" by many professionals. But sedation is not a necessary property of these drugs' antipsychotic actions; there is in fact a general inverse relationship between the potency of various antipsychotic agents and their sedating properties (Munkvad, Fog, & Kristjansen, 1976).

Neurological Effects.   Antipsychotics produce acute postural and motor disorders in almost direct relationship to their clinical potency. In fact, antipsychotic agents are often described as "neuroleptics" in light of these neurological actions. *Acute dystonia* is a rigid spasm of the muscles of the neck, face, and tongue, causing arching of the back and a twisting posture of the neck and body (Cole & Davis, 1969). *Akathisia* involves a feeling of acute discomfort in the muscles of the extremities, producing a reactive fidgeting, pacing, to-and-fro leg movements, and general restlessness. *Parkinsonian* effects mimic the symptoms of Parkinson's disease: muscular rigidity, a degree of tremor, slowed movements and stooped posture, a masklike inexpressive visage, and, sometimes, drooling (Baldessarini, 1977). These often distressing neurological side-effects generally respond well with anticholinergic agents useful in the treatment of naturally occurring Parkinsonism. The development of a non-neuroleptic antipsychotic agent is obviously of high priority. The recently developed dibenzazepine clozapine (Table 6.4) is of great theoretical and practical interest because it is a fairly potent antipsychotic having sedative but few neurological side-effects (Baldessarini, 1977; Munkvad et al., 1976).

Tardive dyskinesia, meaning "late-appearing abnormal movements" is a distressing and embarrassing consequence of prolonged treatment with antipsychotics. It consists primarily of slow, rhythmical movements in the region of the mouth, with protrusion of the tongue, smacking of the lips, and other bizarre muscular stereotypies. Abnormalities of posture, rocking body movements, and choretic movements of the extremities may also be involved. Tardive dyskinesia occurs in approximately 15% of patients receiving antipsychotic medication; elderly and more chronic cases are especially at risk. The syndrome went unrecognized for many years following the introduction of antipsychotic agents, probably because bizarre mannerisms, grimaces, and stereotyped movements had been classically described as catatonic manifestations of schizophrenia.

Tardive dyskinesia is most likely due to a drug-induced supersensitivity of receptors at dopamine-mediated synapses of the nigro-striatal tract (see Figure 3.7). Because of the postulated supersensitivity, the disorder may worsen rather than improve when antipsychotic medication is withdrawn. Although gradual improvement may occur after the withdrawal of antipsychotic medication, many cases appear to be irreversible. There is at present no completely satisfactory treatment for tardive dyskinesia. The symptoms may be controlled by increasing the antipsychotic drug dose, but this threatens an ultimate worsening of the disorder. On the hypothesis that tardive dyskinesia represents a functional imbalance between dopamine and acetylcholine systems in the basal ganglia, agents that increase brain acetylcholine levels have been tested for therapeutic efficacy. Among these, dietary choline, in the form of lecithin, appears to be a particularly promising treatment. The best treatment, however, is prevention through the careful use and early withdrawal of antipsychotic medication where feasible (Baldessarini & Tarsy, 1978; Cole, 1976; Crane, 1973).

Maintenance Therapy.   In addition to their efficacy in controlling both fundamental and accessory schizophrenic symptoms, the antipsychotics also forestall recurrent psychotic exacerbations when administered in maintenance doses to released patients. Maintenance therapy is especially efficacious when combined with aggressive case follow-up in the community. The interaction of drug and social therapy is seen clearly in the results of a major study reported by Hogarty, Goldberg, Schooler, and Ulrich (1974). Discharged schizophrenic patients were assigned to one of four treatment groups: (1) phenothiazine maintenance; (2) a form of intensive social case work known as major role therapy (MRT); (3) both drug therapy and MRT; and (4) placebo administration alone. MRT was aimed at resolving personal and social problems that directly affected patients' vocational roles as homemakers or wage earners. Other MRT objectives ranged from improving the quality of social interaction and reducing social isolation to improving the rudiments of self-care, financial assistance, and medication maintenance. Non-MRT patients received conventional case work consisting of crisis intervention and referral as necessary to other community agencies. Figure 6.1 shows the 2-year relapse rates for the four conditions. Drug therapy was clearly superior to placebo treatment independently of MRT: By 24 months, about 80% of placebo-treated patients relapsed compared with about 40% of drug-treated patients. The lowest relapse rate occurred among drug patients also receiving MRT, the major benefits occurring during the second year following discharge. Other data reported by Hogarty et al. (1974) showed that

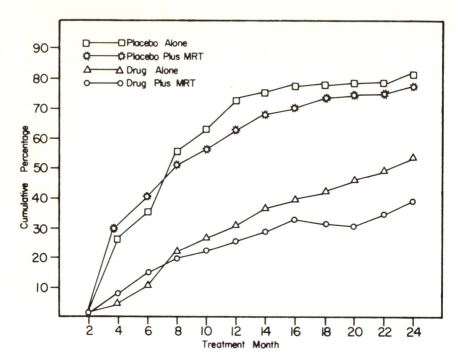

FIG. 6.1.   Cumulative relapse rates over 24 months for schizophrenic patients treated with four combinations of antipsychotic medication, placebo, and intensive social case work (MRT). (From Hogarty et al., 1974.)

among nonrelapsed patients, the quality of social interaction, psychological well-being, and vocational performance was significantly enhanced by MRT.

Some formerly hospitalized schizophrenic patients will survive in the community with minimal follow-up. As Figure 6.1 illustrates, about 20% of patients treated with placebo alone fail to relapse within 2 years. But about 70% of patients treated with drugs and systematic supportive follow-up survive in the community at a reasonably high level of adjustment. These data speak directly to the promise of deinstitutionalization: Community care can work if schizophrenic patients are afforded continuing high-level care combining drug, psychological, and social support. The challenge for community care is to develop even more effective interventions in order to increase the long-term success above the 70% rate possible today and to ensure that such care is routinely available to all schizophrenic patients.

The Unfulfilled Promise of Deinstitutionalization

Figure 6.2 illustrates the impact of deinstitutionalization on patient care in U.S. mental health facilities. In 1955, in-patient services of state and county mental hospitals accounted for one-half of all patient care episodes. By 1973, this proportion had declined to 12%. Over the same period, treatment episodes in the out-patient services of psychiatric clinics, mental hospitals, and general hospitals grew from about one-quarter to one-half of the total. By 1973, in-patient and out-patient facilities of community mental health centers, unrepresented in the 1955 figures, accounted for almost one-quarter of all treatment episodes.

Although the number of patient care episodes tripled from 1.7 to 5.2 million episodes between 1955 and 1973, the absolute number of residential mental hospital patients showed a steady decline from 550,000 in 1955 to less than 200,000 by the end of the 1970s; a number of states reported declines of 80% to 90% (Kohen & Paul, 1976). States began to close and to consolidate mental hospitals. California's plan to completely phase out all hospitals by

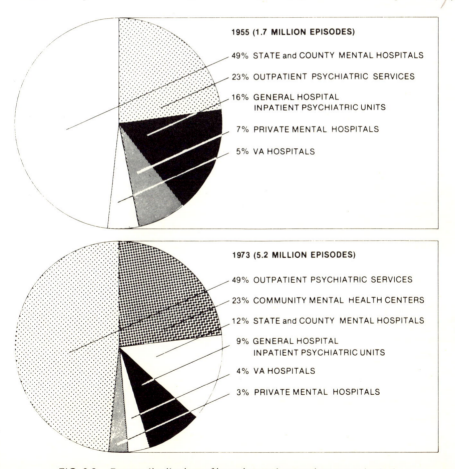

1955 (1.7 MILLION EPISODES)

49% STATE and COUNTY MENTAL HOSPITALS

23% OUTPATIENT PSYCHIATRIC SERVICES

16% GENERAL HOSPITAL
INPATIENT PSYCHIATRIC UNITS

7% PRIVATE MENTAL HOSPITALS

5% VA HOSPITALS

1973 (5.2 MILLION EPISODES)

49% OUTPATIENT PSYCHIATRIC SERVICES

23% COMMUNITY MENTAL HEALTH CENTERS

12% STATE and COUNTY MENTAL HOSPITALS

9% GENERAL HOSPITAL
INPATIENT PSYCHIATRIC UNITS

4% VA HOSPITALS

3% PRIVATE MENTAL HOSPITALS

FIG. 6.2.   Percent distributions of in-patient and out-patient care episodes in mental health facilities, by type of facility: United States, 1955 and 1973. (From Keith, Gunderson, Reifman, Buchsbaum, & Mosher, 1976.)

1977 was aborted only by local community protests against the "dumping" of mental patients and by lobbying by mental hospital employees threatened with unemployment.

Mental patients have been discharged into a variety of settings. Many elderly patients have been placed in nursing homes, a disposition that shifts the financial burden of care from state to federal Medicare programs. Others have been placed in state-supported halfway houses or community residences. A growing number are now discharged into so-called board-and-care facilities licensed by the state but operated by the private sector. Finally, many former patients have been discharged back to families or simply given the opportunity to fend for themselves under state welfare or Social Security programs.

Schizophrenic patients have benefited somewhat less than other diagnostic groups from these trends. As previously noted, a majority of schizophrenic patients continues to receive in-patient care. Of all schizophrenic patients, 40% are treated in traditional mental hospitals; schizophrenic patients continue to account for one-half of all mental hospital residents. However, the average length of stay in mental hospitals has been drastically reduced, and fully 40% of schizophrenic patients are treated in out-patient settings (NIMH, 1977b). The modal approach to the treatment of acute schizophrenic episodes now relies on aggressive in-hospital drug therapy, quick release to out-patient or partial hospitalization status, and eventual discharge or release to community facilities (Klerman, 1977).

The decline of the mental hospital as the primary treatment medium for the schizophrenic patient does not, unfortunately, mean that the average patient is today better off in the community. This is especially true of former hospitalized patients and those who would have become long-term mental hospital residents under the old system. Certainly the mental hospital's contributions to dehumanization, abrogation of civil liberties, and the drift to chronicity have been curtailed by the new treatment policies. But many schizophrenic patients have encountered similar problems in community settings. Deinstitutionalization has not been synonymous with rehabilitation. Although the locus of care has shifted, the care itself has not necessarily improved and may in fact be inferior to that available in most mental hospitals (Kohen & Paul, 1976).

Borrowing from Kirk and Therrien (1975), we may analyze the shortcomings of deinstitutionalization under three "myths" or tenets of the community mental health movement at variance with the realities of the current situation: the myth of rehabilitation, the myth of reintegration, and the myth of continuity of care.

The Myth of Rehabilitation. As we have seen, the community mental health movement was in large part a reaction against the failures of the earlier mental hospital movement. A major assumption was that community care, by eliminating the negative effects of institutions, would allow for a more rapid recovery from the original disability. However, this assumption had been only marginally tested before deinstitutionalization became a reality. Pasamanick, Scarpitti, and Dinitz (1967) had demonstrated the feasibility of treating schizophrenic patients in their homes with a combination of drug therapy and supporting visits by psychiatric nurses. For periods up to 30 months, the rate of relapse was no greater than for a control group receiving equivalent in-patient care. However, these data only demonstrated that home care could be as effective as routine hospitalization, not that it was superior. Indeed, a later follow-up showed a rate of relapse of the original home-care group equivalent to that of the control group when only routine community care was available following project termination. Rather than participating in the community, most of the original home-care patients became increasingly home-bound, withdrawn, and inactive after project termination (Davis, Dinitz, & Pasamanick, 1974).

Community mental health centers have also failed to develop as originally intended. Proposed as an alternative to hospitalization, CMHCs tended instead to respond to a different segment of the patient population, primarily those with acute neurotic, personality, or psychosomatic disorders. CMHC staff are also likely to harbor disparaging attitudes toward former mental patients, to be pessimistic about their rehabilitation, and to offer them few innovative programs (Chu & Trotter, 1974; Kirk & Therrien, 1975).

Finally, community placements of former mental patients can be even less effective therapeutic settings than hospital wards. Kohen and Paul (1976) point out that placements in private extended-care facilities such as nursing homes and board-and-care residences have largely consisted of "administrative releases," which assume chronic patients to be incurable because existing institutional programs have failed to remediate their problem. The effect is simply to transfer custodial care to the community. An Illinois survey found that few former mental patients in board-and-care homes were released to more independent circumstances and that the majority of releases were accounted for by death, transfer to another home, or transfer to more highly supervised nursing homes (Kohen & Paul, 1976).

The Myth of Reintegration.   The community mental health movement also originally assumed that by keeping patients out of the hospital they would therefore be kept in the community. But the very notion of "the community" was never fully thought out. The catchment areas of CMHCs are primarily geographical rather than cultural entities. Former patients, by the nature of their long-term incarceration, may have no particular family, friends, or neighborhood to return to. And neighborhood groups often oppose the establishment of intermediate or extended-care facilities out of a combination of fear of mental illness and fear of declining property values. The result is that community residences often aggregate in deteriorated, isolated or otherwise undesirable areas. Unfortunately, residence "in the community" may be as segregated, dehumanizing, and disparaging as life on a back ward (Kirk & Thierren, 1975).

The Myth of Continuity of Care.   As Braginsky et al. (1969) emphasized, the mental hospital at least provides a less complicated existence than prevails in the outside world. Patients discharged into the community face a bureaucratic morass of service fragmentation and division of responsibility, which is often beyond their ability to cope. The proliferation of approximately 135 federal programs directed at supporting deinstitutionalization has undoubtedly served to exacerbate the situation.

Ideally, a former patient should be followed up by the local community mental health clinic, which should be able to work closely with the public welfare department, the vocational rehabilitation program, the board-and-care operator, and any other necessary support agencies. But service integration has proved extremely difficult to achieve. Not only do agencies bicker over the limits of their responsibility for a particular problem, but already overburdened social services are likely to place former mental patients low on their priority list of applicants (Kirk & Thierren, 1975). A recent government analysis found that there was no over-all federal plan or management system to set forth specific steps to accomplish deinstitutionalization, to define specific objectives and schedules, to define acceptable levels of community-based care, or to provide central direction and evaluation (General Accounting Office, 1977).

Given the psychological disabilities of schizophrenic patients, combined with a tendency to drift into apathy and inactivity with inadequate care, there is a great risk that patients in the community will not even attempt to contact those services at their disposal. Patients require a designated person or team with ultimate responsibility for seeing that their treatment, financial, and rehabilitative needs are met. Each community should have one agency—whether it be the CMHC, the vocational rehabilitation center, or even the local hospital—that will glue disparate services into a comprehensive support system and ensure that clients move through the network in orderly fashion (Herbert, 1977).

Although the National Institute of Mental Health is legally responsible for only a portion of the total range of deinstitutionalization services available to former patients, it may in the future assume primary oversight for all services. The recently announced Community Support Program (CSP) aims to help former mental patients to take advantage of available services in such areas as housing, health, employment, and rehabilitation. Through CSP, the National Institute of Mental Health may grant funds to state mental health agencies, which in turn subcontract to what is called a "core service agency." The designated agency, whether a CMHC or other facility, is then responsible for coordinating all local resources of potential help through the assignment of a case manager for each patient.

Deinstitutionalization is a reality, but its promise is as yet unfulfilled. Community care has replaced mental hospitalization as the treatment medium for a growing number of schizophrenic patients. Yet these patients are not necessarily members of the communities in which they reside nor even better off than they would have been in a traditional mental hospital. These unresolved problems are not inherent in the nature of schizophrenia itself. We know that a combination of maintenance drug therapy and aggressive case follow-up can effectively prevent relapse in the great majority of cases. The next stage of deinstitutionalization will be to provide just such high-quality, integrated treatment to the more than 1 million citizens in the United States alone who each year seek help for the psychological and social burdens of schizophrenia.

REFERENCES

Allen, M. G., Cohen, S., & Pollin, W. Schizophrenia in veteran twins: A diagnostic review. *American Journal of Psychiatry,* 1972, *128,* 939–945.

Altschule, M. D. *The development of traditional psychopathology: A source book.* Washington: Hemisphere Publ., 1976.

American Psychiatric Association. *Diagnostic and statistical manual of mental disorders.* Washington, D.C.: American Psychiatric Association, 1968.

American Psychiatric Association Task Force. *Megavitamin and orthomolecular therapy in psychiatry.* Washington, D.C.: American Psychiatric Association, 1973.

Angrist, B., Sathananthan, G., Wilk, S., & Gershon, S. Amphetamine psychosis: Behavioral and biochemical aspects. *Journal of Psychiatric Research,* 1974, *11,* 13–23.

Anonymous. An autobiography of a schizophrenic experience. *Journal of Abnormal and Social Psychology,* 1955, *51,* 677–689.

Antelman, S. M., & Caggiula, A. R. Norepinephrine–dopamine interactions and behavior. *Science,* 1977, *195,* 646–653.

Arie, T. The decline of duodenal ulcer. In O. W. Hill (Ed.), *Modern trends in psychosomatic medicine.* New York: Appleton-Century-Crofts, 1970.

Ayd, F. J. Jr., & Blackwell, B. *Discoveries in biological psychiatry.* Philadelphia: Lippincott, 1970.

Baldessarini, R. J. Factors influencing S-adenosyl methionine levels in tissue. In H. E. Himwich, S. S. Kety, & J. R. Smythies (Eds.), *Amines and schizophrenia.* New York: Pergamon Press, 1967.

Baldessarini, R. J. *Chemotherapy in psychiatry.* Cambridge, Mass.: Harvard University Press, 1977.

Baldessarini, R. J., & Tarsy, D. Tardive dyskinesia. In M. A. Lipton, A. DiMascio, and K. F. Killam (Eds.), *Psychopharmacology: A generation of progress.* New York: Raven Press, 1978.

Barchas, J. D., Akil, H., Elliott, G. R., Holman, R. B., & Watson, S. J. Behavioral neurochemistry: Neuroregulators and behavioral states. *Science,* 1978, *200,* 964–973.

Bateson, G., Jackson, D. D., Haley, J., & Weakland, J. H. Toward a theory of schizophrenia. *Behavioral Science,* 1956, *1,* 251–264.

Beers, C. W. *A mind that found itself.* New York: Longmans, Green, 1908.

Birnbaum, M. The right to treatment. *American Bar Association Journal,* 1960, *46,* 499–503.

Bleuler, E. *Textbook of psychiatry.* (A. A. Brill, trans.). New York: Macmillan, 1924.

Bleuler, E. *Dementia praecox or the group of schizophrenias.* (J. Zinkin, trans.). New York: International Universities Press, 1950.

Bleuler, M. Some results of research in schizophrenia. *Behavioral Science,* 1970, *15,* 211–219.

Bloom, B. L. *Community mental health: A historical and critical analysis.* Morristown, N.J.: General Learning Press, 1973.

Bowers, M. B., Jr. *Retreat from sanity: The structure of emerging psychosis.* Baltimore, Md.: Penguin Books, 1974.

Bowers, M. B., Jr. Clinical phenomenology in the functional psychoses. In D. X. Freedman (Ed.), *Biology of the major psychoses: A comparative analysis.* New York: Raven Press, 1975.

Braginsky, B. M., Braginsky, D. D., & Ring, K. *Methods of madness: The mental hospital as a last resort.* New York: Holt, Rinehart & Winston, 1969.

Brecher, E. M. *Licit and illicit drugs.* Mt. Vernon, N.Y.: Consumers Union, 1972.

Broadbent, D. E. *Perception and communication.* Oxford: Pergamon Press, 1958.

Broadbent, D. E. *Decision and stress.* New York: Academic Press, 1971.

Carlsson, A., & Lindquist, M. Effect of chlorpromazine or haloperidol on formation of 3-methoxytyramine and normetanephrine in mouse brain. *Acta Pharmacologica et Toxicologica,* 1963, *30,* 140–144.

Carpenter, W. T., Strauss, J. S., & Bartko, J. J. Flexible system for the diagnosis of schizophrenia: Report from the WHO international pilot study of schizophrenia. *Science,* 1973, *182,* 1275–1278.

Carpenter, W. T., Strauss, J. S., & Bartko, J. J. Use of signs and symptoms for the identification of schizophrenic patients. *Schizophrenia Bulletin,* Winter 1974, pp. 37–49.

Cash, T. F., Neale, J. M., & Cromwell, R. L. Span of apprehension in acute schizophrenics: Full-report technique. *Journal of Abnormal Psychology,* 1972, *79,* 322–326.

Chapman, L. J., & Chapman, J. P. *Disordered thought in schizophrenia.* Englewood Cliffs, N.J.: Prentice-Hall, 1973.

Chodoff, P., & Carpenter, W. T., Jr. Psychogenic theories of schizophrenia. In G. Usdin (Ed.), *Schizophrenia: Biological and psychological realities.* New York: Bruner/Mazel, 1975.

Chu, F. D., & Trotter, S. *The madness establishment.* New York: Grossman Publ., 1974.

Cohen, B. D., Nachmani, G., & Rosenberg, S. Referent communication disturbances in acute schizophrenia. *Journal of Abnormal Psychology,* 1974, *83,* 1–13.

Cole, J. O. Phenothiazines. In L. L. Simpson (Ed.), *Drug treatment of mental disorders.* New York: Raven Press, 1976.

Cole, J. O., & Davis, J. M. Antipsychotic drugs. In L. Bellak & L. Loeb (Eds.), *The schizophrenic syndrome.* New York: Grune & Stratton, 1969.

Connell, P. H. *Amphetamine psychosis* (Maudsley Monograph No 5). London: Oxford University Press, 1958.

Crane, G. E. Clinical psychopharmacology in its 20th year. *Science,* 1973, *181,* 124–128.

Creese, I., Burt, D. R., & Snyder, S. H. Dopamine receptor binding predicts clinical and pharmacological potencies of antischizophrenic drugs. *Science,* 1976, *192,* 481–483.

Davis, A. E., Dinitz, S., & Pasamanick, B. *Schizophrenics in the new custodial community.* Columbus: Ohio State University Press, 1974.

Deutsch, A. *The mentally ill in America* (2nd ed.). New York: Columbia University Press, 1949.

Dohrenwend, B. P., & Dohrenwend, B. S. *Social status and psychological disorder: A causal inquiry.* New York: Wiley, 1969.

Dohrenwend, B. P., & Dohrenwend, B. S. Psychiatric disorders in urban settings. In G. Caplan (Ed.), *American handbook of psychiatry* (2nd ed., Vol. 2). New York: Basic Books, 1974.

Donaldson, K. *Insanity inside out.* New York: Crown Publ., 1976.

Dunham, H. W. *Community and schizophrenia: An epidemiological analysis.* Detroit: Wayne State University Press, 1965.

Eaton, W. W., Jr. Residence, social class, and schizophrenia. *Journal of Health and Social Behavior,* 1974, *15,* 289–299.

Engel, G. L. The need for a new medical model: A challenge for biomedicine. *Science,* 1977, *196,* 129–136.

Erlenmeyer-Kimling, L. Studies on the offspring of two schizophrenic parents. In D. Rosenthal & S. S. Kety (Eds.), *The transmission of schizophrenia.* Oxford: Pergamon Press, 1968.

Essen-Möller, E. Psychiatrische Untersuchungen an einer Serie von Zwillingen. *Acta Psychiat. Scandinavica,* 1941, Supplement 23.

Fischer, M. *Genetic and environmental factors in schizophrenia: A study of schizophrenic twins and their families.* Copenhagen: Munksgaard, 1973.

Fish, B. Biologic antecedents of psychosis in children. In D. X. Freedman (Ed.), *Biology of the major psychoses: A comparative analysis.* New York: Raven Press, 1975.

Fleming, P., & Ricks, D. F. Emotions of children before schizophrenia and before character disorder. In M. Roff & D. F. Ricks (Eds.), *Life history research in psychopathology.* Minneapolis: University of Minnesota Press, 1970.

Fontana, A. F. Familial etiology of schizophrenia: Is a scientific methodology possible? *Psychological Bulletin,* 1966, *66,* 214–227.

Foucault, M. *Madness and civilization.* New York: Random House, 1965.

Frank, G. H. The role of the family in the development of psychopathology. *Psychological Bulletin,* 1965, *64,* 191–205.

Freedman, B. The subjective experience of perceptual and cognitive disturbances in schizophrenia. *Archives of General Psychiatry,* 1974, *30,* 333–340.

Freedman, B., & Chapman, L. J. Early subjective experience in schizophrenic episodes. *Journal of Abnormal Psychology,* 1973, *82,* 46–54.

Friedhoff, A. J., Park, S., Schweitzer, J. W., Burdock, E. I., & Armour, M. Excretion of 3, 4-Dimethoxyphenethylamine (DMPEA) by acute schizophrenics and controls. *Biological Psychiatry,* 1977, *12,* 643–654.

Friedhoff, A. J., & Van Winkle, E. The characteristics of an amine found in the urine of schizophrenic patients. *Journal of Nervous and Mental Disease,* 1962, *135,* 550–555.

Garmezy, N. Process and reactive schizophrenia: Some conceptions and issues. *Schizophrenia Bulletin,* Fall 1970, pp. 30–74.

General Accounting Office. *Returning the mentally disabled to the community: Government needs to do more.* Washington, D.C.: U.S. General Accounting Office, 1977.

Gerard, R. W. The nosology of schizophrenia: A cooperative study. *Behavioral Science,* 1964, *9,* 311–333.

Goffman, E. The moral career of the mental patient. *Psychiatry,* 1959, *22,* 123–142.

Golann, S., & Fremouw, W. J. (Eds.). *The right to treatment for mental patients.* New York: Irvington Publ., 1976.

Goldstein, M. J., & Rodnick, E. H. The family's contribution to the etiology of schizophrenia: Current status. *Schizophrenia Bulletin,* Fall 1975, pp. 48–63.

Gottesman, I. I., & Shields, J. Contributions of twin studies to perspectives on schizophrenia. In B. A. Maher (Ed.), *Progress in experimental personality research* (Vol. 3). New York: Academic Press, 1966. (a)

Gottesman, I. I., & Shields, J. Contributions of twin studies to perspectives of schizophrenia. In B. A. Maher (Ed.), *Progress in experimental personality research* (Vol. 3). New York: Academic Press, 1966. (a)

Gottesman, I. I., & Shields, J. Schizophrenia in twins: 16 years' consecutive admissions to a psychiatric clinic. *British Journal of Psychiatry,* 1966, *112,* 809–818. (b)

Gottesman, I. I., & Shields, J. *Schizophrenia and genetics: A twin study vantage point.* New York: Academic Press, 1972.

Grinspoon, L., Ewalt, J. R., & Shader, R. Long-term treatment of chronic schizophrenia: A preliminary report. *International Journal of Psychiatry,* 1967, *4,* 116–128.

Grob, G. N. The state mental hospital in mid-nineteenth-century America: A social analysis. *American Psychologist,* 1966, *21,* 510–523.

Gruenberg, E. M. The epidemiology of schizophrenia. In G. Caplan (Ed.), *American handbook of psychiatry* (2nd ed., Vol. 2). New York: Basic Books, 1974.

Gurland, B. J., Fleiss, J. L., Cooper, J. E., Sharpe, L., Kendell, R. E., & Roberts, P. Cross-national study of diagnosis of mental disorders: Hospital diagnosis and hospital patients in New York and London. *Comprehensive Psychiatry,* 1970, *11,* 18–25.

Hawkins, D. The orthomolecular approach to the diagnosis of schizophrenia. In D. Hawkins & L. Pauling (Eds.), *Orthomolecular psychiatry. Treatment of schizophrenia.* San Francisco: Freeman, 1973. (a)

Hawkins, D. Orthomolecular psychiatry. In D. Hawkins & L. Pauling (Eds.), *Orthomolecular psychiatry. Treatment of schizophrenia.* San Francisco: Freeman, 1973. (b)

Herbert, W. Seeking the missing rungs. *APA Monitor,* July 1977, *8*(7).

Heston, L. L. Psychiatric disorder in foster home reared children of schizophrenic mothers. *British Journal of Psychiatry,* 1966, *112,* 819–825.

Heston, L. L. The genetics of schizophrenic and schizoid disease. *Science,* 1970, *167,* 249–256.

Higgens, J. The concept of process-reactive schizophrenia: Criteria and related research. *Journal of Nervous and Mental Disease,* 1964, *138,* 9–25.

Higgens, J. Process-reactive schizophrenia: Recent developments. *Journal of Nervous and Mental Disease,* 1969, *149,* 450–472.

Hillyer, J. *Reluctantly told.* New York: Macmillan, 1926.

Hirsch, S. R., & Leff, J. P. *Abnormalities in parents of schizophrenics* (Maudsley Monograph No. 22). London: Oxford University Press, 1975.

Hoffer, A. The effect of nicotinic acid on the frequency and duration of re-hospitalization of schizophrenic patients: A controlled comparison study. *International Journal of Neuropsychiatry,* 1966, *2,* 234–240.

Hoffer, A. Biochemical aspects of schizophrenia. In D. V. Siva Sanker (Ed.), *Schizophrenia: Current concepts and research.* Hicksville, N.Y.: PJD Publ., 1969.

Hogarty, G. E., Goldberg, S. C., Schooler, N. R., & Ulrich, R. F. Drug and sociotherapy in the aftercare of schizophrenic patients. *Archives of General Psychiatry,* 1974, *31,* 603–618.

Hollingshead, A. B., & Redlich, F. C. *Social class and mental illness: A community study.* New York: Wiley, 1958.

Inouye, E. Similarity and dissimilarity of schizophrenia in twins. *Proceedings, Third World Congress of Psychiatry* (Vol. I). Montreal: University of Toronto Press, 1963. Pp. 524–530.

Iverson, L. L. Dopamine receptors in the brain. *Science,* 1975, *188,* 1084–1089.

Jackson, D. D. Schizophrenia. *Scientific American,* August 1962, pp. 3–11.

Jacob, T. Family interaction in disturbed and normal families: A methodological and substantive review. *Psychological Bulletin,* 1975, *82,* 33–65.

Jefferson, L. *These are my sisters.* Tulsa, Okla.: Vickers Publ. 1947.

Jencks, C. *Inequality.* New York: Basic Books, 1972.

Joint Commission on Mental Illness and Health. *Action for mental health.* New York: Basic Books, 1961.

Julien, R. M. *A primer of drug action.* San Francisco: Freeman, 1975.

Kallmann, F. J. The genetic theory of schizophrenia: An analysis of 691 schizophrenic twin index families. *American Journal of Psychiatry,* 1946, *103,* 309–322.

Kantor, R. E., Wallner, J. M., & Winder, C. L. Process and reactive schizophrenia. *Journal of Consulting Psychology,* 1953, *17,* 157–162.

Karlsson, J. L. *The biologic basis of schizophrenia.* Springfield, Ill.: C. C. Thomas, 1966.

Katz, M. M., Waskow, I. E., & Olsson, J. Characterizing the psychological state produced by LSD. *Journal of Abnormal Psychology,* 1968, *73,* 1–14.

Keith, S. J., Gunderson, J. G., Reifman, A., Buchsbaum, S., & Mosher, L. R. Special report: Schizophrenia 1976. *Schizophrenia Bulletin,* 1976, *2,* 509–565.

Kendell, R. E. *The role of diagnosis in psychiatry.* Oxford: Blackwell Scientific Publ., 1975.

Kety, S. S. Biochemical theories of schizophrenia: Part I. *Science,* 1959, *129,* 1528–1532. (a)

Kety, S. S. Biochemical theories of schizophrenia: Part II. *Science,* 1959, *129,* 1590–1596. (b)

Kety, S. S., Rosenthal, D., Wender, P. H., & Schulsinger, F. The types and prevalence of mental illness in the biological and adoptive families of adopted schizophrenics. In D. Rosenthal & S. S. Kety (Eds.), *The transmission of schizophrenia.* Oxford: Pergamon, 1968.

Kety, S. S., Rosenthal, D., Wender, P. H., & Schulsinger, F. Studies based on a total sample of adopted individuals and their relatives: Why they were necessary, what they demonstrated and failed to demonstrate. *Schizophrenia Bulletin,* 1976, *2,* 413–428. (a)

Kety, S. S., Rosenthal, D., Wender, P. H., Schulsinger, F., & Jacobsen, B. Mental illness in the biological and adoptive families of adopted individuals who have become schizophrenic. *Behavior Genetics,* 1976, *6,* 219–225. (b)

Keys, A., Brozek, J., Henschel, A., Mickelson, O., & Taylor, H. L. *The biology of human starvation.* Minneapolis: University of Minnesota Press, 1950.

Kidd, A. H. Psychopathology in the backgrounds of normal women. *Journal of Clinical Psychology,* 1974, *30,* 46–48.

Kirk, S. A., & Therrien, M. E. Community mental health myths and the fate of former hospitalized patients. *Psychiatry,* 1975, *38,* 209–217.

Klein, J. I. Mental health law; legal doctrine at the crossroads. *The Mental Health Law Project Summary of Activities,* March 1976, *2*(1).

Klerman, G. L. Better but not well: Social and ethical issues in the deinstitutionalization of the mentally ill. *Schizophrenia Bulletin,* 1977, *3,* 617–631.

Kohen, W., & Paul, G. L. Current trends and recommended changes in extended-care placement of mental patients: The Illinois system as a case in point. *Schizophrenia Bulletin,* 1976, *2,* 575–594.

Kohler, I. The formation and transformation of the perceptual world. *Psychological Issues,* 1964, *3*(4).

Kolata, G. B. Brain biochemistry: Effects of diet. *Science,* 1976, *192,* 41–42.

Kraepelin, E. *Psychiatrie, Ein lehrbuch fur studirende und arzte* (6th ed.). Leipzig: Barth, 1899.

Kraepelin, E. *Clinical psychiatry.* (A. R. Defendorff, Ed. and trans.). New York: Macmillan, 1904.

Kraepelin, E. *Lectures on clinical psychiatry* (2nd ed.). London: Bailliere, Tindall & Cassell, 1905.

Kringlen, E. *Heredity and environment in the functional psychoses.* London: Heineman, 1967.

Kringlen, E. An epidemiological–clinical twin study on schizophrenia. In D. Rosenthal & S. S. Kety (Eds.), *The transmission of schizophrenia.* Oxford: Pergamon, 1968.

Laing, R. D. *The divided self.* London: Tavistock Publ., 1960.

Laing, R. D., & Esterson, A. *Sanity, madness, and the family.* London: Tavistock Publ., 1964.

Landis, C., & Mettler, F. A. *Varieties of psychopathological experience.* New York: Holt, Rinehart & Winston, 1964.

Lang, J. The other side of hallucinations. *American Journal of Psychiatry,* 1939, *96,* 423–430.

Langer, T. S., & Michael, S. T. *Life stress and mental health.* Glencoe, Ill: The Free Press, 1963.

Lidz, T. *The origin and treatment of schizophrenic disorders.* New York: Basic Books, 1973.

Lidz, T., Fleck, S., Alanen, Y. O., & Cornelison, A. Schizophrenic patients and their siblings. *Psychiatry,* 1963, *26,* 1–18.

Lidz, T., Fleck, S., & Cornelison, A. R. *Schizophrenia and the family.* New York: International Universities Press, 1965.

Lopez-Ibor, J. J. The delusional schizophrenic mutation. In A. Burton, J. J. Lopez-Ibor, & W. M. Mendel (Eds.), *Schizophrenia as a life style*. New York: Springer Publ., 1974.

Lorr, M., Klett, C. J., & McNair, D. M. *Syndromes of psychosis*. Oxford: Pergamon Press, 1963.

Luxenburger, H. Vorläufiger Bericht über psychiatrische Serienuntersuchungen an Zwillingen. *Z. ges. Neurol. Psychiat.*, 1928, *116*, 297–326.

MacDonald, N. Living with schizophrenia. *Canadian Medical Association Journal*, 1960, *82*, 218–221.

Maher, B. A. *Principles of psychopathology*. New York: McGraw-Hill, 1966.

Maher, B. A. The shattered language of schizophrenia. *Psychology Today*, November 1968, pp. 30–33.

Maher, B. A. The language of schizophrenia: A review and interpretation. *British Journal of Psychiatry*, 1972, *120*, 3–17.

Maher, B. A. Delusional thinking and perceptual disorder. *Journal of Individual Psychology*, 1974, *30*, 98–113.

Matthysse, S., & Lipinski, J. Biochemical aspects of schizophrenia. *Annual Review of Medicine*, 1975, *26*, 551–565.

May, P. R. A. *Treatment of schizophrenia*. New York: Science House, 1968.

McGhie, A. *Pathology of attention*. Baltimore, Md.: Penguin Books, 1969.

McGhie, A., & Chapman, J. Disorders of attention and perception in early schizophrenia. *British Journal of Medical Psychology*, 1961, *34*, 103–117.

McNeil, T. F., & Kaij, L. Obstetric complications and physical size of offspring of schizophrenic, schizophrenic-like, and control mothers. *British Journal of Psychiatry*, 1973, *123*, 341–348.

Mednick, S. A. A learning theory approach to research in schizophrenia. *Psychological Bulletin*, 1958, *55*, 316–327.

Mednick, S. A. Breakdown in individuals at high risk for schizophrenia: Possible predispositional perinatal factors. *Mental Hygiene*, 1970, *54*, 50–63.

Mednick, S. A., Mura, E., Schulsinger, F., & Mednick, B. Perinatal complications and infant development in children with schizophrenic parents. *Social Biology*, 1971, *18*, 103–113.

Mednick, S. A., & Schulsinger, F. Some premorbid characteristics related to breakdown in children with schizophrenic mothers. In D. Rosenthal & S. S. Kety (Eds.), *The transmission of schizophrenia*. London: Pergamon Press, 1968.

Mednick, S. A., & Schulsinger, F. Factors related to breakdown in children at high risk for schizophrenia. In M. Roff & D. F. Ricks (Eds.), *Life history research in psychopathology*. Minneapolis: University of Minnesota Press, 1970.

Meehl, P. E. Schizotaxia, schizotypy, schizophrenia. *American Psychologist*, 1962, *17*, 827–838.

Meehl, P. E. Why I do not attend case conferences. In P. E. Meehl, *Psychodiagnosis: Selected papers*. Minneapolis: University of Minnesota Press, 1973.

Meltzer, H. Y., & Stahl, S. M. The dopamine hypothesis of schizophrenia: A review. *Schizophrenia Bulletin*, 1976, *2*, 19–76.

Mendel, W. M. A phenomenological theory of schizophrenia. In A. Burton, J. J. Lopez-Ibor, & W. M. Mendel (Eds.), *Schizophrenia as a life style*. New York: Springer Publ., 1974.

Menninger, K. *The vital balance*. New York: Viking Press, 1963.

Mishler, E. G., & Scotch, N. A. Sociocultural factors in the epidemiology of schizophrenia. *Psychiatry*, 1963, *26*, 315–351.

Munkvad, I., Fog, R., & Kristjansen, P. The drug approach to therapy. Long-term treatment of schizophrenia. In D. Kanoli, G. Bartholini, & D. Richter (Eds.), *Schizophrenia Today*. Oxford: Pergamon Press, 1976.

National Institute of Mental Health. *Litigation and mental health services*. DHEW Publication (ADM) 76-261. Washington, D.C.: U.S. Government Printing Office, 1975.

National Institute of Mental Health. *Deinstitutionalization: An analytical review and sociological perspective.* DHEW Publication (ADM) 76-351. Washington, D.C.: U.S. Government Printing Office, 1976.

National Institute of Mental Health. *A citizen's guide to the community mental health centers amendments of 1975.* DHEW Publication (ADM) 76-397. Washington, D.C.: U.S. Government Printing Office, 1977 (a).

National Institute of Mental Health. *Psychiatric services and the changing institutional scene, 1950-1985.* DHEW Publication (ADM) 77-433. Washington, D.C.: U.S. Government Printing Office, 1977. (b)

Neale, J. M. Perceptual span in schizophrenia. *Journal of Abnormal Psychology,* 1971, *77,* 196-204.

Neale, J. M., & Cromwell, R. L. Attention and schizophrenia. In B. A. Maher (Ed.)., *Progress in experimental personality research* (Vol. 5). New York: Academic Press, 1970.

Neale, J. M., McIntyre, C. W., Fox, R., & Cromwell, R. L. Span of apprehension in acute schizophrenics. *Journal of Abnormal Psychology,* 1969, *74,* 593-596.

Noyes, A. P., & Kolb, L. C. *Modern clinical psychiatry* (6th ed.). Philadelphia, Pa.: Saunders, 1963.

Offir, C. W. Civil rights and the mentally ill: Revolution in bedlam. *Psychology Today,* October 1974, pp. 61-71.

Osmond, H., & Hoffer, A. Massive niacin treatment in schizophrenia: Review of a nine-year study. *Lancet,* 1962, *1,* 316-319.

Osmond, H., & Smythies, J. Schizophrenia: A new approach. *Journal of Mental Science,* 1952, *98,* 309-315.

Pasamanick, B., & Knobloch, H. Brain damage and reproductive casualty. *American Journal of Orthopsychiatry,* 1960, *30,* 298-305.

Pasamanick, B., Scarpitti, F. R., & Dinitz, S. *Schizophrenics in the community.* New York: Appleton-Century-Crofts, 1967.

Pauling, L. Orthomolecular psychiatry. *Science,* 1968, *160,* 265-271.

Pletscher, A., & Kyburz, E. Neuroleptic drugs. Chemical versus biochemical classification. In D. Kamali, G. Bartholini, & D. Richter (Eds.), *Schizophrenia today.* Oxford: Pergamon Press, 1976.

Pollin, W., Cardon, P. V., & Kety, S. S. Effects of amino acid feeding in schizophrenic patients treated with iproniazid. *Science,* 1961, *133,* 104-105.

Pollin, W., & Stabenau, J. R. Biological, psychological, and historical differences in a series of monozygotic twins discordant for schizophrenia. In D. Rosenthal & S. S. Kety (Eds.), *The transmission of schizophrenia.* London: Pergamon Press, 1968.

Post, R. M., & Goodwin, F. K. Time-dependent effects of phenothiazines on dopamine turnover in psychiatric patients. *Science,* 1975, *190,* 488-489.

Price, R. H. *Abnormal behavior: Perspectives in conflict.* New York: Holt, Rinehart & Winston, 1972.

Rabkin, J. G., & Struening, E. L. Life events, stress, and illness. *Science,* 1976, *194,* 1013-1020.

Reed, G. *The psychology of anomalous experience.* London: Hutchinson & Co., 1972.

Renaud, H., & Estess, F. Life history interviews with one hundred normal American males: 'Pathogenicity' of childhood. *American Journal of Orthopsychiatry,* 1961, *31,* 786-802.

Ricks, D. F., & Berry, J. C. Family and symptom patterns that precede schizophrenia. In M. Roff & D. F. Ricks (Eds.), *Life history research in psychopathology.* Minneapolis: University of Minnesota Press, 1970.

Rieder, R. O., Rosenthal, D., Wender, P., & Blumenthal, H. The offspring of schizophrenics: Fetal and neonatal deaths. *Archives of General Psychiatry,* 1975, *32,* 200-211.

Rodnick, E. H., & Shakow, D. Set in the schizophrenic as measured by a composite reaction time index. *American Journal of Psychiatry,* 1940, *97,* 214-225.

Rosanoff, A. J., Handy, L. M., Plesset, I. R., & Brush, S. The etiology of so-called schizophrenic psychoses with special reference to their occurrence in twins. *American Journal of Psychiatry,* 1934, *91,* 247–286.

Rosen, G. *Madness in society: Chapters in the historical sociology of mental illness.* New York: Harper & Row, 1968.

Rosenhan, D. L. On being sane in insane places. *Science,* 1973, *179,* 250–258.

Rosenthal, D. *Genetics of psychopathology.* New York: McGraw-Hill, 1971.

Rosenthal, D., Wender, P. H., Kety, S. S., Schulsinger, F., Welner, J., & Ostergaard, L. Schizophrenics' offspring reared in adoptive homes. In D. Rosenthal & S. S. Kety (Eds.), *The transmission of schizophrenia.* Oxford: Pergamon Press, 1968.

Ryle, G. *The concept of mind.* New York: Barnes & Noble, 1949.

Salzinger, K. *Schizophrenia: Behavioral aspects.* New York: Wiley, 1973.

Sameroff, A., & Zax, M. Schizotaxia revisited: Model issues in the etiology of schizophrenia. *American Journal of Orthopsychiatry,* 1973, *43,* 744–754.

Schildkraut, J. J. (Ed.). *Catecholamines and affective disorders.* Bloomfield, N.J.: Health Learning Systems, 1974.

Schopler, E. *Parents of psychotic children as scapegoats.* Paper presented at the meeting of the American Psychological Association, Washington, D.C., September 1969.

Sechehaye, M. *Autobiography of a schizophrenic girl.* (G. Rubin-Rabson, trans.). New York: New American Library, 1970.

Shakow, D. Segmental set: A theory of the formal psychological deficit in schizophrenia. *Archives of General Psychiatry,* 1962, *6,* 1–17.

Shakow, D. Psychological deficit in schizophrenia. *Behavioral Science,* 1963, *8,* 275–305.

Shakow, D. Segmental set: The adaptive process in schizophrenia. *American Psychologist,* 1977, *32,* 129–139.

Shields, J. Heredity and psychological abnormality. In H. J. Eysenck (Ed.), *Handbook of abnormal psychology* (2nd ed.). San Diego: Robert R. Knapp, 1973.

Singer, M. T., & Wynne, L. C. Principles for scoring communication defects and deviances in parents of schizophrenics: Rorschach and TAT scoring manuals. *Psychiatry,* 1966, *29,* 260–268.

Slater, E. Psychotic and neurotic illnesses in twins. *Medical Research Council special report series,* No. 278. London: Her Majesty's Stationery Office, 1953.

Slater, E., & Cowie, V. *The genetics of mental disorder.* London: Oxford University Press, 1971.

Snyder, S. H. The true speed trip: Schizophrenia. *Psychology Today,* January 1972, pp. 42–46; 74–75.

Snyder, S. H. *Madness and the brain.* New York: McGraw-Hill, 1974.

Sobel, D. E. Infant mortality and malformations in children of schizophrenic women. *Psychiatric Quarterly,* 1961, *35,* 60–64.

Spitzer, R. L., & Fleiss, J. L. A re-analysis of the reliability of psychiatric diagnosis. *British Journal of Psychiatry,* 1974, *125,* 341–347.

Spohn, H. E., Lacoursiere, R. B., Thompson, K., & Coyne, L. Phenothiazine effects on psychological and psychophysiological dysfunction in chronic schizophrenics. *Archives of General Psychiatry,* 1977, *34,* 633–644.

Srole, L., Langner, T. S., Michael, S. T., Opler, M. K., & Rennie, T. A. C. *Mental health in the metropolis.* New York: McGraw-Hill, 1962.

Stabenau, J. R., & Pollin, W. Experiential differences for schizophrenics as compared with their non-schizophrenic siblings: Twin and family studies. In M. Roff & D. F. Ricks (Eds.), *Life history research in psychopathology.* Minneapolis: University of Minnesota Press, 1970.

Strecker, E. A., Ebaugh, F. G., & Ewalt, J. R. *Practical clinical psychiatry* (7th ed.). Philadelphia, Pa.: Blakiston, 1951.

Sutherland, N. S. *Breakdown.* New York: New American Library, 1976.

Szasz, T. *The myth of mental illness.* New York: Paul B. Hoeber, 1961.

Szasz, T. *Schizophrenia: The sacred symbol of psychiatry.* New York: Basic Books, 1976.

Task Force on Nomenclature and Statistics. *Diagnostic and statistical manual of mental disorders* (draft 3rd ed.). Washington, D.C.: American Psychiatric Association, 1978.

Tienari, P. Schizophrenia and monozygotic twins. *Psychiatria Fennica,* 1971, 97–104.

Torrey, E. F. Is schizophrenia universal? An open question. *Schizophrenia Bulletin,* Winter, 1973, 53–59.

Torrey, E. F. A fantasy trial about a real issue. *Psychology Today,* March 1977, p. 24.

Torrey, E. F., & Peterson, M. R. The viral hypothesis of schizophrenia. *Schizophrenia Bulletin,* 1976, *2,* 136–146.

Turner, R. J., & Wagenfeld, M. O. Occupational mobility and schizophrenia: An assessment of the social causation and social selection hypotheses. *American Sociological Review,* 1967, *32,* 104–113.

van Praag, H. M. *Depression and schizophrenia. A contribution to their chemical pathologies.* New York: Spectrum Publ., 1977.

Vonnegut, M. *The Eden express.* New York: Bantam Books, 1976.

Wahl, O. F. Monozygotic twins discordant for schizophrenia: A review. *Psychological Bulletin,* 1976, *83,* 91–106.

Wall Street Journal. "Mental attitude. Revised rules reduce involuntary confining of psychiatric patients." January 24, 1978, p. 1.

Watt, N. F., Stolorow, R. D., Lubensky, A. W., & McClelland, D. C. School adjustment and behavior of children hospitalized for schizophrenia as adults. *American Journal of Orthopsychiatry,* 1970, *40,* 637–657.

Watt, N. F., & Lubensky, A. W. Childhood roots of schizophrenia. *Journal of Consulting and Clinical Psychology,* 1976, *44,* 363–375.

Wender, P. H. Dementia praecox: The development of the concept. *American Journal of Psychiatry,* 1963, *119,* 1143–1151.

Wender, P. H. The role of genetics in the etiology of the schizophrenias. *American Journal of Orthopsychiatry,* 1969, *39,* 447–458.

Werner, E., Simonian, K., Bierman, J. M., & French, F. E. Cumulative effect of perinatal complications and deprived environment on physical, intellectual, and social development of preschool children. *Pediatrics,* 1967, *39,* 490–505.

Wing, J. K. A review of "Sanity, madness, and the family." *New Society,* May 1964, pp. 23–24.

Wing, J. K., & Brown, G. W. *Institutionalism and schizophrenia.* London: Cambridge University Press, 1970.

Wing, J. K., Cooper, J. E., & Sartorius, N. *The measurement and classification of psychiatric symptoms.* London: Cambridge University Press, 1974.

Wise, C. D., & Stein, L. Dopamine-β-hydroxylase deficits in the brains of schizophrenic patients. *Science,* 1973, *181,* 344–347.

Wittenborn, J. R., Weber, E. S. P., & Brown, M. Niacin in the long-term treatment of schizophrenia. *Archives of General Psychiatry,* 1973, *28,* 308–315.

Wittenborn, J. R., & Weiss, W. Patients diagnosed manic depressive psychosis-manic state. *Journal of Consulting Psychology,* 1952, *16,* 193–198.

Wyatt, R. J., & Murphy, D. L. Neurotransmitter-related enzymes in the major psychiatric disorders: II. MAO and DBH in schizophrenia. In D. X. Freedman (Ed.), *Biology of the major psychoses.* New York: Raven Press, 1975.

Wyatt, R. J., Schwartz, M. A., Erdelyi, E., & Barchas, J. D. Dopamine-β-hydroxylase activity in brains of chronic schizophrenic patients. *Science,* 1975, *187,* 368–369.

Wyatt, R. J., Termini, B. A., & Davis, J. Biochemical and sleep studies of schizophrenia: A review of the literature, 1960–1970. *Schizophrenia Bulletin,* Fall 1971, pp. 10–66.

Wynne, L. C. Methodologic and conceptual issues in the study of schizophrenics and their families. In D. Rosenthal & S. S. Kety (Eds.), *The transmission of schizophrenia.* Oxford: Pergamon Press, 1968.

Wynne, L. C. Communication disorders and the quest for relatedness in families of schizophrenics. *American Journal of Psychoanalysis,* 1970, *30,* 100–114. (a)

Wynne, L. C. Family dynamics. In J. O. Cole & L. E. Hollister (Eds.), *Schizophrenia.* New York: Medcom, 1970. (b)

Yolles, S. F., & Kramer, M. Vital statistics. In L. Bellak & L. Loeb (Eds.), *The schizophrenic syndrome.* New York: Grune & Stratton, 1969.

Zahn, T. P., Rosenthal, D., & Shakow, D. Reaction time in schizophrenic and normal subjects in relation to the sequence of series of regular preparatory intervals. *Journal of Abnormal and Social Psychology,* 1961, *63,* 161–168.

Zax, M., Sameroff, A. J., & Babigian, H. M. Birth outcomes in the offspring of mentally disordered women. *American Journal of Orthopsychiatry,* 1977, *47,* 218–230.

Zigler, E., & Phillips, L. Psychiatric diagnosis and symptomatology. *Journal of Abnormal and Social Psychology,* 1961, *63,* 69–75.

Zubin, J., & Spring, B. Vulnerability—A new view of schizophrenia. *Journal of Abnormal Psychology,* 1977, *86,* 103–126.

Author Index

Numbers in italic indicate the page on which the complete reference appears.

Subject Index